MW00815195

GRADING FOR GROWTH

GRADING FOR GROWTH

A Guide to Alternative Grading Practices That Promote Authentic Learning and Student Engagement in Higher Education

David Clark and Robert Talbert

Foreword by Linda B. Nilson

Routledge
Taylor & Francis Group

NEW YORK AND LONDON

First published in 2023 by Stylus Publishing, LLC.

Published in 2023 by Routledge
605 Third Avenue, New York, NY 10017
4 Park Square, Milton Park, Abingdon, Oxon OX14 4RN

Routledge is an imprint of the Taylor & Francis Group, an informa business.

© 2023 Taylor & Francis Group

All rights reserved. No part of this book may be reprinted or reproduced or
utilised in any form or by any electronic, mechanical, or other means, now
known or hereafter invented, including photocopying and recording, or in any
information storage or retrieval system, without permission in writing from the
publishers.

Trademark Notice: Product or corporate names may be trademarks or registered
trademarks, and are used only for identification and explanation without intent
to infringe.

ISBN: 9781642673807 (hbk)
ISBN: 9781642673814 (pbk)
ISBN: 9781003445043 (ebk)

DOI: 10.4324/9781003445043

For everyone brave enough to take the first step.

CONTENTS

PART THREE: MAKING ALTERNATIVE GRADING WORK FOR YOU

CASE STUDY LIST

Name	Discipline	Class Size	Modality	Page
Joshua Bowman	Mathematics	25	Face-to-face	51
Robynne Lock	Physics	20–40	Face-to-face	58
Kay C Dee	Biomedical Engineering	20	Online, asynchronous	65
Dustin Locke	Philosophy	15–20	Face-to-face	72
Megan Mahoney	Library Science	15–20	Online, asynchronous	75
Megan Eberhardt-Alstot	Education, Learning Design	30	Hybrid	77
Rebecca Kelly	Environmental Science	20–24	Face-to-face	78
Hubert Muchalski	Chemistry	40–50	Online, synchronous	82
Josh Veazey	Physics	40–60	Face-to-face	89
Jennifer Momsen	Biology	135	Face-to-face	99
Gretchen Bender	History of Art and Architecture	200	Face-to-face	105
Hilary Freeman	Mathematics	36–120 per section, eight sections	Face-to-face	114
Silvia Heubach and Sharona Krinsky	Statistics	25 per section, 80 sections	Face-to-face	120
Renée Link	Chemistry	16–20 per section, 50–75 sections	Face-to-face	124
Gloria Ramos	Physics	25–30	Face-to-face	132
Chris Creighton	Mathematics	32	Face-to-face	142
Betsy Barre	Religion and Philosophy	15–30	Face-to-face	144

We all should be very tired of reading that academia is slow to change. During the past 50 years, universities have gone from relegating teaching to a "custodial" duty to embracing it almost as tightly as it has research for many decades. Suddenly, faculty have had to "teach well," and institutions have been grabbling with the meaning of *well* for the past 20 years. Time was when student ratings alone served the purpose, but not anymore for a host of reasons. Further, good teaching has evolved from choosing and properly implementing the appropriate methods to reaching a myriad of student groups that bring different needs and issues to the classroom—the neurodiverse, the underserved and underprivileged, the first generation, the emotionally challenged, and those from a multiplicity of cultures, as well as students who are developmentally, psychiatrically, or physically disabled.

Now higher education is starting to change one of its most basic functions: grading. We know that our traditional grading system with its points, partial credit, percentages, and the like has been failing us. It hasn't been motivating our students to learn and strive for excellence, nor upholding academic standards, nor fostering intergrader agreement—plus our grades bear little relationship to the "holy grail" of outcomes achievement. Students have refused to assume full responsibility for their grades and have often protested our point allocation decisions. They have told us that they don't know what we expect of them, and they haven't been using our feedback. Too much conflict and stress have marred student–faculty relations. With class sizes and teaching loads swelling, grading has been absorbing more and more faculty time. And, let's face it, this time has been mostly unpleasant. There must be a better way.

Fortunately, we've recently been finding several better ways. Which brings us to David Clark and Robert Talbert's *Grading for Growth: A Guide to Alternative Grading Practices That Promote Authentic Learning and Student Engagement in Higher Education*.

The topic is hardly a new one for Talbert. He has been on the forefront of improving higher education since he started his first blog, *Casting Out Nines*, in 2005. It was consistently so well written and thoughtful that

The Chronicle of Higher Education carried it for years. Over this blog's history, he shared the trials, tribulations, and triumphs of his experiments with flipped learning and alternative grading, especially specifications grading, in his mathematics courses. He coauthors his new blog, *Grading for Growth*, with his colleague David Clark.

In this book, Clark and Talbert offer the finest compilation of the weaknesses of traditional grading, including one on mathematical grounds, that I have ever run across. They then present "four pillars of alternative grading," shared by all the emerging grading systems that their book addresses: standards-based grading, specifications grading, and ungrading. (I am so proud that my work made it into this pathbreaking book!) Among these pillars are clearly defined performance expectations and a focus on encouraging student progress.

Clark and Talbert even move beyond these three systems to all kinds of partial conversions and hybrid variations on them. These are not just hypothetical variants. The authors describe these variants, along with the "pure" forms, as implemented in actual courses that have used them. One variant even integrates student portfolios. These examples come from disparate institutions and encompass a variety of courses: from STEM to humanities, from small to truly large classes, from lecture-based to lab-based to studio labs, from the one-instructor creation to the tightly coordinated multisection type—something for everyone. And something to give courage to everyone who wants to explore alternative grading.

This book makes it easy to dip your toe into the water. One entire chapter is a "workbook" to guide the changeover, and it asks only that you make a partial conversion involving only one or two of the four pillars and just a few aspects of your course. This guidance makes you think deeply about your course in general—what is special about it, why you are teaching it, how it is structured, who the students are, and what different final grades mean. The next chapter answers the questions that probably arose in the course of completing the workbook: How does alternative grading work day-to-day, on-the-ground; what glitches can you expect—and head off; how do your and your students' workloads change; and what have the authors learned by experience?

Returning to the yet undetermined meaning of *teaching well* mentioned at the beginning of this foreword, alternative grading makes inroads into defining good teaching. Certainly, teaching well starts with our setting clear content standards for student work; how can students achieve a misty, murky goal? Good teaching also requires providing actionable feedback that can help students improve their work, along with a mark that signifies their progress toward the goal. Finally, it gives students chances to use this feed-back to revise their work until it meets the clear content standards. In other words, teaching well rests on the four pillars of alternative grading. And they are clear, specific, context-appropriate goals for all of us.

Linda B. Nilson
Clemson University

ACKNOWLEDGMENTS

David would like to acknowledge:

- My wife Sarah for being an amazing partner, sounding board, and rock. There's nobody I can laugh with as hard as her. Ook!
- My parents Robert and Janet Clark, who passed on the teaching bug to me. They are models of caring, compassion, and empathy.

Robert would like to acknowledge:

- My longtime friend and mentor Linda Nilson, for being a guide throughout my career and for writing a book about alternative grading just when I needed it the most.
- All those who have read my blog through the years, from *Casting Out Nines* up to the present day. Your encouragement, incisive comments, and good-faith disagreements have made me a better writer.
- My wife (Cathy) and children (Lucy, Penelope, and Harrison) for keeping me grounded. Last time I wrote a book, I spent too much time writing and not enough being present with you. I hope I did better this time.

Both authors would like to acknowledge and thank everyone we have talked with, interviewed, and sought out for advice while writing this book: Stefanie Austin, Spencer Bagley, Betsy Barre, Gretchen Bender, Debra Borkovitz, Robert Bosley, Joshua Bowman, Matt Charnley, Chris Creighton, Flower Darby, Kay C Dee, Megan Eberhardt-Alstot, Hilary Freeman, Silvia Heubach, TJ Hitchman, Adria Hoffman, Rebecca Kelly, Sharona Krinsky, Owynn Lancaster, Drew Lewis, Renée Link, Robynne Lock, Dustin Locke, Megan Mahoney, Katie Mattaini, Kim McKee, Jennifer Momsen, Firas Moosvi, Hubert Muchalski, Abigail Noyce, Kate Owens, Marney Pratt, Gloria Ramos, Tricia Shepherd, Courtney Sobers, Josh Veazey, and Amy Werman.

Everyone on this list contributed to the ideas in this book, some through full case studies, others through pointing us toward helpful resources or asking pointed questions that made us rethink ideas carefully. All of your ideas are woven through the fabric of this book.

We also both thank our colleagues at Grand Valley State University, and particularly in the Department of Mathematics, for helping us both to grow as teachers and learners, in a uniquely supportive and innovative working environment. Most especially, we thank our students at GVSU, who have been extraordinarily helpful and patient with us as we explore different innovations in our teaching, and who have shown incredible strength through some very difficult times.

PART ONE

WHAT IS ALTERNATIVE GRADING?

I

WHAT THIS BOOK IS ABOUT

"I teach for free; they pay me to grade." It's a simple joke that many of us in higher education have made throughout our careers. And yet it points to a truth that exposes a monumental issue: Grading as we know it is broken, and it's breaking higher education.

If you ask faculty what they love about their jobs, probably none of them will say, "Grading." The never-ending stream of work to be graded sucks away time and energy, and we seem to get little in return. We tend to let it pile up because it is so unpleasant. And when we do get around to grading, we have a term to describe our status: *grading jail*, and we do not get out of jail until we have paid the price. (There seems to be no corresponding notion of "research jail" or "teaching jail.")

When, at last, the grading is done, we move on to something even less pleasant than grading itself: handling student reactions to grades. These run the full gamut of human emotion, often leading to fraught interactions with students who we otherwise love to work with. But we can hardly blame students for how they react. For many years, it has been drilled into them explicitly and implicitly that earning high grades is the purpose and end goal of education. It is perfectly rational from a student's point of view to argue, negotiate, and game the system to attain maximum grades at minimum cost.

When we have honest conversations with students, we find that they, too, dislike grades. They often admit that they'd rather not have grades at all, and that they like and want to learn. But if it comes down to really learning a subject and growing as learners on the one hand, and earning a grade on the other, they know which direction the incentives point.

And perhaps worst of all, grades themselves often have no direct connection to learning. There are false positives, where students manage high grades without corresponding evidence of learning, and false negatives, where students who work hard and demonstrate real learning still earn poor grades. In the end, nobody seems able to look at a grade and say with any certainty what information it conveys about the learner and what they know.

The entire culture built around grades and grading is toxic. The quest for a 4.0, the email requests to "bump up" one's grade, the arguments over points awarded: None of these are actually about learning. But because grades seem to be inextricable from school, there appears to be no other way than the traditions we have.

But what if there *was* a way?

What if there was a way to think about grades built on growth over game-playing, learning over letters and numbers, and productive relationships over adversarial ones? What if we could address, if not entirely repair, so many of these problems, through a quiet revolution in the everyday task of grading?

We believe that this way exists, and that's why we are writing this book. We believe that a fundamentally better approach to grading is possible, and that any higher education faculty can help make it a reality.

Where We're Coming From

The "we" mentioned previously is David Clark and Robert Talbert. We are two professors in the Mathematics Department at Grand Valley State University, a large regional comprehensive public university in Michigan. Grand Valley is a primarily undergraduate, teaching-focused university serving around 23,000 students. In the Math Department, our main focus is teaching (each of us typically has a 3-3 teaching load), we have relatively small class sizes (usually around 30 students), and there are no graduate programs or teaching assistants. However, we have over 50 faculty along with over 1,000 students at any given moment taking our classes. So we do a lot of teaching and a *lot* of grading.

We have used alternative approaches to grading in our classes over the past 10 years, while learning from and helping others do the same. We've collaborated with colleagues in a wide range of disciplines, at many types of institutions and departments, in different professional situations, and with a range of constraints, to highlight and learn from their work and their perspectives. This book represents the best of what we've learned—not just our own experiences (which, being those of white male, tenured professors, are not necessarily representative).

But to help you understand where we're coming from, we'd like to share our origin stories—how each of us got started with alternative grading.

David's Origin Story

In 2010, I was a grad student earning my funding by teaching a lot of Calculus 2. Calc 2 required students to earn a C in its prerequisite, Calc 1. Like many brand-new teachers, I was annoyed when students struggled to use those prerequisites fluently.

I remember thinking about this as I walked across campus on a fresh spring day. What did that prerequisite C even mean? Could a student have learned everything at a mediocre level? Did they knock some things out of the park, but completely miss out on others? The "C" couldn't say. So I day-dreamed up a report card that would list the main topics from Calc 1 and record the student's final level of understanding on each one separately. Then a future instructor (a.k.a. me) could read that report and understand what students knew, and where they needed help.

What a dream! But alas, I was a grad student and definitely couldn't change an entire university's grading system. So I tucked the idea away and got lunch instead.

Fast forward a few summers. I was a new postdoc, and my brain was spinning with an idea I'd just learned about at a conference: "standards-based grading" (SBG). It sounded just like my grad student dream. Three weeks before the semester started, my new department called to beg me to teach a class that needed coverage. Of course, I said "yes" and immediately decided I'd give this SBG thing a try. Three weeks to learn about it and set it up. No problem, right?

So I read everything I could and built a syllabus from scratch. Reviewing that syllabus is an exercise in humility. It was clunky and complex. Worse, it was all about policies, rules, and *my* reasons why *I* wanted to use this strange grading system. Students barely showed up in the maze of rules.

But as class unfolded, I discovered unexpected benefits for students. Because SBG only records a student's eventual level of understanding, students took time to review past failures and learn from them. My office hours became busy, and my discussions with students moved from "Why did I lose a point for this?" to "I'm having trouble with generator matrices; can we talk about them?"

Most unexpectedly, some of my students *begged* me to give them a quiz—on the day before a major holiday break. *They wanted to show me what they knew.* What a dream!

In that first wild semester, I started to see how my grading choices made huge differences in how students experienced my class. Using SBG helped me see how traditional grades hurt students by reinforcing systemic inequity, setting perverse incentives, and encouraging bad habits.

I didn't start by focusing on students, but I grew into it. Just like me, you might be interested in alternative grading for any number of reasons. None of them are "right" or "wrong." But once you start down the rabbit hole, you might be surprised where you end up.

Robert's Origin Story

At the end of fall semester 2014, as I entered course grades, I finally reached the end of my patience with traditional grading. I was angry and ready to burn it all down. And it was because of one student.

On the very first day, she stood out: Excited and engaged, she loved math and wanted to learn. Soon, she was not only seemingly learning rapidly but also helping others.

Then came the first test.

As the hour unfolded, something changed with this student. Her initial nervous excitement turned to frustration. She turned in her test upset, and soon I realized why: Her work was not good at all, and her grade was shockingly low. It was so low that she was mathematically eliminated from earning an A in the course, according to my syllabus.

At the next class meeting, she was different. She took notes and participated, but her energy was gone. But as she worked over the next couple of weeks, I noticed that while her work might initially have a lot of flaws, she eventually understood the content—on a 5- to 7-day delay from my schedule. Which was a problem, since only assessments on my schedule counted.

The second test went about as well as the first. She was knocked out of contention for a B. Her classroom behavior turned disruptive. Once she interrupted class by loudly saying, "I don't know why we're doing this; I'm not going to learn it anyway." After the third test, even a C was impossible. Soon she dropped off the map, and I never saw her again.

As I entered her F in December, I vowed that what happened to her can never happen again. Although the next semester was starting soon and I had already written the syllabi, I decided to delete everything and start over, using a grading system that would not break a student just because they took a week longer to grasp calculus than others.

I had no idea what alternatives were available. But just days after submitting grades, I learned that Linda Nilson (a friend and mentor since my grad school days at Vanderbilt University) had written a book on specifications grading.[1] "Specs grading" was exactly what I needed: a system based on feedback loops, where students have the time and space to grow. I devoured the book in 2 days. Over 2 weeks, I engaged in a crash program to rebuild my next class with specs grading.

I had no idea what I was doing, and it showed. My design was far too complex (e.g., I had 68 learning objectives to assess) and I most definitely was not "saving time," as the subtitle of Nilson's book advertised. But it did actually *work*: Students resonated with having no points and no partial credit, but opportunities to redo anything. They started to relax and focus on learning rather than points. The narrative moved from "What do I need to make on the next test to get a B?" to things like "What can I do to understand vertex colorings better?"

Until ditching traditional grading, I hadn't realized just how much it was working against my professional goal of helping students become lifelong learners. By replacing traditional grading, even with a flawed system, my class became a safe space to make mistakes, an invitation to engage in a feedback loop that makes you a better thinker and problem-solver.

And most importantly, I felt if my calculus student had had this system, she wouldn't have been left behind.

Who This Book Is For, and What's in It

We hope that you resonate with our origin stories. Fortunately, alternative grading can be used successfully at any level, in any situation. The faculty you'll meet in this book come from the STEM disciplines, humanities, library science, and many other places. They work in a wide range of positions and institutions, and they teach classes ranging from tiny to enormous.

This book is intended as a resource:

- for higher education faculty (whether from four-year universities, small liberal arts colleges, two-year institutions, or others) who want something different and better for their students in terms of grades and assessments, and are curious about what's possible
- for faculty who are currently using alternative grading systems and want to improve them or learn more about other options
- for faculty who are skeptical about alternative grading approaches, but who are curious about our claims

Although the focus here is on faculty, anyone interested in these issues will find something interesting and thought-provoking, including students, administrators, and parents.

Here is how the book is structured:

- Chapter 1 is *where you are now*: an introduction to us and our ideas.
- Chapter 2 is about *how we got here*: the history of grades in higher education, and the pros and cons of our current methods.

- Chapter 3 introduces *a framework for alternatives*: the four pillars of alternative grading, based on effective assessment methods in use both in and outside of academia.
- Chapter 4 outlines what *we currently know about the effectiveness of alternative grading*: evidence that supports alternative approaches.
- Chapters 5 through 10 are the heart of the book, where we *put the theory into practice*: detailed examples of how alternative grading practices are used in all kinds of classroom environments and all kinds of institutions. In these chapters, you'll meet real faculty members who share how they use alternative grading, to give you a sense of what's possible and how you can use their ideas.
- Chapter 11 is a *workbook*: a step-by-step process for building a prototype of your own alternatively graded class.
- Chapter 12 gives *practical advice*: how to make your newly planned class work on a day-to-day basis.
- Chapter 13 *looks ahead*: a description of what to expect and identifying open questions.
- Finally, we end the book with an appendix containing answers to frequently asked questions, with references to where each is discussed in more detail.

A Word About Words

Before we continue, we need to say something about the words we'll use in this book.

In the past, we've used a common term to refer to alternative grading practices: *mastery grading*. This has been useful as an umbrella term covering a range of related practices. But there's also been a growing realization that it has issues. In this book, we will not be using the term *mastery grading* except as a historical reference or when quoting other works, and we are moving away from the use of that term in our own practice.

Mastery grading has been used in the past to refer to grading practices that promote growth and individual "mastery" of concepts in a course. Whereas traditional grading audits a student's abilities and leaves it at that, the term *mastery grading* is intended to point toward grading practices that promote continued development of those abilities so that they are eventually honed into comprehensive skill.

The term has done good work for us. It economically describes the idea that *all* students have the ability to grow and develop comprehensive skill in what they are studying. However, as the idea of mastery grading has evolved and its profile has risen, we have more and more frequently run into three major issues with that term.

First, we've seen mastery grading become conflated with other pedagogical ideas that also use the word *mastery*, such as *mastery learning, flipped mastery*, and *mastery-based testing*. These are all ideas with merit, and they have some roots in common with mastery grading. But none of them are what we mean by *mastery grading*.

Second, we've come to believe that the word *mastery* doesn't accurately describe what we're after. Of course we want students to "master" the material they are learning—eventually. But in reality, true mastery of a subject is something that often takes a lifetime to achieve and can look like many different things. Expecting real mastery of a subject in a single course seems unrealistic. It also mitigates against growth, since once you've "mastered" a subject, where do you go from there? It seems more conducive to lifelong learning to say that a successful experience in a course means you've started the journey toward "mastery" and are ready to continue exploring.

Finally, and perhaps most significantly, the word *mastery* carries with it some connotations that are highly charged and harmful. This requires a little more explanation.

There are two similar but very different meanings of the word *mastery* in English usage. One of those is "comprehensive skill" of a human being in a task or a subject of study. One "masters" proof by mathematical induction or the bass guitar, for example. This connotation is found in common academic concepts like the master's degree, mastery learning, and others. In this sense, *mastery* is a deeply human word that encapsulates the dignity and abilities of every learner.

But there is another connotation: the domination of one human being over another. This connotation directly leads to, and comes directly from, the concept of slavery and all other places where a person is the "master" of another person. It is an odious and inhuman concept, the very opposite of what we hope to achieve with "mastery grading." Sadly, this second meaning has found its way into common uses: for example, the term *master bedroom*, or the idea of *master/slave* in computing. Over the past few years, the use of the word *mastery* in those contexts has been stopped; most realtors now call it the *primary bedroom* instead, for example.

We reached out to people in our professional networks who we trust and respect for advice about how to handle the term *mastery grading*. They brought up the three issues we have outlined, as well as the point that words matter. *Mastery* is a harmful word that should not be used if there is a way to avoid it.

In this book, we make no attempt to invent a new term to take the place of *mastery grading*. We have tried, with the help of many others, and none of the proposed replacements captures the essence of what we mean without giving up some other essential aspect or introducing new cultural or linguistic baggage. We will refer to *alternative grading practices* as a whole when we need to.[2] More often, we'll use the names of specific systems like *standards-based grading*, *specifications grading*, and so on. We will focus on the common concepts that drive all of these, rather than trying to come up with a common name.

Notes

1. Nilson, 2014.
2. We realize that by calling these systems *alternative*, we are giving pride of place to the "traditional" grading systems that we are working to supplant. In the words of our collaborator Sharona Krinsky, we certainly hope that alternative grading systems become so well established that someday we can simply call them *grading*. But we also realize that traditional systems are the default in almost every institution, and so this book does indeed describe an alternative.

2

WHY DO WE GRADE?

T his book is about "alternative" grading practices. But alternatives to what? Our origin stories from the previous chapter involved reaching an impasse with "traditional" grading. Perhaps you're reading this book because you are at a similar impasse, and it's time for a change.

But what is "traditional" grading, and how did it become a tradition? In this chapter, we'll walk through the convoluted history of grading to see how and through whom it came to be traditional. We'll end with an honest look at the serious issues with traditional grading that motivate the kinds of changes we want to make.

What We Mean by "Traditional" Grading

With few exceptions, the assessment and grading systems that you have likely experienced look like the following:

- In a given class, students do various kinds of work, especially (but not limited to) timed quizzes and exams, done once with no reattempts allowed.
- Their work is given a point value or percentage by the instructor or a teaching assistant.
- Those numerical scores are run through a weighted average formula at the end of the term and translated into a letter grade for the course— A, B, C, D, or F—with perhaps a "plus" or "minus" attached.

This overall practice—assigning points to one-time assessments and aggregating those points into a letter grade for the course—is what we mean by "traditional" grading.

There are a myriad of variations on traditional grading. Indeed, a look through the syllabi for one student's courses from just one semester will likely reveal significant differences in grade policies. There will be widely varying quantities and types of assessments, different weights on the points for those assessments, and different formulas for determining course grades.

Just as important are two things that are absent from nearly all traditional grading practices:

- *There are no reattempts or revisions of work in traditional grading.* Assessment is "one-and-done": Students turn in the work once, it receives points or a percentage, and that is the end of it. That grade is permanently part of a student's record.
- *Student work does not typically get helpful feedback.* While instructors might give feedback, it is often something like an "X" put through incorrect work, or a one- or two-word interjection. It does not contain much information that tells the student how to improve. Even when instructors give longer feedback, if there are no revisions or reattempts allowed, then there are few ways to actually make that feedback *helpful* by putting it to use.

In other words, traditional grading lacks *feedback loops.* In a feedback loop, a learner makes an attempt to demonstrate their understanding, gets information on their efforts from a trusted source, mindfully analyzes the information, and then incorporates the result into a new attempt. We've outlined this in Figure 2.1.

Figure 2.1. A feedback loop.

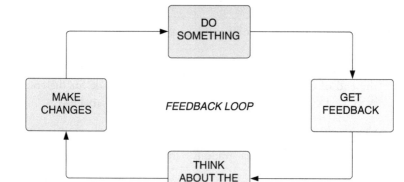

All human learning is predicated on feedback loops. From learning to walk through advanced studies, whatever you know, you know because of your engagement with a feedback loop. But as central as feedback loops are to learning, they are conspicuously absent from nearly all traditional grading systems. They do sometimes appear, for example on writing assignments where students iterate through multiple rounds of drafting and feedback, but the rarity of this approach makes it the exception that proves the rule. More often, feedback loops are at best indirect and ill-defined, with instructors hoping that students will somehow use grades to "do better" in a nebulous future.

When student work gets a grade, students are often in the dark about where the grade came from and what it means. There may or may not be a rubric for allocating points consistently, and if there is, it may not be shared with students. Point values are mysteriously allocated, and it's not clear why certain items are even on the assessment, or what the purpose of the assessment is in the first place.

As a result, traditional grading often is like a black box. The object is to put effort into it and get a number out. The connection between input and output is tenuous, and the outputs themselves are of questionable meaning.

How We Got Here

When taking a critical eye at traditional grading practices, they start to seem arbitrary and outlandish. How did we ever end up with such a system? Many take the existence of traditional grading for granted, as if it were inextricable from higher education itself. Let's look at the story of how traditional grading evolved, starting at the beginning.

Before 1800

The first university (the University of Bologna) was founded in 1088. In the European tradition, students attended lectures and engaged in discussions. Students typically had one examination in their entire college careers, a public oral exam at the very end of their education. A group of instructors, or third parties designated by the university, "graded" the exam simply by approving or disapproving of the student's performance.[1] (We see this tradition today embodied by PhD dissertation defenses.)

The European way of education made its way to what eventually became the United States. As early as 1646, Harvard College (founded just 10 years prior) conferred degrees by public oral examinations involving translation of the Old and New Testaments into Latin and having examinees "resolve them logically."[2] In 1650, Harvard instituted a policy increasing the frequency of examinations to once per year to gauge student progress. Examinations, both in America and in Europe, were at this time exclusively oral, in part because inexpensive writing technologies were still somewhat far off. (For example, lead pencils were not mass-produced until 1866.)[3]

There is no historical record of any formal structures for determining passing or failure on these examinations, and no grades as we now know them.

At Yale, in 1785, we have the earliest record of marks being given to student performance on their examinations. Ezra Stiles, the president of Yale, recorded that students received one of three descriptive adjectives to categorize their performance: *Optimi, Inferiores (Boni),* and *Pejores* ("The best," "Inferior but good," "Worse").[4]

The 19th Century

The structure, or lack thereof, in student examinations at universities led to significant dissatisfaction among professors. Many complained that the examinations were not thorough enough to provide a comprehensive picture of a student's learning. It is likely that in many cases, degrees were conferred on the basis of a student's social standing rather than—or perhaps in spite of—their performance on examinations.

Around the turn of the 19th century, universities began to become more systematic in the way students were evaluated. Advances in written communication technology (remember the pencils?) enabled a shift from oral to written examinations, and it was believed that these would provide more consistent results. Harvard began using written entrance exams in 1851. Other foundational American colleges did the same.

There was also a shift toward giving instructors more autonomy in evaluating student examinations. In 1830, a University of Michigan student publication reported on a proposal in which "examinations in the various branches should take place at the discretion of the professor in charge, and should be rather in the form of a quiz." Written examinations soon became the default at U.S. colleges and universities, and individual instructors had autonomy in giving and evaluating those exams.

The rise of written exams was paralleled by a burst of interest in marking systems. By 1813 Yale had begun marking exam scores on a 4-point scale and recording the average results in a ledger.[5] In the 1830s, Harvard shifted from descriptive adjectives to a 20-point scale used for exams in rhetoric and physics, to a 9-point scale, then a 4-point scale, then a 100-point scale. By 1877, this 100-point scale was used to rank students into six separate divisions, with "Division 1" corresponding to 90 or above, "Division 2" to

75 to 89, and so on. The University of Michigan reverted from numerical scales back to a "Pass"/"No Pass" system; 10 years later, they added a "condit" (for "conditional") modifier, and by 1895 the school had changed systems yet again, this time to a 5-point marking system for exams. Yale, around 1896, apparently had a brief flirtation with a grading scale in which 225 points was "passing."[6]

Sociological changes in the United States created even greater pressure for schools to change. By the end of the Civil War in 1865, grades in schools were commonplace but not standardized or compatible with each other. Owing in part to the creation of child labor laws, compulsory schooling, and an influx of immigrants, enrollments in primary and secondary schools in the United States tripled between 1870 and 1910. Schools began to become less personalized and more bureaucratic. Additionally, children became more likely to change schools frequently. There was therefore a growing need for the ability to communicate pedagogical information not only within a school but between schools using a standardized and scalable measure of student learning.

At the end of the 19th century, two events that are fundamental to our current "traditional" grading system took place. Harvard in 1884 instituted the first recorded use of a letter grade, in a correspondence referring to a student earning a B. Then, in 1896 at Mount Holyoke College, a grading system was introduced that combined letter grades, percentages, and descriptive adjectives. The letter grades were A, B, C, D, and E; Mount Holyoke changed the E grade to F because, it is believed, professors feared students would interpret *E* as meaning "Excellent."[7] In 1898, Mount Holyoke dropped the verbal descriptions from this system, leaving only the now familiar combination of letter grades and percentages.

The 20th Century and the Present

As grading systems became common in the late 1800s, the Second Industrial Revolution took hold in the United States and elsewhere and industrial ideas invaded education.

Foremost among those ideas was an obsession with scientific measurement. Dozens of psychological tests, such as the IQ test, were invented to measure intelligence, based on assumptions not only that a person's intelligence is fixed but also that different groups have higher innate intelligence than others. (Subsequently, the supposed objectivity of those measurements was used to justify racism and eugenics.) At the same time, the principles of scientific management (or "Taylorism"), wherein workers are given instructions to perform highly specialized tasks in specific ways to maximize efficiency, became popular. Grades became a popular metric for the "scientific" measurement of student abilities. Numerous studies appeared focusing on the ideal theoretical distribution of grades, such as the normal or "bell" curve.[8]

However, by the 1940s, a small but vocal body of writers began to emerge that pushed back on grades as a means of scientific measurement[9] and as a means of categorizing students. In one memorable publication in 1945, Dorothy De Zouche wrote:

> By the time that Jim [a student] has been told for twelve years that he is inferior, for that is what the I's on the report card mean to him regardless of what they mean to us, he finally comes to believe it, and if we have not succeeded in getting algebra or Spanish or world history across to him, we have at least succeeded in pounding into his head that one idea: he's inferior. And we put a diploma into his hand, grudgingly, mumbling apologies to each other as we do so, and send him out into the world to begin his battle already convinced that he is a failure.[10]

Instructors continued to question the purpose and effectiveness of grades into the second half of the 20th century. During the Vietnam War, in particular, students' military draft deferment was partially based on being a "student in good standing." Grading therefore became, literally, a life-or-death decision for instructors, and grade inflation became a concern. During this time, two important books were published that advocated the dismantling of grading systems altogether: *Teaching Without Grades*[11] and *Wad-ja-get?: The Grading Game in American Education*.[12] Some colleges founded during this period such as New College of Florida (1960)[13] and Evergreen State College (1967)[14] eschewed traditional grades in favor of narrative evaluations.

Today, despite nearly a century of growing objections, traditional grading practices persist, more or less unchanged since 1897. They have remained, not because they have stood the test of time and are the logical endpoints of centuries of mindful refinement, but primarily because they are useful—efficient, scalable, and interoperable—particularly so for the large bureaucracies that educational systems have become. But in order to attain that usefulness, grades have lost what pedagogical meaning they once had.

In recent years, some faculty have turned to alternative means of grading, including "ungrading," in search of a better way. In particular, the work of Alfie Kohn (particularly his seminal essay "The Case Against Grades")[15] has galvanized educators at all levels to think critically about traditional grading practices. A growing belief that traditional grading might not be best for students (or for instructors) along with a realization that traditional grading is not a sacred, unwritten law of higher education leads us to the present.

What's Good About Traditional Grading

You might be surprised to see this section. We'll go into detail on specific issues with traditional grading soon enough. But first it's worthwhile to highlight a few jobs that it does well, or at least which can be perceived as positive features.

First, as we have noted, traditional class grades help different schools communicate about a student's work. It's quite common today for college students to earn a degree through a patchwork of credits from different institutions. This is generally a positive development, given the complex lives of students. It's difficult to see how this would be possible if different colleges used different systems. Indeed, one of the most common criticisms against of grade alternatives such as narrative evaluations is the difficulty of transferring credits.

Second, traditional grading at the assignment level lets students calculate their "current grade" in a course at any time, giving a sense for "where they are at in the class" and whether they need to adjust their efforts. Whether the calculations for this purpose are meaningful, or even correct, is a separate question. But the "transparency" afforded by points and grade formulas gives students at least the perception of meaning and validity in their grades.

Third, traditional grading is the default, including and especially in learning management systems, which are almost universally designed to use numerical points and nothing else. Whatever flaws one might find in traditional grading, having to hack the gradebook is not one of them.

Fourth and finally, in a traditional grading system, points are fungible. This means that 1 point is 1 point, whether it was earned on a final exam or a homework set or through attendance or extra credit. Therefore a student can make up for poor performance in one part of a course by earning more points in another part. We note strenuously, though, that although students usually perceive this as positive, it's not clear at all that this promotes learning.

So traditional grading isn't all bad. But let's be honest: It also has serious issues that cannot be overlooked. Otherwise, we wouldn't be writing a book about alternatives. Like so many things in life, a story can help us uncover the issues and see how serious they are.

The Story of Alice and Bob

Alice and Bob are students in a class with a traditional grading setup: The course grade is determined entirely by two midterm exams and one cumulative final exam. The midterms are worth 100 points each, and the final is worth 200 points. There are no do-overs or revisions available; it's all one-and-done. Table 2.1 shows Alice and Bob's results at the end of the semester.

Clearly, these two students haven't followed the same path. Alice got off to a slow start, but she has grown, and, if the cumulative final is to be believed, she has come to understand the course content thoroughly. Bob, on the other hand, seems to be in the same state as he was at the beginning, and not an especially great state at that.

Alice and Bob are on very different trajectories. And yet if we use the traditional method of computing course grades—averaging all the scores together—they both end up in the same place: 60%, which in most courses is barely passing.

Traditional "weighted average grading," in which all of a student's points are averaged together to determine a final grade, doesn't reveal these differences. In fact, it buries them. Alice's early struggles have doomed her to the same barely passing grade as Bob, even though she's aced a cumulative final. Not even the individual scores on the exams tell the whole story.

What *is* Alice's story here? Did she struggle early with the material and then gradually came to understand it, through perseverance and practice? Did she have a strong grasp on the content all along, but was sick on exam days and not at her best? Did she have to miss the first exam to take care of a family member or be present at a job? Did the exams require extensive written work, but English is not her first language? We don't know, and the grade isn't talking.

And what about Bob? What do his "60%" scores mean? Did he learn 60% of the topics in the course extremely well but had no clue on the other 40%? (If so, which of those 60% are critical topics, and which aren't?) Or did he learn a little bit of everything at a mediocre level and attained his grade through partial credit, even though he doesn't truly understand anything well? Or, like Alice, did he actually have a strong grasp on most of the content, but something unrelated got in the way? Again, we don't know, and the grade is silent.

Like a black hole whose gravity is so strong that not even light can escape, the grading system collapses all of the information about student learning into a single number, and no information about Alice or Bob emerges.

TABLE 2.1
Alice and Bob's Grades

	Midterm 1 *(100 pts)*	*Midterm 2* *(100 pts)*	*Cumulative Final* *(200 pts)*	*Total* *(400 pts)*
Alice	0	40	200	240 (60%)
Bob	60	60	120	240 (60%)

Alice and Bob are not the same. And yet, from the standpoint of the grading system, they *are* the same. Growth is, literally, not part of the equation.

The Problems With Traditional Grading

Alice and Bob's story points to several important issues with traditional grading systems. These may not be surprising, but let's examine them in detail to see just how harmful they can be.

Traditional Grading Misrepresents Learning

As we saw with Alice and Bob, a grade of "60%" on an exam or in a course tells us nothing about what a student has learned or needs to work on. It only tells us that the student earned six tenths of the maximum amount of points available. This is nice if our primary interest is filling out a gradebook. But if we want students to *grow* in their learning, it's not useful at all.

The fact that most if not all of the information about student learning and growth is hidden by traditional grades makes traditional systems prone to two types of errors:

- *False positives.* These occur when a student earns a grade that overstates their actual level of learning. In traditional grading, false positives can happen because points are fungible, and therefore a student can mask poor skill in one (potentially crucial) area of a course by earning more points in another (less crucial) part of the course or through partial credit, causing the grade to become disconnected from learning. This might be what happened with Bob.
- *False negatives.* These occur when a student earns a grade that understates their actual level of learning, as likely happened with Alice. In traditional grading, false negatives can happen because of the focus on one-and-done assessments and averaging, which permanently penalizes students for not performing on the instructor's terms. Even if any helpful feedback is given on these assessments, there is no means of acting on the feedback to improve one's skill. This, too, causes a disconnect between the grade and learning.

Traditional Grading Misuses Statistics

Typically, traditional grading systems use points to evaluate student work. Those points are, of course, numbers, and we average those numbers to determine a course grade. Here we encounter a technical but serious issue: Although grades are numbers, they are not numerical data, and averaging them leads to nonsensical results.

Data come in two basic varieties: numerical and categorical. Numerical data are the results of a measurement or a count, while categorical data are names or labels. For example, the number of words in this chapter is numerical information, but the ZIP code of the location where it was written is categorical.

Notice that not all numbers are numerical data. ZIP codes, for example, are numbers. But they are categorical, not numerical. We can average all the ZIP codes in the state of Michigan, if we wanted. The answer is 48982.7354, which rounds to 48983. There is no location in Michigan with a ZIP code of 48983; even if there were, it wouldn't necessarily be at the "center" of Michigan.

And there's the problem with grades: Grades, while numbers, are not numerical data but rather categorical. We typically grade with categories in mind and, perhaps using a rubric, translate those categories into points. For example, in a 50-point assignment we might say that a total of 50/50 is in the "excellent" category, a 40/50 is "good but not great," and so on. Or we might grade that assignment by having a rubric that allocates 10 points for the introduction to an essay, 10 points for grammar and spelling, and so on, and then totaling up the points earned on each part. In either case, the instructor is either granting or withholding points based on whether the student did or didn't do something in the professor's view. So the points are labels that represent quality, not the result of a measurement; and that makes them categorical data.

As labels, points can have meaning (although the same meaning can be conveyed much more clearly in words). But as inputs to mathematical calculations, they don't. Computing averages of the categorical data called *grades* makes no more sense than averaging ZIP codes.

Traditional Grading Is Inequitable

Equity in grading means ensuring that students have access to the same opportunities to learn and succeed, and particularly involves removing barriers to learning that can be presented by grading systems. Joe Feldman's book *Grading for Equity*[16] provides three clear criteria that equitable grading systems must meet: They must be *accurate*, *bias-resistant*, and *motivational*. We'll dig into these in chapter 4, where we argue that alternative grading is well aligned with these criteria.

Traditional grading, however, is anything but equitable. We've already seen how it is inaccurate: Student learning is hidden behind a mash-up of points, partial credit, and averaging. Remember Alice and Bob: Do their grades accurately reflect what they've learned? Traditional grading disproportionately benefits students who learn fast, or more likely, who've already learned the material or know how to "play the game" due to their educational or family background.

Traditional grades are also bias-prone. By including points for nonacademic factors like extra credit, attendance, participation, or meeting deadlines, traditional grades can reflect a student's environment and behavior rather than what they actually know. Making decisions about participation points, deadline extensions, and other such items reflects an instructor's implicit assumptions and unconscious biases rather than a student's actual knowledge.

Finally, traditional grading is demotivating and discourages students from learning for its own sake. This is especially visible in the permanent penalty incurred by averaging early attempts, while a student is first learning. This penalizes students like Alice who need time to learn and rewards speed and prior knowledge. The "one-and-done" approach to assessments discourages students from engaging in a feedback loop. Instead, it leads to a familiar outcome after handing back exams: Half of them end up in the trash bin on the way out the door. It shouldn't be surprising that students aren't motivated by a system that reduces their efforts to a single numerical score that can easily fail to show their real learning, and with no opportunities for improvement.

It's actually even worse than that: A classic study by Butler and Nisan[17] often replicated, showed that students who received grades on an activity, even when paired with feedback, were less intrinsically motivated on subsequent activities. One possible reason is that students see grades as a judgment about their own selves. This is easily visible in students' reactions to poor grades.

The practice of "curving" grades by adjusting them to a fixed distribution, usually a normal distribution or "bell curve," is also demotivating and inequitable. Rooted in the Taylorist ideologies and scientific measurement craze of the early 1900s, grade-curving concerns itself with comparing one student to another, not with determining what a student has learned. It assumes that there is such a thing as an "average" student and a predetermined "ideal" distribution centered around that average. As Benjamin Bloom wrote in 1968,

> We have for so long used the normal curve in grading students that we have come to believe in it. . . . There is nothing sacred about the normal curve. It is the distribution most appropriate to chance and random activity. Education is a purposeful activity and we seek to have the students learn what we have to teach. . . . In fact, we may even insist that our educational efforts have been unsuccessful to the extent to which our distribution of achievement approximates the normal distribution.[18]

Traditional grading as a whole suffers from many problems that amount to penalizing students who've received unequal opportunities.

And More!

It gets worse: Traditional grading promotes unhealthy student–faculty relationships, as any instructor who has ever argued with a student about a grade can attest. It also promotes unhealthy relationships between students through its emphasis on competition and ranking. For the same reasons, traditional grading also promotes academic dishonesty; the system promotes earning the maximum amount of points with the minimum amount of effort. Finally, traditional grading can be a tremendous waste of time for faculty, who are consigned to spending hours splitting hairs over whether a student should earn 7 points or 8 points out of 12. That's time that would be much better spent actually helping students grow.

Summary

Traditional grading, with its focus on one-and-done assessments graded with points which are converted into letter grades using points-based statistics, is a mess.

Traditional grading is more a result of uncontrolled faculty experiments, the influences of early 20th-century capitalist ideology, and sheer imitation than any sort of mindful practice. Traditional grading is shot through with critical flaws including a detachment from learning, anomalous statistical processes, demotivation, and conflict. You can likely think of even more problems for this list. And in a time where equity in higher education is receiving long-overdue attention, traditional grading violates any reasonable standard of equity.

Perhaps most damning of all is the apparent fact that nowhere in the history or practice of traditional grading do students and their growth make any contribution, or even an appearance, except as those upon whom this deeply flawed system is inflicted.

If traditional grading were on trial, there would be more than enough evidence to convict it. The need to replace it with something better has never been stronger. The good news is that we *can* replace it with grading methods that are better in every sense. In the next chapter, we'll explore what this can look like.

Notes

1. Smallwood, 1935.
2. Smallwood, 1935.
3. Coles, 1999.
4. Durm, 1993; Smallwood, 1935.
5. Smallwood, 1935.
6. Durm, l993.
7. Palmer, 2010.
8. Becker, 2003.
9. For an example, see Crooks, 1933.
10. De Zouche, 1945, pp. 339–340.
11. Marshall, 1968.
12. Kirschenbaum et al., 1971.
13. New College of Florida, n.d.
14. Evergreen State College, 2023.
15. Kohn, 2011.
16. Feldman, 2018.
17. Butler & Nisan, 1986.
18. Bloom, 1968, p. 2. See Bowen & Cooper, 2021, for an even more detailed breakdown of how curving is inequitable.

3

A FRAMEWORK FOR
ALTERNATIVE GRADING

W e ended the previous chapter by examining the flaws in traditional grading systems. It's now time to start thinking about how to do better and build a system of grading that promotes learning and growth. In this chapter, we'll isolate key elements of "better" grading systems and see how these elements are already used outside of traditional classrooms. We'll then introduce some existing models of alternative grading that will appear throughout the rest of the book: standards-based grading (SBG), specifications grading, and ungrading. Finally, we'll distill all of the characteristics that make these alternative systems work into a framework we call the four pillars of alternative grading.

How to Improve Grading

The simplest formulation of how to build a better grading system might be to look at all the flaws of traditional grading from chapter 2 and do the opposite. When we do so, we find two main areas where we can rapidly improve:

- *Make grades meaningful by connecting them directly to demonstrated learning, using clear criteria for what is expected and what is satisfactory.* Traditional grading has lots of false positives and negatives and serious issues with demotivation because grades are disconnected from learning and growth. Instead, we should remove the guesswork. The purpose of each assessment and each item on an assessment should be understood, the requirements for student success should be clear and easy to understand, and the results should speak directly to what went well and what needs more work.

- *Put feedback loops at the center.* Humans fundamentally learn through feedback loops, but traditional grading keeps students out of such loops. Instead, a student's grade should be the result of good-faith attempts, followed by feedback and opportunities to continue the feedback loop.

If this approach to grading sounds like a fantasy, there is good news: It's not. In fact we've seen it before, all around us.

We've Seen This Before

Methods of evaluating student work that use these basic ideas not only exist but are common both in and outside of education. Here are just a few examples that should be very familiar to you.

Kindergarten Report Cards

Let's start at the beginning: kindergarten. Kindergarten report cards are a model of the grading system we are trying to construct. A typical one, in part, might look like Table 3.1.

Notice that the criteria, or "standards," for what kids should be able to do is clearly stated using plain descriptive language that a kindergartner can understand: *I can count to 100 by 10s.*

So are the descriptions of the kids' current statuses with those standards: "Does with help," "Does independently," "Needs assistance," and so on. There's not much left to the imagination, which is helpful to the kids and their parents.

Docs it seem likely that kids in kindergarten are given only one shot to recite the alphabet in order, and the results of that attempt are what's on the card? No, kids work on these skills every day, and the report card shows the results of either their most recent attempt or their best attempt. It shows what the kids have eventually been able to do, through regular engagement in a feedback loop.

TABLE 3.1
Part of a Kindergarten Report Card

Skill	Status	Notes
I can recite the alphabet in order.	Does independently	Sings the alphabet song during station time
I can count to 100 by 10s.	Does with help	Needs frequent prompting

Peer Review

Stepping forward a few decades, most instructors in higher education are intimately familiar with the process of submitting articles to research journals to be peer-reviewed. This process, too, models the kind of "grading" system we wish to see.

Most journals have sections of their websites with clear standards for what constitutes an acceptable publication, with specific criteria for word count, font size, structural elements, and so on. Certainly, following these instructions doesn't guarantee publication. But the minimal standards for publication, at least, are clear and easy to access.

Peer review is also the epitome of a feedback loop. The vast majority of journals do not assign numerical grades to submitted manuscripts. Instead, submissions are given labels that indicate what needs to happen next: "Rejected," "Major Revision," "Minor Revision," or "Accepted," for example. Unless the response from the journal is "Rejected," the submission process isn't one-and-done. After getting the initial review, the authors use feedback from the reviewers to improve the work and resubmit it, as many times as needed until it's "good enough."

Personnel Evaluations

Finally, personnel evaluations, both in academia and in the "real world," also follow this model.

As long as the organization isn't dysfunctional, each employee has a clear job description listing their responsibilities. There may also be a curated list of additional criteria describing what all employees need to do (and not do) in order to get a positive review. That list does not include nonwork-related items, because including those introduces tremendous bias. At review time, the employee gets a 360-degree review from (among others) their managers, who give a thorough verbal or written report on their progress. These almost exclusively do not use points, nor are the results used to rank employees. (Systems that do use points, and then use points to rank—and fire—employees, such as the notorious "rank and yank" system,[1] have fallen into almost universal disrepute.) And as with other examples, annual review is not one-and-done. The purpose is to invite the employee into a feedback loop where the results of the last evaluation are productively enacted before the next one.

Models of Alternative Grading

Meaningful, feedback-loop-based evaluation methods are not only common outside of formal educational coursework (minus kindergarten), they appear to be the default. Only in school (or school-like settings such as certification exams), it seems, are individuals evaluated by "traditional" assessments, despite the fact that these are rarely seen in the real world for which we supposedly prepare students.

But in fact, even the use of traditional methods inside formal schooling is beginning to change. Three broad models of assessment and grading have risen to prominence in recent years, each aiming to connect grading to learning, and learning to feedback loops. They play a major role in the remainder of this book, and so we'll describe each of them by name here.

Standards-Based Grading

SBG is a system that can be used in both K–12 and higher education. In SBG, the instructor creates a list of clear *standards* that describe specific things a student will learn to do. Each assignment is aligned with one or more of these standards, and each standard is assessed multiple times, offering multiple attempts to meet the standards without penalty. Rather than using points or percentages, the instructor reports progress on meeting each standard and gives clear, helpful feedback on student work. Marks for each standard typically take forms such as "Meets this standard" or "New attempt required." An instructor's gradebook records a student's history of progress on each standard, across all assignments. Final grades are based on how many, or which, standards a student has met by the end of the semester, regardless of whether it took few or many attempts to meet them. SBG can be used in many kinds of classes, but is especially useful in courses where there are distinct skills to be learned and practiced. We'll examine case studies of classes that use SBG in chapter 5.

A variation that applies the ideas of SBG only to tests or exams is called *standards-based testing*. SBT is an excellent first step into using alternative grading. Because it involves changing only how tests or quizzes are graded, it can be added into an already-built class without much fuss. We'll see an example of SBT in chapter 10.

Specifications Grading

"Specs" grading is another approach to providing students with clear criteria and actionable feedback. Linda Nilson developed "specs grading" and describes it in a book of the same name.[2] Instructors create a list of *specifications* that describe the qualities and characteristics of a successful submission for an assignment. Student work is graded holistically based on those specifications, earning a single mark: "Satisfactory" or "Not Yet." Students have the chance to use feedback by revising and resubmitting for full credit. Specifications grading is especially useful with projects, portfolios, essays, and other assessments where process and communication are key.

Some other assessment systems that are organized in similar ways include contract grading and labor-based contracts.[3]

Ungrading

Ungrading rejects grades entirely (or at least to the extent that is possible). Ungraded classes eliminate grades from as many assignments as possible and focus on feedback. Philosophically, ungraders focus on reducing the trauma that can be associated with traditional grades by attempting to refocus power dynamics in their classes. Instructors often provide a list of criteria or a narrative description for final grades, and some instructors build this list collaboratively with students, leading to an increasing common name: "collaborative grading." Ungraded classes often involve two key features: First, instructors hold periodic meetings with students (or ask students to write reflective essays) in order to come to an agreement on a student's current level of progress. Second, students construct a final portfolio of work that shows how they have grown and/or met key course objectives. It is possible, and often desirable, to include ungraded aspects in most courses by removing grades from some assignments to help refocus attention on feedback. In this book, we will highlight some opportunities to reduce the presence of grades in this way. If this intrigues you, an excellent resource for ungraded classes is Susan Blum's *Ungrading*.[4]

The Four Pillars of Alternative Grading

The general ideas and examples we've seen so far may seem enticing. But how do you turn them into a syllabus and make them work for you and your students? Here we'll distill the key ideas we've identified for an ideal grading system into a general and actionable framework for alternative grading practices: a map that stakes out and identifies the overall ideas that unify all the different approaches we've seen, with room for interpretation and flexibility.

Four distinct common elements, which we can apply to grading, emerge from these approaches:

1. *Student work is evaluated using clearly defined and context-appropriate content standards for what constitutes acceptable evidence of learning.* Our examples of effective evaluation practices are effective in part because both the person doing the work and the person assessing it are clear on what matters. Everyone is aware of what sort of learning or growth needs

to be evident, as well as the evidence that needs to be presented. The standards used in evaluation make these clear; and the standards are professionally appropriate and scaled to the level of the student. In addition, these standards should be *taught* and *practiced* in the class as content, rather than behaviors or ideas that we expect students to already know or assume they will pick up without help.[5]

2. *Students are given helpful, actionable feedback that the student can and should use to improve their learning.* Feedback is the beating heart of all of these practices, and helpful feedback that drives a feedback loop is at the center. To be helpful, feedback must inform students about what was good in their work as well as what they need to work on, and how to act on that information. In alternative grading, students' work opens up a conversation and initiates a feedback loop.

3. *Student work doesn't have to receive a mark, but if it does, the mark is a progress indicator toward meeting a standard and not an arbitrary number.* We will often use the word *mark* in this book, instead of *grade*, to mean "an indicator of progress placed on student work." In traditional grading, the mark is typically a percentage or point value; in other systems, it might be a brief description ("Satisfactory," "Needs Revision," etc.) or a character symbol ("S," "R," "☺").[6] Alternative grading practices acknowledge that marks, if given, are merely at-a-glance summaries of the feedback indicating the progress students have made toward meeting the clear standards previously described. They are there primarily for convenience and for entry into a gradebook and augment, rather than replace, feedback.

4. *Students can reassess work without penalty, using the feedback they receive, until the standards are met or exceeded.* Feedback loops are at the center of alternative grading practices. There is no loop without the iteration provided by reassessments of work that doesn't meet the standards. In fact, the defining ingredient of all effective learning processes—from kindergarten to the tenure and promotion process—is the feedback loop, enabled by the ability to reattempt work that would benefit from it. Learners' growth resides in the act of *trying again*. And we don't penalize this, because who penalizes growth?

Rather than point to these four common elements and devise a new grading system with a cool name, we think it's more beneficial to set up a big tent with a lot of room underneath for anybody who wants to implement these elements in their grading processes, no matter what they call it. However, we'll give the tent itself a cool name: *the four pillars of alternative grading* (see Figure 3.1).

Figure 3.1. The four pillars of alternative grading.

This work is licensed under a Creative Commons Attribution-ShareAlike 4.0 International License.

The four pillars model shows the components of a grading system (or any kind of assessment process) that centers on the growth of the learner: *grading for growth*. The four pillars (and the "roof" that indicates the centrality of feedback loops) provide us with guideposts for making grading better. They show us how to move away from the ineffective methods of the past and into grading processes that are more humane, more informative, and more effective at enabling real lifelong learning. The rest of this book works out the details of what the four pillars model looks like in actual practice, and how you can make it work for yourself.

Before we proceed, a very important note. Not everyone is able, in their specific professional situation, to implement a grading system that invokes all four pillars. For example, you might be in a position where you *must* use points to grade student work, or you can't build reassessments without penalty into the course. Maybe the institution prohibits it; maybe you just don't have the time or energy. Whatever your case is, even if you focus on just one of the four pillars in your classes, you are doing great work and helping students. If the only thing you can manage right now is giving feedback that's more helpful, or clarifying your standards and making those more visible, this is a major step in the right direction.

Again: *You do not have to go all-in on the four pillars in order to drastically improve your grading system.* As you continue to read about instructors who have changed their grading, simply ask the question *What can I do, given my situation and the time and tools at my disposal?* Improving grading to make it focus on growth can be done in small increments.

These four pillars are, we hope, ideas that can carry you as far into this world as you would like. Any changes you can make that are in alignment with them help move the needle in the right direction and bring some good into the world. You don't need to jump in wholesale. You also don't need to do things just so; as you'll see in the case studies, there are as many ways to adopt these principles as there are instructors, including partial implementations and mixtures of many ideas.

Indeed, you may notice that some of the case studies that form the core of this book include elements that seem to go against our advice or ignore one of these pillars. In each case, the instructor has made a deliberate choice to use what works best for them and their students. We hope that you always feel free to do what is best in your situation, inspired by the principles we've outlined here.

The Prime Directive

In the *Star Trek* science fiction universe, there's one rule that can never be violated: the Prime Directive, which states that Starfleet personnel and spacecraft cannot interfere with the normal development of any alien society they encounter.

In addition to the four pillars, we think there is an unofficial but extremely important "fifth pillar" for alternative grading, a guideline that can make or break any attempt to implement alternative grading practices in real life. It's our own Prime Directive for alternative grading, and it states:

Keep It Simple

In our experience, the greatest enemy of grading for growth is *complexity*. Our origin stories from chapter 1 share the experience of first attempts at alternative grading that were unwieldy and overcomplicated. Make no mistake: As you learn about alternative grading, you'll be tempted to create a system that tries to do too much, and if you're not careful, the resulting complexity will defeat the purpose of the system.

Observe the Prime Directive and *keep it simple*:

- If you are starting from a completely traditional grading system, rather than doing a full redesign right now, consider implementing small, concrete steps that address some but not necessarily all of the four pillars. For example, you might write a short list of two or three standards before your next class meeting that describe the intended learning outcomes of the class, and share those with students. Or you might allow students to reattempt or revise one important assignment. As James Lang powerfully argued in his book *Small Teaching*,[7] small but purposeful changes can make a big difference.

- If you are committed to doing a complete redesign of your grading system, examine your work at regular intervals and ask yourself what you could *remove* from it rather than add to it. Do you need students to complete 10 essays, when five would do? Do you really need to have 68 content standards? And so on.

- Always look at your course from the students' point of view, and if it feels overcomplicated from that standpoint, it is.

Leonardo da Vinci said that "simplicity is the ultimate sophistication." It's also the ultimate life hack for taking on a big project, like changing your grading system, without overwhelming yourself. And in the end, simplicity is the ultimate way to build trust with your students as you take them on this journey with you.

Notes

1. If you're not familiar with "rank and yank," check out http://performance-appraisals.org/faq/rankyank.htm.

2. Nilson, 2014.

3. Inoue, 2019.

4. Blum, 2020.

5. Some experts are dubious about this level of structure in the evaluation of work (e.g., see Kohn, 2006). However, in any form of assessment, even if you're not using a rubric, you still have a sense of what matters and are making decisions accordingly. Those decisions aren't just made by "gut feel" but through standards that you, as a content expert, believe are appropriate for determining quality. In other words, we're all using standards, and it's simply beneficial for students if we are transparent about the standards that we are using.

6. The word *grade* can be confusing because it has different but related meanings: It could mean the mark on student work ("I got a grade of 87 on the exam"), the final result of a course ("My grade in the class was B–"), or a student's academic level ("My son is in the eighth grade"). We adopt the term *mark* to mean the first of these.

7. Lang, 2016.

4

DOES ALTERNATIVE GRADING WORK?

Now that you've been introduced to the four pillars of alternative grading and seen a few general frameworks, you might be wondering: Does this work? If I change how I assess and grade, will the benefits outweigh the costs? And is there any research backing up these ideas, or is it all hype?

We'll address these questions now, starting with a general overview of research on learning, motivation, anxiety, and emerging research on grading and alternative approaches. Since questions about research often arise in criticism of alternative grading, we'll give some research-backed responses to common objections to alternative systems. We end with a detailed discussion of one of the most important and salient features of alternative grading approaches: *equity*.

A Word About Research

In this chapter, we'll provide short summaries of the most relevant and immediately useful results. The notes provide references for those interested in digging deeper.

At the time of this writing, peer-reviewed research on alternative grading is still emerging. It is mostly "action research" focusing on practical experiences on a small scale. This work is useful for learning and inspiration and hints at significant future results. However, since the field is relatively new and still developing, we will focus on the research from much larger and well-studied areas such as motivation and self-regulation. This work arises from psychology and related fields and provides clear and compelling arguments for alternative grading.

What Research Says About Academic Performance

Do students learn more, and "perform better," in an alternative grading system than in a traditional one? To think about this question, it's helpful to look at research on specific practices that improve learning and see how alternative grading, guided by the four pillars, supports them. For more information on these and other practices, we recommend *Make It Stick: The Science of Successful Learning*.[1] We will examine three practices in particular.

Retrieval practice takes place when you attempt to recall information you have learned, without prompts or materials. This can be done, for example, by self-quizzing. The benefits of the "testing effect" that result from retrieval practice are well established in cognitive science.[2] Among those benefits are improvements to long-term memory,[3] exam performance,[4] and the ability to transfer knowledge.[5]

Spaced repetition is the practice of engaging in repeated review sessions of content, spread out over time. The opposite of spaced repetition is *massed practice*. Research showing the superiority of spaced repetition over massed practice, particularly for long-term memory, dates back to the late 19th-century work of Hermann Ebbinghaus, famous for the "Ebbinghaus forgetting curve" (see Figure 4.1). That model shows that while human memory decays exponentially (the leftmost curve), we forget things at a slower rate, and retain more of what we learn, when we practice recalling it repeatedly (subsequent curves).[6]

Figure 4.1. The Ebbinghaus forgetting curve.

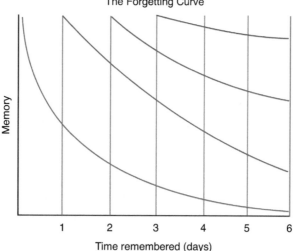

Interleaving, also known as *mixed practice*, takes place when different topics are part of the same practice or review session, as opposed to sessions being focused on a single area (known as *blocked practice*). Like retrieval practice and spaced repetition, interleaving benefits learning and performance in many different forms and settings.[7] Interleaving has been shown to have benefits beyond even the spaced repetition that it naturally causes.[8]

All three of these powerful learning practices are supported by the feedback loops that lie at the heart of alternative grading systems that use the four pillars. In these classes, students constantly engage in feedback loops, causing them to revisit and reflect on their past work (retrieval practice) at different points in time during the semester (spaced repetition). Students typically study new topics and reassess older ones simultaneously (interleaving). In short, the four pillars naturally incentivize some of the best practices for learning.

Feedback loops also support other effective learning practices. These include *elaboration*, in which the learner reflects on and specifies the relationship between what they know and what they are about to learn,[9] and *calibration*, where the learner rectifies what they think they know with what their work and feedback actually reflect.[10]

By contrast, traditional grading systems disincentivize these beneficial practices, primarily because of one-and-done assessments and the absence of reassessment. But by placing feedback loops at their center, alternative grading systems not only support positive learning practices, they invite and normalize them.

We address academic performance in the sense of final grades later in the section on grade inflation.

What Research Says About Motivation

Another question often asked about alternative grading is whether it improves student *engagement*. That term, while extraordinarily common, is devilishly hard to define. A related term with a longer and more solid pedigree in psychology research is *motivation*. If *engagement* is a state of committed involvement in which one is "entirely present and not somewhere else,"[11] then *motivation* is the psychological force that compels people to enter that state.

The body of published literature on motivation is vast, and we will focus on the work of Edward Deci and Richard Ryan on self-determination theory (SDT),[12] which proposes that human beings have three basic psychological needs: competence, autonomy, and relatedness. *Competence* refers to "the experience of behavior as effectively enacted"[13]—in other words, knowing that one has done well in performing a task. *Autonomy* is "the experience of behavior as volitional and reflectively self-endorsed"[14]—for example, when one willingly devotes time and effort to one's studies. Finally, *relatedness* refers to an experience of belonging, of being connected to other people and to the contexts in which one is learning.

According to SDT, satisfaction of these three basic needs promotes optimal motivation. And it is from SDT that we get the concepts of *intrinsic* and *extrinsic motivation* that describe performing a task for its own sake or because one is motivated by external factors, respectively. The more fully the fundamental psychological needs are satisfied, the more likely intrinsic motivation becomes.

Even a superficial look at alternative grading might convince you that it promotes motivation. Establishing clear standards and encouraging reassessment until the standards are met supports competence. On the other hand, in traditional grading, partial credit leads to partial understanding without real underlying competence (remember the issues with false positives we saw in chapter 2). Giving students the ability to choose their own path for how and when they assess supports autonomy, unlike in traditional grading where a fixed assessment schedule and averaging can sink a person's grade due to one bad test score. And the tendency of alternative grading to enable healthy professional relationships between students and the professor builds relatedness.

But research says much more about the connection between grades and motivation. Perhaps the most iconic study in this area is by Ruth Butler and Mordecai Nisan.[15] Their study took 261 sixth-graders and gave them two tasks: the first, referred to as a "quantitative" task, involved constructing words in various ways. The second was more "qualitative," leading students through some items from a divergent thinking test. The students were randomly assigned to three groups: one that received only written feedback on their work, another that received numerical grades, and a third that received neither feedback nor numerical grades.

At the end, all students completed a questionnaire asking intrinsic motivation–related questions. Butler and Nisan found that the group receiving only written feedback showed significantly higher expressed interest in the tasks than either the numerical-grade group or the no-feedback group and were much more willing to volunteer for further tasks. Additionally, students in the numerical-grade group were less likely to attribute success to their own skill than the other groups. Finally, the majority of students, including over three fourths of the numerical-grade group, said they preferred getting feedback instead of numbers or nothing. In other words, feedback without numerical scores promoted intrinsic motivation, while numerical grades (or the absence of feedback altogether) suppressed it. Students getting feedback also happened to perform better on the tasks than either of the other two groups. In fact, there was no statistically significant difference in performance between the group getting only numerical scores and the group getting nothing.[16]

What Research Says About Educational Environment and Student Well-Being

The features that make alternative grading effective at improving learning and motivation can also support student well-being by promoting student-centered learning environments and reducing stress and anxiety.

Student-Centered Learning Environments
At their best, alternatively graded classes aren't just about grades. They also foster a more student-centered learning environment. Buckmiller et al. noticed that teachers who used SBG in K–12 classrooms also used the grading to improve instruction:

> Teachers in such environments recognize that regular formative feedback improves instruction and guides student growth. There is also a constructivist element to SBG; understanding the role that learners' ever-changing mental schemas play in cognitive growth can powerfully inform educational practice, and instructors' abilities to respond effectively to these evolving needs can be enhanced by adopting such assessment models.[17]

The four pillars enable this ability to respond to student needs. By framing progress in terms of clear standards, instructors can easily identify which topics individual students or the class as a whole need to review. For students, feedback and reassessment give them a chance to improve, thereby making even a "summative" exam into a formative chance to learn more.

Thus, alternative grading lets the instructor achieve what Alley called for:

> Assessment is far too undervalued as a potentially active tool of quality student-centered learning. More than merely an instrument for measuring student mastery, it can and should be woven into the basic fabric of the teaching and learning process so that it both reflects and enhances learning.[18]

A desire to use evidence-based practices to improve student learning and well-being is one of the reasons that we also often see alternative grading paired with active learning pedagogies that are shown to have large effects on student learning.[19]

Stress and Anxiety

One thing is crystal clear from implementations of alternative grading: Students self-report lower stress in classes that use alternative grading than those using traditional practices. Nearly all of the published articles on alternative grading mention self-reported lower stress, usually on student evaluations of teaching.[20]

The phenomenon of lower self-reported stress makes logical sense: When students know that there are multiple chances to reassess without penalty (via the fourth pillar), then each assessment has lower stakes, and hence there should be lower stress. This reasoning is often seen in comments on student evaluations.

We also have empirical data to support those perceptions. In one study,[21] students took instructor-created surveys at different points in the semester. They self-reported how much anxiety they felt before exams in an SBG class versus other classes, and also self-reported how their anxiety changed throughout the semester. Students in SBG classes overwhelmingly reported less anxiety before exams compared to traditionally graded classes. Furthermore, students in SBG classes started the semester significantly more anxious but ended significantly less anxious, compared to their counterparts in traditionally graded classes. The latter result is likely due to SBG students being unfamiliar with the system itself and their anxiety declining once they got comfortable with it.

A particularly well-studied form of anxiety is *test anxiety*, an all-too-familiar state induced by potential negative consequences resulting from performance on a timed assessment. Test anxiety has a huge range of symptoms: difficulty concentrating, panic attacks, racing thoughts, and headaches are just a few of the more common ones. These can happen both before and during assessments.

It's well established that students who have higher test anxiety perform worse than those who don't.[22] It's also known that female students tend to have higher levels of test anxiety than male students, although this doesn't necessarily correspond to lower performance, due to a variety of confounding factors.[23] There is debate about why this happens, but students regularly report that the symptoms directly interfere with their ability to think, understand, and recall.

In a study of early curriculum math classes taught using SBG, Lewis administered validated pre- and postclass surveys that measure test anxiety. Students took the postsurvey twice: once with instructions to complete the survey as it applied to their SBG class and once as it applied to their non-SBG classes. The results were impressive. On the postsurveys, students showed much lower test anxiety in the SBG classes than in their other classes.

In the SBG classes, test anxiety decreased throughout the semester, while for non-SBG classes, it increased. Female students reported higher test anxiety on the presurveys, but the postsurveys showed that "the difference [in test anxiety] between male and female students was eliminated in the SBG course but persisted in students' other courses." [24]

Lewis found that asking students to think separately about their SBG and non-SBG classes was critical: If students weren't asked to think separately about the classes, then the test anxiety instrument showed higher test anxiety throughout the semester. It's possible that the students' test anxiety in their non-SBG classes was responsible. [25]

Responding to Common Criticisms About Alternative Grading

Questions about research often arise from criticisms of, or concerns about, alternative grading. In this section, we give research-based responses to several of the most common concerns about alternative grading.

Does Alternative Grading Lead To Academic Dishonesty?

You might wonder if grading systems that follow the four pillars lead to greater academic dishonesty. Perhaps reassessments allow more chances for cheating, or students fail to take more flexible grading systems seriously. But, instead, instructors report *less* academic dishonesty.

Research in achievement goal theory explains this. Achievement goal theory provides a framework that divides the ways individuals perceive their competence into two categories: as improvements in personal mastery (called *mastery goals*) or in terms of superior performance compared to others (*performance goals*). Elliot and McGregor expanded this dichotomy into a 2×2 framework, with mastery and performance goals on one axis and "approach" or "avoidance" orientation on the other (see Table 4.1). [26]

A key difference between the goals and orientations in the 2×2 model is that performance goals, especially performance-avoidance goals, tend to encourage "maladaptive behaviors" (including cheating) as students try to avoid appearing incompetent or looking bad rather than focusing on developing deep understanding: "One of the strongest and most consistent findings

TABLE 4.1
Types of Goals in Achievement Goal Theory

	Mastery	*Performance*
Approach	Mastery-approach goal	Performance-approach goal
Avoidance	Mastery-avoidance goal	Performance-avoidance goal

in the literature on cheating is that students are less likely to cheat when they hold mastery goals or *perceive a mastery goal structure* [emphasis added]."[27]

In other words, if students are aware that an instructor values and supports deep learning, this tends to disincentivize cheating. Research results in achievement goal theory provide two practical pieces of advice along these lines. First, "provide students with opportunities to remediate and possibly retake exams or rewrite assignments to improve." By doing so, the instructor "sends an unambiguous message to students that the goal in the classroom is mastery of content; if students can redo their work until they attain mastery, cheating does not serve a purpose." Second, use "a detailed rubric or other means" to communicate standards, which helps prevent students from developing "low-outcome expectations" that support cheating. Notice that both of these messages are directly supported by the four pillars (particularly *clear standards* and *reassessment without penalty*).[28]

The theoretical expectation of reduced cheating is confirmed in published research, where many authors point out that they have seen less cheating, even in online classes or with unproctored take-home exams or quizzes. This reduction is often ascribed to reduced anxiety from lower-stakes assessments and reassessments, which we learned about previously, and less interstudent competition due to the connection between grades and learning.[29] For the same reasons, we expect similar results in the context of concerns about student use of artificial intelligence tools.

Linda Nilson also explained why alternative grading systems should actively discourage cheating. In her evaluation of specifications grading, Nilson wrote:

> [Specifications grading] discourages cheating by reducing students' motivation and ability to cheat. It is more difficult to cheat on assessments that are authentic and that focus on higher-order cognitive skills and creativity. Moreover, students will find cheating less appealing when they want to learn and excel and can choose aspects of their assessments and their grades.[30]

To summarize, achievement goal theory provides a strong research foundation to explain that the four pillars disincentivize cheating. Meanwhile, instructors don't report cheating as a significant issue in alternatively graded classes.

Does Alternative Grading Promote Grade Inflation?

Because the four pillars ensure that students have multiple chances to demonstrate learning without a grade penalty, a common concern is that alternative grading leads to grade inflation. *Grade inflation* in this context is often defined as the tendency to award progressively higher grades for work that would have received lower grades in the past.

Although you might think that having clear standards, helpful feedback, and (especially) reassessment without penalty would result in higher grades as a matter of course, the actual results are not so clear:

- Average grades often, but not always, increase under alternative grading. Some instructors have found a statistically significant increase in final grades compared to traditionally graded classes, usually in the range of about 0.3 to 0.6 grade points on a 4-point scale.[31] A meta-analysis found that setting clear standards led to a 21% improvement in achievement scores overall.[32] But some authors report no change in final grades at all.[33]
- Often, more students pass alternatively graded courses, and DFW rates (the percentage of students earning D or F or withdrawing) drop.[34] In K–12 classes using "equitable grading procedures" like SBG, the percentage of students earning a D or F dropped by one third.[35] But some instructors see fewer A's and more B's compared to departmental averages.[36]
- Grade distributions may become bimodal. Many articles indicate both that more students earn higher grades *and* more students earn lower grades. In other words, middle grades (usually the C range) become less common.[37]

Some of the variety shown here is due to different types of classes, institutions, and student backgrounds. For example, many of the studies that found increased grades are in STEM fields, and include introductory courses that traditionally have very low grade averages and high DFW rates (pejoratively referred to as "weeder courses"). Implementing alternative grading helps reduce negative effects that typically pervade those courses.

On the other hand, several of the instructors we interviewed for this book are in departments that experienced grade inflation in traditionally graded classes. The inflation was ascribed to student expectations of high grades (and corresponding pushback about any low grades). After converting to alternative grading, the number of A's sharply deflated, but students generally reported greater ownership of their work and less displeasure with their grades.

In general, instructors who see increased grades ascribe the increase to a common reason: Clear standards and reassessments remove penalties for early struggles, which makes a student's final grade into a more honest indicator of their actual level of understanding. Conversely, students who don't take advantage of reassessments end up with lower grades.

This leads us back to grade inflation. Grade inflation does not simply mean "higher grades" or even higher grades than what students may have earned in the past. A more useful definition is: higher grades *without* better learning. In an alternative grading system, grades are directly tied to what students actually learn, and reassessments make those grades more accurate. So when you see higher grades, it means more learning. That's not "inflation"; it's real growth.

Does Alternative Grading Lower Academic Standards?

Instructors who use alternative grading sometimes get pointed questions about reassessments: By allowing students multiple attempts without penalty, doesn't that lower academic standards? In other words, aren't alternatively graded courses "less rigorous"?

We will not attempt to define *academic standards* or *rigor*, since indeed there appear to be no accepted definitions. However, even if we accept those terms as they are commonly used, alternative grading literature reports exactly the opposite: many authors have reported "greater rigor" and setting "higher academic standards" in their classes after changing to alternative grading.

Leading this pack is Linda Nilson, who put "restoring rigor" in the subtitle of her book and described how instructors "uphold high academic standards"[38] by setting the criteria for acceptable work at a B level or better. Instructors report being able to set higher standards, and ask harder questions, while noting that students are more likely to reach those high bars.[39] Students also notice this: "You do a lot more work with [SBG] because you have to prove that you met the standard."[40]

The four pillars support higher, not lower academic standards. Students in alternatively graded classes must complete work that is fundamentally correct, without partial credit, thus setting a high bar. Their grades are directly connected to what they have learned (the first pillar) and are more accurate due to reassessments (the fourth pillar). In particular, reassessments maintain high standards, because students must always meet the same high bar to earn credit.

A related concern, as we saw previously, is that the higher grade distribution that may occur in an alternatively graded class represents lowered standards. But this reflects a mistaken belief that grades are a limited resource. The first pillar directly implies that grades represent learning, not competition or comparison between students. There is no "giving" grades in alternative grading; students earn grades through honest, substantive learning experiences that are documented through assessments. Traditional practices that rely on comparisons between students, such as "curving" grades, do not create a meritocracy.

Equity and Alternative Grading

One of the greatest strengths of alternative grading is the possibility to make assessments and grading more equitable for students. By *equitable*, we mean actively working to provide students access to the same opportunities to learn and succeed. This means not only working to remove barriers to that access but also identifying and changing practices that disproportionately advantage some students, and disadvantage others, based on their backgrounds.

In chapter 2, we outlined ways that traditional grading is inequitable, using Joe Feldman's *Grading for Equity* framework.[41] Here we'll examine how alternative grading can promote equity, using that same framework.

Feldman noted that "grading is a critical element to affirmatively promote equity, to stop rewarding students because of their wealth, privilege, environment, or caregivers' education and to prevent us from punishing students for their poverty, gaps in education, or environment."[42]

By design, alternative grading systems respect the ways that humans actually learn, rather than enacting barriers and discouraging learning. But improving equity is also an *intentional* activity that must be implemented with care for the underlying principles and the people involved.

As a reminder, Feldman identified three "elements" that describe the characteristics of equitable assessment, which we'll focus on in this section: accuracy, motivation, and bias resistance.[43]

Accuracy

Grades should validly describe a student's level of knowledge. Alternative grading systems do this in several ways:

- *Clear content standards* (the first pillar) give grades concrete meaning in terms of what students have learned, rather than their environment or behavior.
- *Reassessment without penalty* (the fourth pillar) ensures that grades more accurately represent a student's current level of understanding.
- *Marks that indicate progress* tie each mark to a specific meaning in terms of learning.

Each of these items avoids penalizing students who need time to engage in a feedback loop. In addition, they avoid benefiting students who work "fast," usually due to previous educational experience (which in turn tends to depend on which school they attended, and hence where their parents could afford to live).

Motivation

Equitable grading practices should be motivational, encouraging students to "strive for academic success, persevere, accept struggles and setbacks, and to gain critical lifelong skills."[44] Feldman described motivational practices as ones that "lift the veil" by making the expectations and processes of assessment clearer to all students. Systems based on the four pillars strongly promote motivation:

- *Helpful feedback* is critical to motivating students, as we saw in the earlier discussion of Butler and Nisan's study. Feedback "lifts the veil" by helping students understand what they need to do and giving concrete advice on how to do it.
- Opportunities to use that feedback through *reassessments* motivate students to view learning struggles as waypoints on the road to success rather than as permanent failures.
- *Marks that indicate progress* give clear purpose and meaning to grades and help students understand where grades come from.

However, motivation is not automatic in alternative grading, and instructors must intentionally work to build student trust. For example, feedback that simply lists errors, or seems to attack a student or their work, is demotivating; so is being left in the dark if aspects of the grading system (e.g., what it means to "meet" a standard) are left unexplained. This work includes pruning out contradictory parts of the system, such as endorsing reassessments but then having draconian deadline policies. It's crucial to make the system clear and coherent to all students, especially first-generation students and those unfamiliar with the "hidden curriculum" of higher education. We'll say much more about this in chapter 12.

Bias Resistance

A *bias* in grading is an assumption or belief that affects our interpretation of a person's work. Bias-resistant grading practices are those that work to prevent biases from corrupting grades.[45] Like motivation, bias resistance is not a foregone conclusion in alternative grading, but some common features of alternative grading systems can promote it:

- *Basing grades on learning only.* The first pillar requires that alternative grading systems use clear content standards, and by implication, grades are based *only* on evidence of having met the standard. That is, grades should not include items that reflect behavior, which can be affected by the instructor's personal biases or a student's environment. In particular, "engagement" factors such as participation are generally viewed through an instructor's unstated or unconscious expectations about what "engagement" looks like, often in ways that are aligned with the dominant culture. As we will see in the case studies and in chapter 12, "soft skills" *can* be factored into alternative systems, but they must be taught and practiced with feedback, just like any other course content.

- *Using reassessments instead of extra credit.* Traditional grading systems frequently involve extra credit for doing extra work or completing nonacademic tasks. This disproportionately benefits students who have the time and personal schedules to complete it. Alternative grading typically does not use extra credit (or "credit," for that matter), instead relying on reassessments that are directly connected to course content. However, reassessments can likewise disproportionately benefit students who have the time to complete them. An equitable implementation of alternative grading requires viewing reassessments as a regular part of the course's workload, and carefully building time for reassessments into the schedule.

- *Focusing on eventual understanding.* Instructors should avoid grading formative work. Formative assessments (like traditional homework) are part of the process of learning. Recording grades for formative work—as is often done in traditional systems—penalizes students who need practice in order to learn, and benefits those who've previously seen the ideas (perhaps due to their family or educational background). However, summative assessments are meant to evaluate a student's level of understanding *after* they have had a chance to practice. Reassessments effectively allow any assessment to remain formative, not penalizing the student, until the student and instructor are satisfied with their progress, at which point a grade is recorded. Reassessments also help reduce anxiety about high-stakes summative assessments, as we saw earlier.

Building bias resistance in any course is a process that requires careful attention. Even in an otherwise carefully implemented system, bias can creep in via what the instructor chooses to assess. For example, an instructor might implicitly expect students to write in "academic English," which is the product of centuries of white, male, and Western institutions. The instructor's unspoken assumptions about writing style then silently affect student grades. The instructor could choose to explicitly teach "academic English" and have students practice with it, in which case it could be considered part of the course content. But if the focus of the class is not on this specific type of writing, the instructor must be careful not to assess it. Moreover, this could open the door to creativity and flexibility by allowing students to choose other forms of communication like videos, posters, or podcasts.

There are many other issues to consider when designing a bias-resistant system; we've only touched on some of the biggest ones here. We strongly encourage the interested reader to find a copy of Feldman's *Grading for Equity* to learn more.

Summary

In this chapter, we've argued that alternative grading does, indeed, "work." The published research, not only the results of studies focusing directly on alternative grading but also those from studies on effective learning in general, all point to positive outcomes. Replacing traditional grading systems with alternatives that rest on the four pillars leads to greater student success, better long-term learning habits, higher levels of motivation, lower stress, improved goal orientation, and a learning environment that overall is more centered on student success. If that weren't enough, the four pillars strongly promote, and make concrete, notions of equity that are so critically needed in education.[46]

But you still may not be convinced that alternative grading works in practice. For that, we'll need to see how real instructors make alternative grading work for them.

Notes

1. Brown et al., 2014.
2. See Roediger & Butler, 2011, for a detailed survey.
3. Karpicke & Roediger, 2008.
4. Lyle & Crawford, 2011.
5. McDaniel et al., 2013.
6. See Carpenter et al., 2012, for more information on spaced repetition.
7. For example, see Carter & Grahn, 2016; Mayfield & Chase, 2002.
8. Taylor & Rohrer, 2010.
9. Hamilton, 2012.
10. Stone, 2000.
11. Axelson & Flick, 2010, p. 40.
12. Ryan & Deci, 2000.
13. Niemiec & Ryan, 2009, p. 135.

14. Niemiec & Ryan, 2009, p. 135.
15. Butler & Nisan, 1986.
16. Other studies have found similar results in higher education. Lipnevich & Smith, 2008, is a direct example. Going further, Chamberlin et al., 2018, found that students from the nontraditional-grading universities had significantly higher levels of intrinsic motivation and "autonomous" motivation than students in traditional universities.
17. Buckmiller et al., 2017, pp. 151–152.
18. Alley, 1996, p. 53.
19. Freeman et al., 2014.
20. For just one example, see Elsinger & Lewis, 2020.
21. Harsy et al., 2021.
22. See, e.g., Schwarzer, 1990, who reported a correlation of –0.21 between test anxiety and final grade. Using a different approach, Cassady & Johnson, 2002, reported that cognitive test anxiety accounts for 7–8% of variance in exam scores.
23. Hembree, 1988.
24. Lewis, 2022, p. 74.
25. Lewis, 2020.
26. Elliot & McGregor, 2001.
27. Anderman & Koenka, 2017, p. 97.
28. Anderman & Koenka, 2017, p. 99; see also McCabe et al., 2001.
29. See, e.g., Barth & Higginbottom, 2021; Elsinger & Lewis, 2020; and Bowman's case study in chapter 5. In one survey of college students, Baird, 1980, indicated that the most common reason for cheating was "competition for grades" (p. 516).
30. Nilson, 2014, p. 129.
31. Chen et al., 2022; Harsy & Hoofnagle, 2020.
32. Marzano, 2003.
33. Blackstone & Oldmixon, 2019; Harsy et al., 2021; Ring, 2017.
34. Boesdorfer et al., 2018; Chen et al., 2022.
35. Feldman, 2019.
36. Toledo & Dubas, 2017.
37. Arnaud, 2021; Harsy et al., 2021.
38. Nilson, 2014, p. 9.
39. Shields et al., 2019.
40. Buckmiller et al., 2017, p. 154.
41. Feldman, 2018.
42. Feldman, 2018, p. 14.
43. Feldman actually called these elements *pillars*, but we've chosen to use *elements* to reduce confusion with the four pillars of alternative grading.
44. Feldman, 2018, p. 71.
45. Feldman, 2018.
46. For an extensive review of literature on SBG in particular, see Townsley & Buckmiller, 2016.

PART TWO

WHAT ALTERNATIVE GRADING CAN LOOK LIKE

In the next few chapters, you'll read detailed case studies of alternative grading systems. You'll meet instructors from a wide variety of disciplines and institutions, teaching classes small and large, online and face-to-face, introductory and senior-level. In short, you'll see concrete, practical, and *real-life* examples of how grading can be improved in almost any setting.

The first chapters each address one type of grading: standards-based grading (chapter 5) and specifications grading (chapter 6). We address hybrids of the two in chapter 7. Next we focus on special settings: large classes (chapter 8), lab classes (chapter 9), and classes that focus on only one or two of the four pillars (chapter 10). These chapters are independent; feel free to pick the most interesting topic and start there. Each chapter ends with notes about special considerations, and a summary of the key ideas in that grading method or setting.

As you read through these case studies, keep a few things in mind:

- *Keep it simple!* If you're new to alternative grading, don't try to use everything you read in this book. Simplicity will make everything better. You can change or add new ideas in a future semester (see chapter 12 for some suggestions on how to do this).
- *There isn't just one way to do it.* While we've worked to highlight especially well-designed grading systems, you should never feel that you *must* use exactly the same system as someone else, or that you must implement a certain item exactly as described here. No approach to grading is "perfect" and there is no single ideal way to implement alternative grading. *Find what works for you (and be willing to revise).* We've described many options and some of the reasons to choose one over another. Pick whatever makes the most sense for you and your students, and feel free to mix and match aspects from different systems. Indeed, trying to copy somebody else's

system is likely to lead to a poor fit. Embrace the idea that any course is always a work in progress: Be ready and willing to change your approach as you plan, and revise it in future years.

- *You don't have to change everything.* If you aren't ready to dive in head first, or if you face constraints on what you can change, we've included examples of courses that are partially converted to alternative grading. These include courses that are highly coordinated, have required labs, or include common final exams.

A careful reader will notice that some case studies include elements that seem to go against our advice or ignore one of the pillars. "Wait, they can't do that!" you may exclaim. These examples illustrate that *there isn't just one way to do it*, and show how instructors have found what works for them. In each case, we've worked to include the instructor's reasoning for these departures. You should also feel free to pick, choose, modify, and remix where it makes sense for you and your students. First understand the reasoning for our advice, and look to your underlying principles to help guide any departures.

After you've read some case studies, you'll likely be excited to start planning your own class. Excellent! Our workbook (chapter 11) will step you through the process of making a thorough and thoughtful plan for your first alternatively graded class. Chapter 12 gives advice for making your plan work on a day-to-day basis, and chapter 13 looks ahead to what you might do beyond that first implementation.

5

STANDARDS-BASED
GRADING

Our first case studies use standards-based grading (SBG). Recall from chapter 3 that SBG classes are organized around a list of clear standards, and assessments are graded based on which standards have been met successfully.

Calculus 1 With Multiple Types of Standards and a Final Exam

Joshua Bowman is an assistant professor at Pepperdine University in Malibu, California. Its undergraduate liberal arts college has about 3,500 students. Bowman has refined an SBG system that he has found to be especially flexible in extreme circumstances.

Each of Bowman's Calculus 1 classes has around 25 students. Students take part in group discussions, activities, and whiteboard exercises. Calculus 1 is a common introductory course that is required for many STEM majors.

Everything in the class centers around one or more *tasks*. That's Bowman's name for standards, and it does a good job of describing what students do: They complete tasks, consisting of one or more related problems, that demonstrate their ability to use the tools of calculus in various ways.

The tasks are divided into three categories: Core tasks cover fundamental ideas in calculus, including both calculations and concepts. Auxiliary tasks focus on an understanding that goes beyond the basics and can range from interpretation up through complex problems that involve multiple skills. Modeling tasks involve creating, interpreting, or analyzing mathematical models using techniques from calculus.

There are 37 tasks total, a high number for an SBG class, although this number varied as Bowman refined his system. Other standards-based classes typically vary from 20 to 30 standards. Here are some examples, along with the short "code" that helps identify them on assessments.

Core Tasks (14 total)

C.1: Find and interpret the average rate of change of a quantity.

C.7: Find derivatives (including higher order) of a polynomial function.

C.14: Find particular values of the antiderivative of a given function, by using integrals.

Auxiliary Tasks (20 total)

A.9: Estimate a derivative by approximation using a table or chart.

A.10: Determine the units and physical interpretation of a derivative in an applied context.

A.16: Solve a related rates problem.

Modeling Tasks (all three)

M.1: Determine how a quantity varies over time (increase, decrease, periods of constancy, points where maximum or minimum value is reached) given its rate of change.

M.2: Identify the objective function and constraints in a situation involving maximization or minimization; find and interpret conditions under which the desired extreme value occurs.

M.3: Find and interpret the total amount of change in a quantity over time from its instantaneous rate of change function.

Bowman's assessments of these tasks look fairly traditional, primarily using in-class exams. However, once you start looking at the details, you can see how Bowman uses SBG to build in opportunities for reflection and growth.

As in many alternatively assessed classes, there are more exams than you might expect: five exams throughout the semester, plus a final exam. Having several smaller exams spreads out the workload, reduces test anxiety, and gives students multiple opportunities to show their learning. Each exam covers eight to 11 tasks, with each task being assessed by one or two related questions. One of the exam periods is dedicated to the gateway exam, which we describe later.

Figure 5.1 shows an example of how task C.14 (which we saw previously) might be assessed on an exam.

Figure 5.2 shows an example of how Bowman has assessed task A.9.

Figure 5.1. An example assessment for core task C.14.

C.14 "Find particular values of the antiderivative of a given function, by using integrals"

The graph of g(x) is shown on the left. Sketch a graph of $G(x) = \int_{-2}^{x} g(t)\,dt$ on the right.

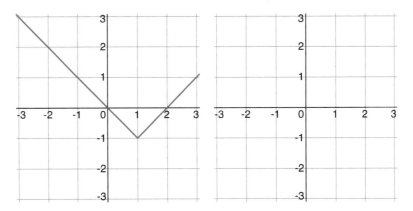

Identify the critical points and local extreme values of G (<u>not</u> g).

Figure 5.2. An example assessment for auxiliary task A.9.

A.9 "Estimate a derivative by approximation using a table or chart"

Below is a table of some values for the function A(x).

x	2.0	2.2	2.6	3.4	4.0
A(x)	5.0	5.5	6.0	6.7	7.0

Using this table, estimate the values of A'(2.2), A'(2.6), and A'(3.4).

An assessment of modeling task M.2, about optimization problems, may be quite long, and so we leave out a detailed example here. A typical question would begin by asking students to read a narrative description of a physical situation, and then ask them to find the largest or smallest value of some physical quantity. It would end by asking students several questions that lead to their creating and analyzing appropriate functions using the tools of calculus.

The previous examples include a full description of the task for our convenience. In a typical exam, Bowman labels each problem only with the short "code" for the task (e.g., "A.9") and includes the code and full description of each task on the back of the cover page. Thus there is no mystery about what is being assessed.

Students don't receive an overall grade on an exam. Instead, they earn a mark on each task separately, as well as detailed feedback. These marks indicate progress: "Successful," "Minor Revisions Needed," "New Attempt Required," or "Incomplete/Insufficient." Marks are assigned based not only on the final answer but also on the student's work and explanation. These marks are also recorded on the back of the cover page, in the list of task descriptions.

Only "Successful" marks count in the final grade. The rest of the marks, together with feedback, indicate what the student's next step should be.

Tasks that earn "Minor Revisions Needed" have a small arithmetic error, a miscopied value, or a similar error that should be fixed but is not central to the student's understanding of the task. Bowman says that "a minor revision should correct a mistake that, if I were watching the student work on the solution in real time, I could simply ask 'Are you sure?' and they would fix it." He also mentions that such errors are often related to prerequisite knowledge that "can degrade under the cognitive load of new content" and so students are quick to recognize and fix them.

Many instructors might call this level of progress "Successful," but Bowman chose instead to make minor revisions very easy for students to complete. He says that this helps him be consistent when grading.

Anything that earns "Minor Revisions Needed" can be revised once. Students have 3 days to submit a "Revision Form" in which they explain their errors and how to correct them. In addition to asking for the task being revised, the form has two prompts:

1. Here's the mistake I made on my last assessment of this task: (Be thoughtful in your response; don't just list the error, explain the thinking process that led to it.)
2. Here's my correction of the solution, and how my understanding has improved by making this revision:

If the student satisfactorily addresses these prompts, their mark becomes "Successful." If not, this is usually because they have revealed a deeper misconception, which turns the mark into "New Attempt Required." This illustrates an important point, as Bowman puts it: "[Minor Revisions Needed] is not partial credit." Only "Successful" counts at the end.

A mark of "New Attempt Required" indicates that a student made some useful progress, but their work has an important error. "Incomplete/Insufficient" is reserved for solutions that don't show enough work to evaluate.

Students can make new attempts on two tasks per week during office hours, a process that involves submitting a request 24 hours in advance.

Bowman also offers a "reassessment day" in the middle of the semester, and another one at the very end. These are class days where students can reattempt any tasks that they need to. The days also act as a break from new content.

As we will see later, many instructors choose to include new attempts on future exams, to help manage office hour traffic. Bowman doesn't do this. Each exam includes new tasks only, except for the two reassessment days. He instead focuses on "live" reattempts, which give a chance for an interactive conversation and guiding questions. He notes that this can overwhelm office hours. Bowman found that preselecting the new problems before the semester begins, and having copies of them ready in a folder, has made this a workable system for him.

This distinction between *revision* and *new attempt* helps students understand the relative importance of mistakes. New attempts guarantee that students can solve problems from scratch without important errors. Revisions save time and effort by focusing only on minor fixes.

Students typically need to complete a task with a mark of "Successful" once to earn credit for it. However, the final exam is a "recertification" of 10 of the core tasks that everyone must attempt. This is a common approach to final exams and checks that students have retained core skills. (Later, we'll see ways to incorporate common final exams.) In some semesters, Bowman chooses the 10 required tasks and announces them in advance. In others, he offers questions covering all 14 core tasks and requires students to choose 10 of them. Instructors could also survey students to see which tasks they most want to appear, or base the choice on which tasks most students still need to complete.

In any case, this recertification approach tends to make the final exam higher stakes, and Bowman tells students that he broadens the definition of "Successful" on the final exam to include minor errors (since revisions won't be possible). Completing a certain number of these "recertified" core skills on the final exam is a requirement for higher grades, as we will see in the following. Another option could include making the final exam simply one last chance to meet each standard, with no special recertification requirement.

Students also complete a "gateway exam" that focuses on rote computations. These computations are separate from tasks which assess higher-level skills. The gateway exam consists of 10 rote computational questions that are important for later problem-solving in calculus. The gateway exam is graded "Pass" or "Not Yet": Students must complete nine out of 10 problems correctly to earn "Pass." Students have five attempts to earn "Pass", and after the first time, new attempts are done outside of class. Each attempt contains a new set of questions. This is in the spirit of our fourth pillar: reassessments without penalty. Gateway exams are a way to ensure that students are fluent in computational skills that form the basis for higher-order work. In Bowman's Calculus 1, students must "pass through the gateway" in order to earn a grade of B– or better.[1]

The last component in Bowman's assessment system is homework, which is effectively ungraded. Homework assignments include many problems and give students some choice, such as "choose 5 problems that you need to practice, from #1–20 in the textbook." Homework is purely formative and gives students a chance to practice with ideas from class before they are assessed on an exam. Because different students need to practice different things, the instructions are intentionally flexible.

Students don't necessarily submit their work. Instead, they submit a "homework report" that describes which problems they attempted, why they chose those, and any remaining questions they have about them (in which case they would submit their work on a relevant problem as well). Bowman or a grader responds to the questions. The only thing recorded is whether the report was completed; the problems themselves are not graded. The goal is both to give students practice without pressure and to encourage metacognition. (It's often a good practice to provide students with an answer key after homework is due.)

Bowman says, "These reports get students to keep up with practicing the material, and the attention they get from the grader is targeted to the specific questions each student has." He also reports that this system is more effective than making homework purely optional.

The syllabus includes a list of requirements for each letter grade, and *all* requirements must be satisfied to earn that grade. For example, to earn an A, a student must do the following:

- pass the gateway exam
- submit 20 homework reports (typically out of 22–24)
- complete all 14 core tasks
- complete all 20 auxiliary tasks
- complete all three modeling tasks
- complete nine core tasks on the final exam

This is a high bar. An A indicates excellent work. Students will stretch to reach a high bar like this, given support and encouragement. To earn a B, students must do the following:

- pass the gateway exam
- submit 15 homework reports
- complete 12 (of 14) core tasks
- complete 17 (of 20) auxiliary tasks

- complete two (of three) modeling tasks
- complete seven core tasks on the final exam

To earn a C, students must do the following:

- submit 10 homework reports
- complete 10 (of 14) core tasks
- complete 15 (of 20) auxiliary tasks *or* pass the gateway exam and complete 11 auxiliary tasks
- complete one (of three) modeling tasks
- complete five core tasks on the final exam

"In-between" results lead to a "plus" or "minus" grade, and the rules for applying these are spelled out in the syllabus. For example, "if all criteria for a letter grade are met as well as two of those for a higher letter grade, then a plus will be added." It's important to include specific policies in your syllabus like those listed, to describe what happens if students are "in-between" grades. Intervene early with students who seem to be progressing unevenly in one category, since they may be expecting some sort of "average" to happen.

These grade criteria demonstrate some common choices for instructors using SBG. Grades can be based on how many standards are completed, but they can also be based on which standards are completed, thus focusing higher grades on specific skills. Bowman does this by requiring students to earn "Successful" on specific numbers of core, auxiliary, and modeling tasks.

It is also possible to base final grades on how often students demonstrate each standard. Bowman requires students to earn only one "Successful" mark per standard. This is simple, but as a result each assessment must thoroughly address the requirements of the task. Another choice, which we will see later, is to require multiple demonstrations of each standard. A mix of these options is also possible.

How well does this system work? Bowman reports three major benefits. First, the tasks give students greater *clarity* about the instructor's expectations, how they can meet them, and how each assignment fits in with these expectations. Specific feedback on tasks and homework helps direct student studying.

Second, the assessment system drives higher *quality* conversations with students. Office hour and email conversations are focused on the content of the course and specific ways to improve, rather than concerns over partial credit. The language of the tasks and feedback help students ask better questions. Bowman says, "The reassessments themselves and the discussions they provoke can probe quite deeply into the relevant topics, which is a boon regardless of whether or not an individual attempt succeeds."

Finally, the system is *flexible* under exceptional circumstances. In fall 2018, wildfires forced Pepperdine into 2 weeks of remote classes. Pepperdine also moved online in March 2020, as the Covid-19 pandemic took hold. In both cases:

> Having a list of tasks helped me determine what was critical—and even what was possible—to cover during this period of remote instruction. . . . At times of crisis, having a list of standards or tasks makes it much easier to sort out what must be kept and what can be trimmed for the sake of guiding students to the essential elements of the course.

The flexibility of SBG can help even in less extreme circumstances. Bowman mentions that, on some occasions, he has dropped an auxiliary task from the list if he judges that students need more time to focus on the core and modeling tasks. He clearly communicates these changes to students, including how they affect the final grade requirements.

Many other instructors we interviewed reported similar benefits from SBG during the "great pivot" of March 2020: The flexibility and clarity of the system helped them make decisions.

The assessment system we just saw is an excellent example of SBG. All of the assessments in the class are aligned with clear standards ("tasks"), with built-in opportunities for formative assessment and feedback. Bowman's assessment system also demonstrates how SBG can assess multiple levels of student learning. The gateway exam, core tasks, auxiliary tasks, and modeling tasks each assess steadily higher levels of Bloom's taxonomy.

Cross-Cutting Standards and Study Skills in Physics

There are many ways to structure a class using SBG. In this case study, rather than describing the entire class, we will focus on a particular aspect that makes it unique: standards that assess problem-solving skills and other cross-cutting topics.

Robynne Lock is an associate professor who teaches University Physics 1 at Texas A&M University–Commerce. This course is taught at the first-year level and is a prerequisite for many other STEM classes. The size of the class is typically 20 to 40 students.

Lock organizes her standards into several groups, as shown in Table 5.1. The number of standards in each group is given in parentheses.

"Physics Content" covers traditional content standards. "Cross-Cutting Content" includes ideas that are used throughout many physics topics. Finally, "Thinking Skills" includes four groups of standards not explicitly

TABLE 5.1
Groups of Standards for Robynne Lock's University Physics 1

Standards		
Physics Content	*Cross-Cutting Content*	*Thinking Skills*
1. Momentum and impulse in one dimension (10) 2. Dynamics Part 1 (12) 3. Dynamics Part 2 (13) 4. Work (9) 5. Energy (9) 6. Kinematics (10) 7. Kinematics in two dimensions (10)	1. Units (4) 2. Vectors (6)	1. Problem-solving process (7) 2. Synthesis of concepts (4) 3. Learning strategies (4) 4. Learning community (4)

related to content. In this case study, we will focus on how Lock teaches and assesses cross-cutting standards and thinking skills.

We'll begin by using the "Problem-solving process" group of thinking skills as an example. Within this group, students learn, practice, and are assessed on standards like "Represent and describe a physical situation with a sketch and detailed labeled diagram" and "Estimate a reasonable answer before solving." These are cross-cutting standards that apply to many different types of assessments.

Lock introduces these skills throughout the semester, and students have chances to practice with them during class and get feedback. This helps make these thinking skills into content standards for the course. In order to assess these sorts of thinking skills, it's necessary to teach them, not just to assume that students already have them. Otherwise, you won't be helping students learn these skills but will disproportionately benefit students who come from backgrounds where they already learned them.

There are no assessments dedicated to just these thinking skills. Instead, some problems include multiple standards—for example, both content and problem-solving skills. Or a problem-solving skill may be assessed across all work on an exam. Lock tells students that they should use each problem-solving skill whenever appropriate on an assessment. Then students earn a mark for each problem-solving standard that they demonstrate in addition to marks for content skills. SBG makes it possible to assess multiple standards per problem, independent of each other.

Another of Lock's groups of standards includes cross-cutting content such as "Label values with the correct SI units" and "Use correct metric prefixes." Like problem-solving standards, these cross-cutting content standards are also assessed independently of the physics context in which they appear.

For example, students might demonstrate thorough understanding of a particular physics concept, but fail to include units. In this case, they would earn credit for the physics content standard, but not for their use of units. The opposite is also possible: A student "can have a major conceptual error in the problem, but if the units they use are consistent with their process, they get credit for units but not content."

Critically, in addition to giving students opportunities to learn about and practice with all standards before being assessed, Lock's cross-cutting skills are written to be clearly defined and observable. For example, it is straightforward to observe whether a student has "estimate[d] a reasonable answer before solving" a problem. All standards, including those for thinking skills, should be formulated with simple language and clear action verbs that avoid vague or unobservable behaviors. For example, "Make sense of problems" is well-intentioned but hard to assess (although this might be a good course- or program-level goal). Lock's problem-solving skill 8.6, "Determine which laws of physics are relevant to a problem," is an improvement, since it is an observable way to make sense of a problem. We'll say more about how to write standards in chapter 11, "A Workbook for Alternative Grading."

Common Questions About SBG

After reading these case studies, you might have some questions or concerns about how SBG works. In this section, we address some common questions and suggest ways to address the issues.

The Dead Frog Problem

By dividing a class into discrete standards and assessing them separately, don't we risk missing the big picture? This idea is sometimes called the "dead frog problem": If a person attempts to understand a frog by dissecting it and examining each piece separately, then they have also destroyed the living, cohesive being. Likewise, if you dissect a course into many separate standards, you risk losing sight of the interconnected whole.[2] There are several ways to address this problem, some of which we've already seen:

- Joshua Bowman uses "auxiliary" and "modeling" tasks to assess big-picture skills. For these, students complete a significant problem that incorporates multiple lower-level and higher-level skills. They earn credit for the task only if the work as a whole is correct and complete.
- Robynne Lock's cross-cutting standards provide another model. Students demonstrate their proficiency with thinking and process skills

alongside content skills. We will see more examples of this kind of standard in chapter 9.

- Kate Owens, a senior instructor in mathematics at the College of Charleston, shows another way to emphasize the interconnectedness of standards. Owens groups her standards into "Big Ideas" that correspond to four or five modules in her class (see Figure 5.3 for one example). She describes these Big Ideas as "an organizational tool that helps structure the course." This helps Owens address the concern that SBG systems could subdivide skills to such an extent that students "can't see the forest for the trees." She observes, "I think the Big Ideas help remedy this; it makes it easier to point out in class, 'While we are looking today at this individual tree, don't forget we are in the forest of [whatever idea].'" The Big Ideas have "helped students see the link between various topics."

Finally, specifications grading, described in the next chapter, is another way to focus on the interconnectedness of multiple ideas.

Giving Away the Solution

The first of the four pillars insists that we clearly tell students what we are assessing. But doesn't that "give away" how students should solve a problem? That is, if we tell students we're assessing Standard X, doesn't that tell students how to solve it?

Yes, and whether this is an issue or not depends on what you're trying to assess. For example, "I can use integration by parts to evaluate an integral" is a clearly stated task, and it explicitly tells students which method to use in their work. This isn't an issue if what you are trying to assess is whether students can correctly execute integration by parts. It is an issue if you are trying to assess students' ability to select integration by parts from among several techniques.

Figure 5.3. A "big idea" from Kate Owens's algebra class.

Big Idea: Linear functions and models

- I can graph a linear function.
- I can determine whether a linear function is increasing, decreasing, or constant.
- I can determine the average rate of change of a linear function and use it to identify linear functions.
- I can build linear models from verbal descriptions and use linear models to establish conclusions.

In the latter case, you are actually assessing a different skill, which involves a different standard, such as: "I can select an appropriate technique for evaluating an integral," that directly addresses what you want to assess.

Selection of the method is one standard, and *using* the method correctly is another, separate standard. Both standards could be assessed separately through different questions, or you could reasonably assess both standards in the same problem by asking students to select and then apply the method. (However, this is a place where the "dead frog problem" can rear its head, as noted previously.)

When Is a Standard "Met"?

Another common question is: When is a standard considered "met"? There are really two questions: First, *how often* should students demonstrate understanding, and second, *which* of those demonstrations should we use as evidence of learning?

On the first question, Bowman requires one successful completion of a task because his assessments are individually quite thorough. Others, such as Hilary Freeman (see chapter 8), require two to four shorter completions, to get a 360-degree view of what a student knows. Which approach you might take depends on your context. But completion of a standard should represent thorough, comprehensive understanding regardless of the specifics.

Which attempts should we use? Suppose a student needs to complete a standard twice. In three attempts, they have earned "Satisfactory," "Not Yet," and "Satisfactory," in that order. Which two attempts, from this inconsistent data, should we count? There are several options. One option, supported by Feldman (author of *Grading for Equity*),[3] is to count only a student's most recent attempts on a standard. In this case, this student would not yet have met the standard, because their work has been inconsistent. An advantage of this method is that it guarantees a student's grade represents their most up-to-date level of understanding. However, this can be demotivating for students and can be hard for instructors to record.

A more common option is to consider a standard "met" as soon as students have completed the required number of successful attempts, even if they were separated by unsuccessful attempts. The big advantage of this method is its simplicity. An issue with this approach is that it may give false positives: Students might be able to reach enough demonstrations by brute force.

Another option is to count only successful attempts, but also require recertification at a later point. For example, Joshua Bowman uses the final exam to require students to reattempt some important tasks. In this approach, students must not only complete a standard at some point in the course but also show that they have retained that understanding.

Key Ideas

A course organized around SBG contains a list of discrete standards that describe specific things a student will learn to do. These standards can cover anything that matters: specific content, computations, concepts, synthesis, problem-solving, and more. Each assessment is aligned with one or more standards. The instructor assesses and reports progress on each standard separately, so students might demonstrate proficiency with one standard, but not another, even on the same work. There are multiple opportunities to earn credit for standards. Final grades are based on how *many*, how *often*, or *which* standards a student has met by the end of the semester, regardless of whether it took few or many attempts to meet them.

- Standards can be grouped into categories, such as "core" and "auxiliary" skills, that count differently in the final grade. Standards can be cross-cutting, require synthesis, or represent problem-solving skills. As always, everything in a standard should be taught, practiced, and given feedback before being formally assessed. More categories or types of standards allow more precision in determining student understanding, but also result in a more complex (and therefore hard to understand) assessment system.
- Standards may require one or more successful attempts to earn credit. Multiple attempts help show student understanding over time, while single attempts are often easier to manage logistically. Instructors often require recertification of a few core standards. Some instructors track only a student's most recent attempts, while others count a student's best attempts.
- Reassessments can take many forms. Students may be able to revise work with minor errors or may be required to make new attempts if there are major issues. Marks can distinguish between these. New attempts may be included for "free" on subsequent assignments, or work may be revised or reattempted during office hours.
- Other items can be included in final grades as well as standards. We saw this in the lists or "grade tables" in this chapter. It is always worth considering whether an assignment needs to be graded at all—and if it is graded, *completion* is often an appropriate standard for practice and preparation work.

If you're interested in reading more examples of SBG, see Hilary Freeman's large multisection coordinated Calculus class, which appears in chapter 8. References to more examples are given in the notes.[4] SBG classes tend to use exams, quizzes, traditional problem sets, and online homework. In future chapters, we will see how SBG can be combined with specifications grading, which opens the door to more options such as essays, projects, portfolios, and others.

Notes

1. For more information about gateway exams, see Barth & Higginbottom, 2021.
2. Beatty, 2013.
3. Feldman, 2018.
4. More articles that give examples of SBG, organized by discipline:
   - Chemistry: Boesdorfer et al., 2018; Toledo & Dubas, 2017
   - Communications: Elkins, 2016
   - Educational leadership: Townsley, 2019
   - Engineering: Post, 2014
   - Math: Brilleslyper et al., 2012; Elsinger & Lewis, 2020; Linhart, 2020; Selbach-Allen et al., 2020
   - Music theory: Duker et al., 2015
   - Physics: Beatty, 2013; Rundquist, 2012 (including voice-based assessments)

6

SPECIFICATIONS GRADING

Our next case studies focus on *specifications grading*, which originated with Linda Nilson.[1] In "specs" grading, instructors create a list of "specifications" for each assignment that describe the qualities of a successful submission. The entire assignment is graded holistically based on those specifications, earning a single mark: "Satisfactory" or "Not Yet." (Specs grading differs from SBG by assessing an entire assignment for meeting all specifications, rather than comparing work to individual standards.) Students have opportunities to revise or reattempt work, if needed, in order to meet the specifications. Final grades are based on completing "bundles" of assignments that group related work together. Higher grades can be earned by completing more, or more advanced, bundles.

An Online Senior-Level Biomedical Engineering Course

Kay C Dee is a professor of biomedical engineering and associate dean of learning and technology at Rose-Hulman Institute of Technology, a teaching-intensive STEM-focused institution in Terre Haute, Indiana.

We will focus on Dee's class Regulatory Affairs—Medical Devices. This is a senior-level undergraduate class for biomedical engineers that was designed to be taught online from its very first offering. The class usually has around 20 students. Its catalog description states: "Through this course, students will build a fundamental understanding of how the FDA regulates medical devices in the United States, with an emphasis on pathways to market."

Dee designed the course to be extremely practical:

> I believe it is important for the students to be navigating the FDA's (voluminous and circuitous) websites and databases to find and use information, guidance, interpretations, templates and forms, etc., just as a professional does. They don't need lectures on how to do that, or to be led

step-by-step by a professor—they need a set of instructions, and then an interesting problem to solve as a motivation to explore and learn.

The course is asynchronous (no scheduled class sessions), and interaction happens in many ways, including discussion assignments, peer-review assignments, online office hours, and email communication. By creating the course to be offered asynchronously online, freeing up lecture time, Dee gained more time to focus on "giving students feedback on their work, beyond just a simple '8/10 good.'"

The class is organized around 10 weekly modules. Content for each module is posted on the course's learning management system (LMS). Here is an outline of one module on "design controls."

1. Watch a short instructor video describing the basic "design controls" required by the Code of Federal Regulations in medical device development.
2. Take an auto-scored comprehension quiz (this is only a self-check, not for a grade).
3. Watch a short corporate-produced YouTube video on common design control mistakes.
4. Read two online articles about design controls written by industry experts.
5. Read a trade publication article about design control violations at a well-known medical device manufacturer.
6. Read the FDA's FAQ on a form used to report design control violations.
7. Optionally, read about the legal troubles of the well-known medical device manufacturer and its leadership after discovery of the design control failures.

There are two "activity packages" tied directly to each module's content. These are collections of assessments that share a similar level in Bloom's taxonomy.

- Level I activity packages focus on basic proficiency and fundamental concepts in each module, including reading quizzes and traditional homework assignments.
- Level II activity packages "let students demonstrate that they can apply information and skills from that module to situations of varying levels of realism."

There are also Level III activity packages, which are major projects that cut across modules. They are designed to let students showcase deep understanding of course material and "[the] ability to relate course material to current events, professional development, societal issues, scientific research, etc."

Each activity package includes several assignments, such as a reading assignment, a quiz, and homework. Dee provides specifications for the entire package that describe what it means for all of a student's work in a package to be "Satisfactory." To complete a package, *all* specifications must be met.

We'll begin by looking at an example of a Level I activity package for the design controls module outlined previously. There are two assignments within this package. The first is a "Design Controls Assignment" that asks students to obtain the most recent guidance document on design controls from the FDA's website. Students use this guidance document to complete several tasks, such as in the following example:

> Page 28 of this guidance [document] states that "In practice, design review, verification, and validation overlap one another, and the relationship among them may be confusing. As a general rule, the sequence is: verification, review, validation, review." Please use your own words to write a detailed explanation of the differences between design review, verification, and validation, and give hypothetical examples of each.

The second assignment in the activity package is a "Level 1 Quiz" with basic questions on design controls. Table 6.1 shows the specifications for the package. Dee marks each item as either completed or not. Her main focus is detailed feedback, which Dee sees as a major benefit of using specifications grading.

TABLE 6.1
Specifications for the Level I Activity Package

Requirement and Specifications	Completed?
Complete the Design Controls assignment. *Specs:* • All questions are fully answered. • Design review, verification, and validation are correctly explained in the student's own words, and hypothetical examples of each are logically consistent with the explanations.	
Pass the module's Level 1 Quiz by the deadline with a final score of 90% or more.	
Pass overall?	

If all specifications for an activity package are completed, then the student earns a "Pass" mark. Note that the specifications aren't instructions for the assignment but a description of success.

A Level II activity package for a different module consists of a single multipart assignment called the "MAUDE [Manufacturer and User Facility Device Experience] Databases Assignment." In the module, students have examined a case study about designing a specific insulin infusion pump. The assignment begins with a basic task designed to familiarize students with the MAUDE database:

> Use the Product Classification database [. . .] to search for infusion pumps in general, and then to find information about insulin infusion pumps.
>
>   a. How many different product codes are there for infusion pumps in general?
>   b. What is the most likely product code of the specific device in our case study?
>   c. What is the citation for the regulation in the CFR that governs this specific product code?
>   d. What class of medical device is our case study pump most likely to be?

The assignment continues with a task that involves more complex database use:

> Use the MAUDE database to learn about problems that have been reported with currently marketed insulin infusion pumps. [Details about how to search in various ways.]
>
>   a. From the reported adverse events, what are the likely top three problems that the currently marketed devices are experiencing—and so are three problems that our case study team would want to pay extra attention to as they finalize their design?
>   Briefly describe the search(es) and analyses you performed to come to the conclusions [noted previously].

Table 6.2 shows the specifications for this package, which describe the qualities of a successful submission. Some specs focus on basic tasks, while others focus on higher-level cognitive activities. Level II packages address higher levels of Bloom's taxonomy than Level I packages and are intended to demonstrate application of skills in a variety of contexts.

Finally, there are six Level III activity packages, each a major project. Completion of at least three is required for a course grade of B; at least four are required for an A. Dee says, "Choice is valued by students. We tend to

TABLE 6.2
Specifications for the Level II Activity Package

Requirements and Specifications	Completed?
Complete the Product Classification and MAUDE Databases assignment. *Specs:* • All the parts of all the questions are answered. • There are no more than two grammatical/typographical errors in the entire document. • The proposed product code for the device accounts for specific use, instead of treating it as a generic pump. • The correct product class for insulin pumps is given. • The justification for the choice of predicate device logically relates the specific uses of the proposed predicate and the device, rather than simply choosing a generic pump. • The description of the search and analysis process/results makes it obvious that the student actually downloaded data from the MAUDE database and analyzed, rather than simply skim-reading information from the database online.	
Pass overall?	

work harder and enjoy learning more when we are tackling a topic that interests us." Each Level III package can be completed during a specific 3-week time window staggered throughout the course, allowing students to choose how to arrange their work while also keeping them working consistently.

Dee provides a short summary of each Level III package at the beginning of the class, which helps students plan their workload. Here is one example:

Name. ISO14971 Project—Risk Management in Medical Device Design = Safety by Design

Time available to work on package. Weeks 4–7

Creativity. Low

Immediate career practicality. High

Major activities. This project is simulation-intensive, requiring the ability to handle ambiguity, create detailed analyses, and apply broad principles to specific examples. Simulation/Ambiguity: Independently learning about and summarizing Negative Pressure Wound Therapy systems (NPWT). Ambiguity/ Detailed Analyses/Application: Using ISO14971 to create a detailed risk assessment and a comprehensive risk management plan for NPWT; self-assessment of work.

Detailed instructions are given on the LMS. The project includes filling in a risk management plan and a "risk assessment spreadsheet," a skill practiced during the semester. Students can submit a draft that receives detailed feedback before the final submission. Table 6.3 shows the specifications for the project.

If the specifications for a package aren't met, students may use a *token* to revise. Tokens are a form of imaginary currency that allow students to break a course policy in a prescribed way. In Dee's class, students can use tokens to revise packages and extend deadlines without penalty. We'll describe tokens in more detail at the end of this chapter.

Final grades are determined by *which* and *how many* activity packages a student passes:

- A: Complete all 10 Level I activity packages, all 10 Level II activity packages, and at least four Level III activity packages.
- B: Complete at least nine Level I activity packages, at least nine Level II activity packages, and at least three Level III activity packages.

TABLE 6.3
Specifications for a Level III Activity Package

Requirement and Specifications	*Completed?*
All ISO 14971 hazard categories must be addressed when creating the draft risk assessment spreadsheet.	
The written reflection on the risk assessment document comparison must include reflection on, at a minimum: What was similar? What was different? Why? What have you learned about these documents?	
If submitting a revised risk assessment spreadsheet, it should be an improvement on the draft spreadsheet, providing more complete and more detailed information.	
When filling in the risk management plan template, each deliverable mentioned in the template should be described in the completed plan: • its purpose • how it will be produced • how it will be used	
The overall impression of the completed risk management plan, reflection, and risk assessment spreadsheet should be one of professionalism and attention to detail.	
Pass overall?	

- C: Complete at least nine Level I activity packages, and at least eight Level II activity packages.
- D: Complete at least nine Level I activity packages.
- F: Fail to meet the requirements for earning a D.

In Dee's system, students can choose not only the course grade they wish to earn but also the particular path they take to earn it. For example, no student has to complete all six Level III packages; a student who wishes to earn a B just needs to complete their three favorite ones. As a student's desired course grade increases, they need to complete "more hurdles" and "higher hurdles" to do so (using Nilson's phrasing). Dee writes:

> Students who aren't aiming to earn an A don't need to waste their time (and my grading time) turning in every single course assignment performed at a poor level. I'd rather be confident that students who passed my course with . . . a grade of C showed mastery of the fundamentals, than say that they consistently did poorly on assignments.

Dee cites four major benefits to specifications grading. First, grading with a two-level rubric takes much less time than traditional grading. There's no concern about whether an error should cost 1 point or 2.

Second, the structure lets Dee engage deeply with students about their Level III packages, "giving richer feedback and responding to what students have written as if we were having a conversation—which, often, we do end up continuing in person."

Third, Dee can set high standards. To pass *any* package, students must do what she describes as at least "B+/A--level work," rather than getting by with consistently poor work and partial credit. And because she sets high standards, she finds that students meet them. Students "produce higher-quality work when the quality standards are clear and the consequence of being sloppy or procrastinating could be a 'fail.'" Built-in opportunities for reassessment help students reach the high bar. Dee reports that, in general, she's noticed a shift to slightly higher final grades since changing to specifications grading. Because of the high standards she sets via the specifications, Dee knows that whatever work a student completes satisfactorily is of high quality.

Finally, the process of writing specifications and organizing the activity packages forced Dee to prioritize learning goals. "I have to determine what goals are critical enough that an assignment should fail if they are not met, and I have to commit to following through with the specifications I set."

"Leveling Up" in an Introductory Philosophy Course

Part of the beauty of specifications grading is that it works in many settings. In our next case study, we will see how specifications grading works in a different context than we've seen so far.

Dustin Locke is an associate professor in the Philosophy Department at Claremont McKenna College, a small private liberal arts college in California. In his introductory philosophy course, Locke uses a variation on specifications grading that he calls the "Levels system." Locke notes that this system has been used by colleagues across many types of institutions.[2]

The assignments in Locke's introductory philosophy courses are primarily essays focused on identifying, explaining, analyzing, and critiquing arguments made by others. Locke defines four "Levels" for essays (called "Level 1" through "Level 4"), each of which requires and builds on the skills developed in the level before it.

Throughout the semester, each student writes short essays on a regular schedule, beginning with a Level 1 essay and "graduating" to Level 2 only when they have successfully met the specifications for Level 1. Then they write Level 2 essays until successfully meeting the Level 2 specifications, and then graduate to Level 3, and so on.

Every student begins by writing a "Level 1" essay, a basic assignment focused on identifying logical arguments and placing them into a standard form studied in class. The Level 1 specifications include several items, but the critical ones are the following:

- Find a medium-sized argument in a passage from a reading assigned for one of your nonphilosophy courses and put it into "standard form" (a skill that has been studied and practiced in class).
- By *medium-sized*, I mean that once in standard form, the argument contains between five and 10 numbered steps.
- Your standard form should be clear, concise, accurate, and easy to follow.

These blur the line between "instructions" and "specifications." In general, *instructions* are directions, and *specifications* describe what successful completion of the directions looks like. These can often contain the same information, phrased differently.

Level 1 essays are marked "Complete" or "Not Yet." As always, the standard for "Complete" is *not* perfection, but whether the student's work demonstrates sufficient proficiency with the goals of the level. Locke describes "sufficient proficiency" to mean that any remaining issues are "unlikely to seriously hinder their efforts to develop the additional skills required" to succeed at the next level.

A key feature of the Levels system is that the levels build on each other: By successfully completing an earlier level, students have demonstrated a skill that is important for success at the next level. If a student earns "Complete" at Level 1, then their next regularly scheduled essay will be done at Level 2, which has a more advanced set of specifications. If they instead earn "Not Yet" on Level 1, then their next essay will be done again at Level 1 but must be based on a different reading. That is, the next attempt at a Level 1 essay is indeed a wholly new essay on a new topic, but with the same instructions and specifications for successful completion at Level 1.

This process continues, with students writing new essays at the same level until they earn "Complete," and then writing the next essay at the next higher level. There are four levels, with Level 4 representing an advanced explanation and criticism of an argument. There are seven scheduled essays, and so students have seven attempts to work their way up to the highest level they can reach.

Here's a sample of Locke's specifications for a Level 4 assignment. The specifications begin with some clear instructions:

> Choose one particular argument from the readings assigned for this class since the last attempt was due and clearly and accurately explain and criticize that argument in a short paper.

Other specifications involve "mechanical" attributes, including a word count, style, formatting, and citation formats. We leave these out since they are quite familiar.

Finally, the specifications describe the key qualities of a successful Level 4 essay:

- Your criticism must be *focused*; you are making exactly one criticism of exactly one premise or inference.
- Your criticism must be *original*; you may draw on ideas others have put forward, but ultimately your criticism must contain some central idea that you came up with.
- Your criticism must be *plausible*; your criticism does not need to persuade me, but your criticism has to be plausible enough to be taken seriously. (For example, if your criticism simply assumes that "The Earth is flat," or some other outlandish idea, it is not plausible enough to be taken seriously.)
- At the end of your paper, discuss at least one possible objection to your criticism and respond to it. This will give you the opportunity to clarify and defend your argument.

- At the beginning of your paper, include an introductory paragraph (or two) that briefly introduces the topic, explains what your paper is going to be about (including what criticism you will make), and explains how your paper will proceed.

Students have a choice of topics for each essay. If a student has not yet succeeded at a particular level, their new essay must be written using the same specifications as the previous essay. This is Locke's main form of reassessment: Students receive detailed feedback on their previous essay, written in terms of the specifications. They use the feedback to improve their work on the next one. However, this new attempt is *not* a revision of a previous essay. Locke says:

> A student who submits an excellent paper after revising it in light of instructor feedback may have simply mastered the skill of *revising in light of instructor feedback* . . . While revisions primarily improve the paper, retries [new attempts] primarily improve the writer.

Students give peer feedback on drafts of papers during a "workshop day" held shortly before each essay is due. Locke provides suggestions, comments, and clarifications as needed, and he reminds students about the specifications.

A student's final is based on the highest level that the student has successfully completed, with modifications based on the quality of their last attempt. The basic requirements for each grade are straightforward:

A: A successful Level 4 essay
B: A successful Level 3 essay
C: A successful Level 2 essay
D: A successful Level 1 essay

In the seventh and final essay, Locke makes slightly more detailed notes about a student's progress. The final attempt is graded with marks of "Complete," "Almost," "Some Progress," or "Not Yet," which are used to determine plus or minus grades. For example, if a student successfully completes a Level 2 essay, their essay grade is at least a C. But this would become a C+ if the student made a solid but incomplete attempt at a Level 3 essay ("Some Progress"), or a B– if the student nearly passed the Level 3 essay ("Almost").

Locke has seen many benefits from the "Levels" system. He points out that most of the assignments are essentially "ungraded" and focus entirely on feedback, which in turn helps students focus on learning and growth.

He gives each essay only one brief mark ("Complete" or "Not Yet"), the effects of which Locke describes this way:

> Since this mark makes no further assessment of the quality of the student's work, it very likely has a different psychological impact on the student than does a traditional grade. To put it roughly, where a traditional paper grade looks *backward*, and any accompanying comments tend to be seen as justification for that grade, a mark of "Complete"/"Not Yet" on a level attempt looks *forward*, and any accompanying comments tend to be seen as guidance for future attempts.

Locke also finds the system easier to manage than a more traditional philosophy course with a few longer essays. Student writing consistently improves, and the total amount of writing (and hence grading) is relatively small in comparison. By having seven regularly scheduled essays, the workload both for Locke and for his students is predictable and moderate.

This Levels approach works well in a course that naturally includes assessments in a "hierarchy," each a prerequisite for the next one in increasing levels of complexity. Locke compares this hierarchy to two things: first, the traditional system of prerequisite courses in higher education, in which it is assumed that students have learned prerequisite content before continuing to a more advanced course, and second, video games, where players can only advance to the next "level" when they have reached a sufficient level of proficiency with the previous level. If they aren't there yet, they can try again, having learned useful lessons along the way.

In chapter 10, we'll see an example of how to use the Levels system as one element within a traditional points-based system.

More Examples of Specifications

In this section, we focus on detailed examples of assignments and their specifications in a variety of contexts. When reviewing these, keep in mind that specifications should include everything that really matters, and nothing more. Every specification is a commitment to assess that item; everything left out is a commitment *not* to assess it. Our case study faculty told us over and over that it's important to cut back and decide what really matters. Should a project be assessed for beautiful grammar and perfect punctuation and spelling, or should it be merely good enough? Either could be appropriate.

Specifications in a General Education Library Sciences Course

Megan Mahoney is a tenure-track instruction and reference librarian at Emporia State University, a master's-degree-granting, public liberal arts college. She regularly teaches UL 100: Research Skills, Information and Technology, a general education course that focuses on "concepts and skills needed to locate, evaluate, and use information in a manner that contributes to academic, professional, and civic success." This course is offered in an asynchronous online format and is typically taken by 15–20 students who range across majors and years in college.

Here is a typical "science literacy" assignment whose goal is to "practice applying an evaluation tool to information . . . outside of [the student's] comfort zone." Students must find two scientific articles on the same topic and analyze them using PACT, a specific framework for analyzing arguments that is studied in class.

Mahoney includes specifications, in Table 6.4, below the assignment's instructions. To pass this assignment, a student must complete all of the specifications.

Mahoney's course includes several common assignments required across all sections of UL 100. While these aren't designed to use specifications grading, Mahoney takes the requirements for each and creates her own specifications for them.

TABLE 6.4
Specifications for the Science Literacy Assignment

Specifications	Completed?
Sources Two sources on the same topic are used. One is a popular science article and the other is a scholarly science article.	
Citations An APA citation is provided for each source. The citations are complete with minimal errors.	
Summary A summary is provided for each source. It is communicated in plain, everyday English in the author's own words.	
Evaluation Each source is evaluated using PACT as a guide. The evaluations are thorough and provide evidence of critical thinking.	
Discussion The discussion of the student's experience is thoughtful and shows evidence of reflection.	
Mechanics Written work consists of complete, well-written sentences without any errors in spelling, grammar, or punctuation that impede understanding of the work.	
Complete overall?	

Specifications in a Methods Class for Preservice Elementary Teachers

Megan Eberhardt-Alstot is a learning designer for the Teaching and Learning Innovations unit at California State University–Channel Islands. She teaches a second-semester literacy methods course for preservice elementary teachers. Her 30-student class consists of a combination of graduate and undergraduate students who are pursuing teacher certification in California.

Eberhardt-Alstot's assessments are projects that give her students opportunities to customize their work to their future careers. The assessments mirror the requirements of California's Teaching Performance Assessment, which students will take as part of their certification requirements.

Assignments are shared via a document that each student duplicates and fills out. Each part of this document has clear and detailed specifications. Students choose the grade they intend to earn on each assignment, which then adjusts which specifications the students need to follow. An example of part of a lesson plan assignment is shown in Figure 6.1.

Figure 6.1. Specifications for part of a lesson plan assignment.

Directions: To meet criteria for the lesson rationale be sure to completely answer each question in each prompt. You will type your responses in the boxes below each prompt.

Met Criteria:
All responses must include:
- Complete sentences
- Be written in first person narration (e.g., I will . . .)
- Have minimal typos (reread to make sure your message is clear)
- Use discipline-specific vocabulary when appropriate

If submitting for a C+:
- Completely answer questions 1 and 2.

If submitting for an A or a B:
- Completely answer questions 1–5.
- Question 5 is about the resource you've created for this lesson. You will be asked to include a link to your resource or insert image(s).

1. **(Grade A/B/C+) Vocabulary Development and/or Academic Language:** Explain how your lesson supports students' vocabulary knowledge and/or academic language. Which vocabulary words or language function do you expect students to understand by the end of the lesson? How does your lesson support students' progression through the stages of listening, speaking, reading, and/or writing?

To help students know whether they are meeting the specifications before submitting their work, Eberhardt-Alstot dedicates class time for peer reviews of drafts and asking the instructor questions.

Specifications in an Introductory Geographic Information Systems Course

Rebecca Kelly is an associate teaching professor and director of the Environmental Science and Studies Program for undergraduates at Johns Hopkins University. She teaches an Introduction to Geographic Information Systems (GIS) course with 20–24 students.

In Kelly's class, students complete a series of projects. The specifications for each project include a combination of global requirements that apply to all projects (such as a focus on general map-making skills) and requirements specific to the individual project.

Here is a summary of the instructions for one project from Kelly's course:

> For this project, you will be working on a research question of your own design with your choice of datasets from online GIS data sources. The layouts you create for the project will be designed to address the research question in a visual way that would enable the map reader to understand the information you are trying to convey and to come to their own conclusions about it.

Table 6.5 shows a selection of Kelly's specifications.

Kelly describes how specifications grading helps students self-critique and learn to accept helpful criticism. As a result, specs grading "creates a more realistic or 'real world' environment for learning GIS and simultaneously improves the quality of student work."

Tokens

In Kay C Dee's case study, we saw our first example of "tokens." Tokens are an imaginary currency that students can use to "buy" exceptions to the rules of the course. Linda Nilson describes tokens as follows:[3]

> You allocate between one and five tokens to each of your students at the beginning of the course, and they are free to exchange one or more of them—it is your currency to control—for an opportunity to revise or drop an unsatisfactory piece of work, to take a makeup exam or retake an exam, or to get a 24-hour extension on an assignment.

TABLE 6.5
Specifications for a GIS Project

Specific to This Project	
Datasets	Three or more spatial data layers or data tables are used in the project, including any additional layers needed for geographic context on the base map.
Map Frames and Layouts	At least two different maps are displayed on a total of one or two layouts that include all appropriate map elements.
General for All Projects	
Map Projection	A cartographically appropriate map projection is consistently used for all maps, taking map type/use, geographic location, and scale into consideration. The projection arranges the base map in an attractive and, perhaps, familiar shape.
Alignment	All map frames and other map elements are neatly aligned without any visually jarring overlaps or irregularities.
Flow and Use of Space	Space is used well throughout the layout with no big empty spaces. Map elements are sized to fit together well and be easily read. A neat line is used to draw the map elements together on the page. The layout has a nice flow that draws the reader's eye across it in a logical and informative way. The most important elements are featured prominently, and the least important are the least eye-catching. Margins are sufficiently wide for printing and provide an even frame around the page.

Tokens shift power in the course from the instructor to students by providing a tangible means of control over the course requirements. When students want to deviate from the rules of the course, tokens are a simple way to say "yes."

Token "exchange rates" are usually stated in the syllabus, and instructors may choose to add additional ways to use tokens during the semester if needed. Because tokens are limited to specific uses, and are available only in limited quantities, they also help keep this flexibility manageable for instructors.

You can also allow students to earn extra tokens. For example, you could give a token if a student submits a revision of work in the first 2 weeks of class or completes a syllabus quiz. Extra token opportunities should be accessible to all students, including those who attend class remotely, have family obligations, and so on.

More information about tokens and other options for adding flexibility can be found in chapter 12.

Key Ideas

In specifications grading, each assignment has a list of "specifications" that clearly describe what a successful submission will involve. The entire assignment is graded holistically and earns a single mark: Either the specifications are met satisfactorily or not.

- Specifications can range from specific to broad, and procedural to conceptual. Many instructors include specifications such as "use proper grammar, spelling, and punctuation" at the lower end of this scale, but specifications are most often used in situations where higher-order thinking is required.
- Students have opportunities to revise or otherwise redo work until it meets the specifications.
- Final grades are determined by specifying which (or how many) assignments a student completes satisfactorily. These requirements can group together into "bundles" of related work, or work related to specific course learning objectives. Higher grades can be earned by completing more, or more advanced, work.
- Linda Nilson recommends that specifications be written to describe B-level work. In particular, specifications should be set at a high level, but *not* at perfection.

If you feel that the previous two chapters, on SBG and specifications grading, share a lot of similarities, you are right. SBG and specifications grading share much of the same philosophy, differing mainly in *what* is assessed: individual standards or entire assignments. In the next chapter, we will see how to combine aspects of SBG and specifications grading to tailor your assessment system to your needs.[4]

Notes

1. Nilson, 2014.
2. For full details of the "Levels" system, see Locke, 2022.
3. Nilson, 2014, p. 65.

4. More articles that give examples of specifications grading, organized by discipline:

- Chemistry: McKnelly et al., 2021
- Dietetics: Pope et al., 2020
- Information literacy: Shields et al., 2019
- Math: Prasad, 2020; Williams, 2018 (Be careful: "Specifications-Based Grading" is abbreviated "SBG")
- Political science: Blackstone & Oldmixon, 2019

7

HYBRID SYSTEMS

The previous chapters demonstrated "pure" implementations of SBG and specifications grading. These two approaches to alternative grading have different strengths, and you might see that elements from both could be useful in your own classes. SBG is a good fit for assessing discrete skills, while specifications grading works well in assessing longer work that integrates multiple skills. Most classes have a mixture of both.

There is not just one "right" way to implement alternative grading. Many successful systems include elements of both SBG and specifications grading. In this section, we will take a look at two "hybrid" or "mixed" assessment systems that combine these approaches to assess different types of work.

Standards, Specifications, and a Portfolio in Organic Chemistry 2

Hubert Muchalski is a tenured professor in the Department of Chemistry and Biochemistry at Fresno State, a primarily undergraduate institution in the California State University System. His Organic Chemistry 2 course is taken both by chemistry and biochemistry students, as well as students in prehealth majors. He typically has 40–50 students in each of his classes. In its most recent iteration, Muchalski taught Organic Chemistry 2 in a synchronous online format through Zoom sessions. His assessments were completed offline.

As Muchalski says, "Organic chemistry is modular. We begin by learning simple low-level skills which get assembled into high-level skills." His assessment system helps students understand where they are in terms of assembling these skills. To ensure that students see the big picture as well as the details, Muchalski uses a combination of standards and specifications on different types of assessments.

Students demonstrate progress on basic skill standards via quizzes called "checkpoints." Synthesis and cross-cutting skills are assessed on "application/extension problems" (AEPs). These represent more challenging and integrated work at the high end of Bloom's taxonomy, and are graded using specifications. To show their understanding of a key overarching concept, students construct a "mechanism portfolio" throughout the semester that is also graded using simple specifications. Muchalski's class includes a points-based final exam that is required by his department, consisting entirely of multiple-choice questions.

The basic skills tested on checkpoints are covered by 15 standards, six of which are "core." These standards are relatively broad: Each chapter in the class's textbook corresponds to one or two standards. Each checkpoint assesses several standards using what Muchalski describes as one "multilayered problem" per standard. Here are some examples of these standards:

- (CORE) I can use the Brønsted-Lowry theory to explain pKa trends of organic acids and correlations between structure and thermodynamic stability of organic bases.
- (CORE) I can use curved arrow notation to draw mechanisms and explain reaction pathways involving aromatic compounds.
- I can solve synthesis problems involving conjugated pi systems.
- I can use the retrosynthesis method and solve synthesis problems involving functional group interconversions and aromatic substitution reactions.

On checkpoints, each standard is marked "Pass" or "No Pass." Students must pass each standard twice during the semester to earn credit. Earning credit on all core standards is a requirement to earn a B or higher. Standards can be reassessed by attempting a new problem on a subsequent checkpoint. Each checkpoint includes problems assessing the most recently covered standards, plus new problems assessing all previous standards.

Muchalski notes that he used to ask multiple questions per standard on each checkpoint, with "Pass" requiring, for example, three out of four questions to be completed correctly. Moving to a single, carefully chosen question but requiring each standard to be completed twice on different checkpoints is one of his biggest improvements:

> It was difficult to write quizzes that contain a balanced set of questions. For example, in a four-question quiz, one of them was asking students to write the mechanism. But, if they nailed the first three questions and had no clue about mechanism, they could get an A in the course and have zero

clue how to write a sensible mechanism (disqualifying for A in my view). By asking students to answer a single problem two times, I eliminated "one and done" lucky passes.

Checkpoints are given asynchronously: Muchalski designates a class day to be a "checkpoint day" and doesn't hold any class session that day. Students can work on the checkpoint during any 3-hour window within the 24-hour day, with no invasive remote proctoring. The 3-hour window is enforced by the course's LMS. To begin, students submit a "dummy assignment" on the LMS that asks them to agree to an honor pledge (e.g., "By submitting my work, I certify that I have only used permitted resources as described in the instructions") and asks if they want to use a token to extend the window by 1 extra hour. Once submitted, the LMS makes a PDF of checkpoint questions available and begins a timer. Muchalski writes several different versions of each question, so students don't all see the exact same set of questions. Students use phones or a scanner to upload electronic copies of their work to the LMS.

Muchalski reports virtually no academic dishonesty with this system. Having multiple versions of problems helps with this. But more importantly, the reduced stress of this sort of assessment also reduces the incentive to use improper resources. When in doubt, he can ask a student to come to an office hour and rework a problem "live."

Figure 7.1 gives an example of a checkpoint problem for the core standard "I can use the Brønsted-Lowry theory to explain pKa trends of organic acids and correlations between structure and thermodynamic stability of

Figure 7.1. A checkpoint problem.

Criteria for *satisfactory* score

The acidity trend must be correctly identified and explained. Drawings must be used as part of the answer. Drawings alone, without commentary and context, don't sufficiently communicate the answer.

Problem

Arrange the following protons (A, B, and C) from the weakest to strongest Brønsted–Lowry acid (strongest = 1). Use the ARIOS conceptual framework to explain the reasoning behind the trend.

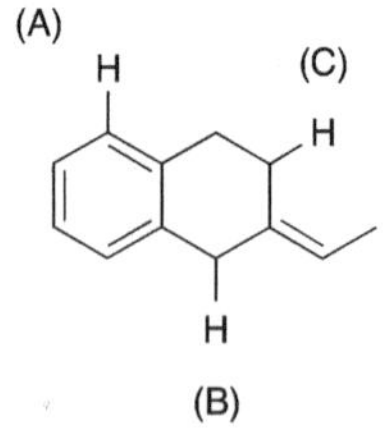

organic bases." In particular, notice the specifications for "Pass" that are listed above the question.

Muchalski's AEPs are specifications-graded assignments, somewhat like miniprojects, that assess higher levels of Bloom's taxonomy. As Muchalski says, "The goal is to stretch students' understanding and ask them to use skills that cannot be siloed into a single chapter." Muchalski posts a new AEP periodically, related to recent topics. Each AEP remains available for several weeks. Students can choose to complete any AEPs that they want. None are required, since these are optional ways to earn a higher grade. Students can submit one new AEP, or a revision of a previous one, each week.

Here is the introduction and specifications page from one AEP:

Purpose

The objective of this assignment is to demonstrate the depth of your knowledge of chemical transformations and synthetic planning. This assignment is also an opportunity for you to practice the following skills that are essential to your success in professional life beyond school:

- precise use of language and specific terminology
- synthesizing prior knowledge with new content knowledge
- communicating complex abstract ideas in a clear way that's free of jargon
- thinking like a scientist (i.e., explaining observations and interpreting data)

Criteria for Success

Clear communication and presentation are just as important as the answer to the problem. A well-presented and correct solution should be good enough to be used as a handout in the course. For multipart problems, answer each problem on a separate page. The answer can be typed or handwritten. If you choose to write everything by hand, make sure it is legible and at a size that allows for reading the text without zooming in. All drawings of structures, reactions, and mechanisms must be drawn by hand.

If the answer is prepared using a mobile device that captures handwriting, only very minimal use of copy/paste and assisted geometry is allowed. Chemical drawings must be valid Lewis structures (octet rule, valence, geometry, formal charge). All calculations and graphics should be appropriately labeled and annotated for the benefit of the reader.

The AEP question itself is in Figure 7.2. Detailed specifications are given in each AEP. General requirements for acceptable work are given as part of a common four-level rubric, the EMPX rubric: "Excellent," "Meets

Figure 7.2. An AEP question.

Design synthesis

Propose a feasible synthesis of the target molecule (TM, Fig. 1) from the indicated starting material (SM). The proposal should contain the following:

- retrosynthetic analysis that includes general transformations
- forward synthesis that aligns with retrosynthetic plan and includes all reagents needed to accomplish each transformation
- curved arrow mechanism of one of the steps

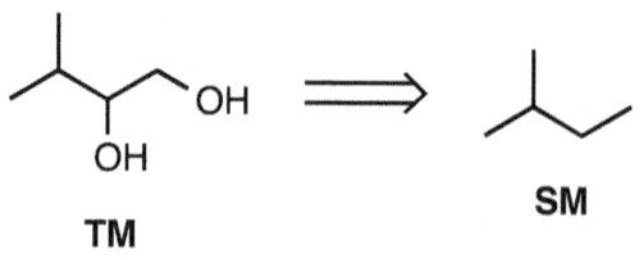

Figure 1: Synthetic target

Expectations," "Progressing," or "Not Assessable." This in turn is a variation on the EMRF rubric ("Excellent," "Meets Expectations," "Revisable," "Fragmentary").[1]

The EMPX rubric can be used to assess work both for correctness and communication quality. While both "Excellent" and "Meets Expectations" earn credit, "Excellent" shows a higher quality of communication. Illustrating it as a flowchart, as in Figure 7.3, helps students understand the instructor's grading decisions.

Each AEP assignment earns one mark for the overall level of work. Each individual AEP assignment has its own instructions and specifications, and so "the work demonstrate[s] thorough understanding of the concepts" and "the work meet[s] the expectations outlined in the assignment" in the EMPX rubric refer to these assignment-specific requirements.

Students can revise one AEP solution each week, and Muchalski grades and returns it with detailed feedback. However, AEPs that earn an X (indicating severely incomplete or fragmentary work) can only be revised if the student spends a token, described in the following. Since these are significant assignments with a high standard, students may need to revise multiple times. Reflecting this, Muchalski requires only one AEP at the "Meets Expectations" level to earn a B, and one additional AEP at the "Excellent" level to earn an A.

Another assessment in Muchalski's class is the mechanism portfolio. This demonstrates an especially useful type of assessment: a collection of work, assembled over time, that gives students a chance to show learning and growth in topics throughout the semester. In particular, the mechanism portfolio allows students to demonstrate their understanding of processes that

Figure 7.3. The EMPX rubric.

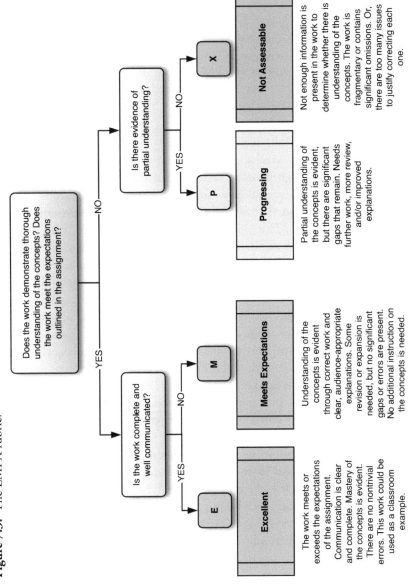

Does the work demonstrate thorough understanding of the concepts? Does the work meet the expectations outlined in the assignment?

— YES —

Is the work complete and well communicated?

— YES —

E

Excellent

The work meets or exceeds the expectations of the assignment. Communication is clear and complete. Mastery of the concepts is evident. There are no nontrivial errors. This work could be used as a classroom example.

— NO —

M

Meets Expectations

Understanding of the concepts is evident through correct work and clear, audience-appropriate explanations. Some revision or expansion is needed, but no significant gaps or errors are present. No additional instruction on the concepts is needed.

— NO —

Is there evidence of partial understanding?

— YES —

P

Progressing

Partial understanding of the concepts is evident, but there are significant gaps that remain. Needs further work, more review, and/or improved explanations.

— NO —

X

Not Assessable

Not enough information is present in the work to determine whether there is understanding of the concepts. The work is fragmentary or contains significant omissions. Or, there are too many issues to justify correcting each one.

explain certain chemical reactions, which are cross-cutting ideas in organic chemistry. As Muchalski says:

> In organic chemistry we "tell stories" [about] how chemical reactions occur. A reaction is a series of bond-breaking and bond-forming events that can be communicated using mechanisms. Mechanisms also help explain unexpected reaction outcomes. [. . .] Many students find it easy to memorize reactions, before and after (reactant → product), but could not explain how it works.

The mechanism portfolio is a collection of explanations of reactions that use specific mechanisms. Mechanisms are first discussed during class. Students are given weekly assignments to review a past mechanism and then explain how it functions in several new situations. These explanations must be error-free and are graded "Pass"/"Fail." The collection of explanations is the mechanism portfolio. The number of fully correct items in it is part of the final grade requirements. Rather than revisions or reassessments, students can submit drafts for feedback before each explanation is due.

Muchalski finds that these portfolio assignments are helpful in many other parts of the class, since mechanisms are so central to organic chemistry. He says that "the assignment is equivalent to 'doing the reps'" as you might in a gym. He believes that the practice of rereading the textbook and practicing with mechanisms helps students on checkpoints in particular, which often use mechanisms as part of the solutions. Muchalski's portfolio problems are, effectively, a form of spaced repetition.

The final exam is multiple choice, provided by the American Chemical Society. This exam is common across not just sections of this course but across organic chemistry courses at multiple institutions. The score on this points-based final exam is simply another requirement in the final grade. In Muchalski's grade table, Table 7.1, notice that the requirements for the final exam are fairly light: It is the only traditional, high-stakes exam in the class, in an unfamiliar format, with no opportunity for reassessment.

In addition to everything mentioned, Muchalski's class is flipped, so he uses the online tool Perusall to help students annotate and discuss preclass readings. Their work is assessed only for completion and effort. Many of our case studies use active learning, flipped classes, and inquiry-based models that align well with the spirit of alternative grading.

Table 7.1 shows how final grades are determined. As usual, an F is earned by not fully completing the requirements for any other letter grade. There are no "half" or partial grades at Fresno State, so these are all possible grades.

To provide flexibility, Muchalski uses a token system. Students begin the semester with five tokens, and their current total is recorded in the LMS

TABLE 7.1
Final Grade Table for Hubert Muchalski's Organic Chemistry 2 Class

	Standards Completed (15)	All Six CORE Standards Complete?	AEP Marks	Mechanism Portfolio (Number Completed)	Perusall Points	Final Exam Score (70)
A	13	Yes	1 E and 1 M+	32	15	42
B	11	Yes	1 M+	26	12	35
C	9	No	none	20	9	28
D	7	No	none	14	6	21

gradebook. One token can be used at any time to submit a second AEP revision in a given week, revise an AEP that earned an "X," or extend a checkpoint deadline by 1 hour. These tokens require no permission and give students flexibility when they need it.

Muchalski has seen some major benefits from using this "hybrid" system. Students report less stress around assignments in general. As Muchalski says, "Some don't believe me that they can retake a quiz." The revision and reattempt system, as well as the AEPs, ensure that students reengage with earlier material that they haven't fully understood, rather than leaving it behind. Students report thinking deeply about chemistry in a way that they haven't done before. Muchalski's efforts made such an impact that one of his students nominated him for a teaching award, which he won.

Engineering Physics With a Lab

Josh Veazey's Engineering Physics class is a second semester of calculus-based physics. It typically enrolls 40–60 sophomore engineering students. Veazey teaches at Grand Valley State University, a regional university in Michigan, and began his career in a nontenure-track teaching stream before moving to a tenure-track position.

The building of problem-solving skills is a central goal in Veazey's Engineering Physics class (in addition to discrete analytical and computational skills, lab skills, analysis skills, and many others). Veazey says, "I want to design courses that showcase to students the value of revising their thinking in response to feedback." He aims to build feedback loops for as many parts of the course as possible. To support these goals, Veazey uses a hybrid system that incorporates elements of SBG and specifications grading.

Veazey uses many types of assignments, all of which interlock and support each other. Some of the assignments are graded using standards while others are graded using specifications. In brief, exams assess core standards that represent a few major problem-solving skills, short quizzes called "waypoints" assess supporting standards, lab reports are assessed using specifications that describe both content and writing quality, and regular practice is provided by weekly video problem solutions and ungraded online homework. The class is flipped, and so students are also expected to complete preclass prep work and come to class ready to take part in activities and group work.

Across all types of assessments, Veazey uses the same four marks: "Exemplary," "Satisfactory," "Progressing," and "Incomplete"—or E, S, P, I. These marks may look very similar to those we saw in SBG rubrics, but here they are effectively specifications. For each type of assignment, Veazey creates a detailed description of what each mark requires. These specifications differ between different types of assignments, reflecting their different roles and goals.

The main summative assessments are five midterm exams, where eight "core" standards are assessed. The core standards are broad, each representing an entire category of multistep problems that are central to the class—for example, "C.1: I can apply vector superposition to find the electric field of a continuous charge distribution."

Figure 7.4 shows an example of an exam question that assesses the standard C.1.

Notice how Veazey labels the problem with the standard name (C.1) and includes prewritten E, S, P, and I's that can be easily circled when grading. Each problem on an exam covers exactly one standard. Veazey gives detailed feedback on all assignments, to aid in reassessments.

Figure 7.4. An exam question assessing core standard C.1.

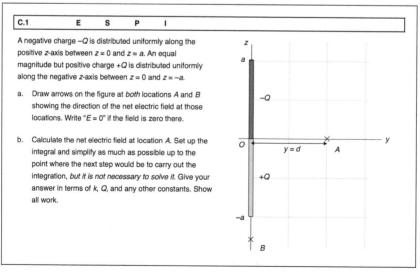

C.1   E   S   P   I

A negative charge $-Q$ is distributed uniformly along the positive z-axis between $z = 0$ and $z = a$. An equal magnitude but positive charge $+Q$ is distributed uniformly along the negative z-axis between $z = 0$ and $z = -a$.

a. Draw arrows on the figure at *both* locations A and B showing the direction of the net electric field at those locations. Write "$E = 0$" if the field is zero there.

b. Calculate the net electric field at location A. Set up the integral and simplify as much as possible up to the point where the next step would be to carry out the integration, *but it is not necessary to solve it.* Give your answer in terms of k, Q, and any other constants. Show all work.

Table 7.2 shows the detailed specifications for earning each mark. Much like Muchalski's EMPX rubric, these are general specifications that apply to *each* core standard.

To distinguish between levels of student work on exams, Veazey builds in recognition for excellent work on core standards, and these "Exemplary" marks can only be earned on core standards. This is in line with their focus on complex, multistep problems as well as their role as a largely summative assessment. By the time students complete an exam, they will have had many chances to practice with these core ideas and receive feedback. Assessing

TABLE 7.2
Specifications for Core Standards on Exams

Exemplary (E)	<ul><li>Demonstrates a clear understanding of the physical phenomena and how to apply them to solving the problem.</li><li>Everything is completely correct, or there is a creative insight communicated.</li><li>Physical reasoning is explained where appropriate. All work is clear and legible.</li><li>Results are plausible, including being the correct order of magnitude and correct dimensions.</li></ul>
Satisfactory (S)	<ul><li>Demonstrates a clear understanding of the physical phenomena and how to apply them to solving the problem.</li><li>Work may contain minor errors that are computational or tangential to the core issue of the problem.</li><li>Physical reasoning may not always be clearly explained, but it should be clear enough to figure out. All work is clear and legible.</li><li>Results are plausible, including being the correct order of magnitude and correct dimensions.</li></ul>
Progressing (P)	<ul><li>There is one or more significant conceptual errors impeding the correct solution.</li><li>Work may contain minor errors that are computational or tangential to the core issue of the problem.</li><li>Physical reasoning is not explained, nor is it clear after a careful look at the work.</li><li>Results are not plausible.</li></ul>
Incomplete (I)	<ul><li>There is not enough information in the solution to be able to assess the work.</li><li>It may be incomplete or too illegible to read.</li></ul>

work for "Exemplary" qualities only on a summative assessment gives room for students to focus on deep understanding when first learning, without fear that their work needs to be "perfect."

Core standards can be reassessed by trying a new problem on a later exam. Exams are cumulative, including both new standards and new problems for old standards. Students only complete the problems that they need, or feel confident attempting. However, students must "unlock" the right to reassess by practicing with related online homework problems before attempting a new exam question.

Veazey notes that he keeps a student's best mark on each core standard. He used to record the most recent mark, but ran into a common side effect: Students avoided reassessing if they knew that their mark might drop (especially below "S"), and this limited the benefits of reviewing and reassessing. He compromised by adding the requirement to attempt online homework problems. The goal is to ensure that students have made a genuine effort to prepare before reassessing.

There are also "supporting" standards that are assessed on short in-class quizzes called "Waypoints." These supporting standards cover a wide range of auxiliary skills, from selecting an appropriate method for a problem, to direct computations, to conceptual reasoning. Here are some examples of supporting standards:

- S.2: I can solve conceptual questions about polarization of conductors and insulators.
- S.9: I can apply relationships between amplitude, period, and frequency with equations of the fields in an electromagnetic wave.
- S.13: I can predict the polarization of light before or after passing through polarizing filters.

Supporting standards can be revised by submitting a video that corrects and reflects on errors in the original solution.

Figure 7.5 gives an example of an assessment for supporting standard S.9. To demonstrate how the specifications vary between types of assessments, here is the description for "Satisfactory" on Waypoints:

Satisfactory: Shows good-faith attempt at solving the problem correctly. Work reflects a student who is clearly intellectually engaged. Physical reasoning is clearly explained. Work does not necessarily need to be all correct, but it should be mostly (~80%) correct, and it should be plausible.

Compare this with "Satisfactory" for core standards. These assessments have different goals, and so the specifications differ.

Figure 7.5. A waypoint assessment of supporting standard S.9.

S.9. An electromagnetic wave traveling in an unknown medium has magnetic field:

$$\vec{B} = (3.0 \times 10^{-8}\ \text{T})\hat{\jmath}\ \cos[(2.4 \times 10^{7}\text{m}^{-1})x + (3.7 \times 10^{15}\text{s}^{-1})t]$$

a. The magnetic field vector is aligned along the:
- i. x-axis
- ii. y-axis
- iii. z-axis
- iv. 45 degrees between the x- and y-axes
- v. 45 degrees between the x- and z-axes
- vi. 45 degrees between the y- and z-axes
- vii. Not enough information. Explain: _____

b. The electric field vector is aligned along the:
- i. x-axis
- ii. y-axis
- iii. z-axis
- iv. 45 degrees between the x- and y-axes
- v. 45 degrees between the x- and z-axes
- vi. 45 degrees between the y- and z-axes
- vii. Not enough information. Explain: _____

c. What is the speed of this wave in the unknown medium? Show all work.

The course includes a lab component, which is graded using specifications rather than discrete skill standards. Veazey teaches the labs connected to his section of the course, and he has full control over their structure and grading system. Chapter 9 will be dedicated to alternative grading in lab classes, and so we give only a brief overview here to illustrate a simple and streamlined example of how to handle grading in a lab.

Labs involve filling in a guided worksheet, with prompts for data and analysis. The worksheet is graded holistically, using three general specifications for every lab. "Satisfactory" is defined as work that meets all three of these specifications:

1. *Clarity.* All work is clear and legible. Physical reasoning is explained where appropriate.
2. *Plausibility.* Experimental data are plausible, or there is an explanation for why they are not plausible, specifically what went wrong.
3. *Mostly Correct. Most* of the work is fully correct. Depending on the lab, *most* may be as low as 70% or as high as 100%. (This is described in more detail on each set of lab instructions.)

Veazey notes that he tries to actively work against the expectation that there is only one "correct" dataset to be found in each lab. While correctness is important, the goal of "plausibility" in these specifications is for students to "actively evaluate their results and make needed adjustments." This also helps reduce a form of lab cheating, where students copy experimental data from one student who they believe has the "correct" results.

Labs can be revised, either by reanalyzing incorrect responses or recollecting data (when that is possible). If "plausibility" is the key issue, students are permitted to write a reflection that suggests a reason why the implausible data were collected, supported by evidence from their lab notes. This encourages students to practice acting like scientists as they evaluate their work.

Another assignment, a weekly video, is a type of homework: Each student records themselves solving a brief computational problem. This video is shared with the rest of the class, and both the instructor and classmates can comment on others' videos. The specifications here focus on a balance between correctness and effort:

> Satisfactory: Shows good-faith attempt at solving the problem correctly. Work reflects a student who is clearly intellectually engaged with new material. Physical reasoning is clearly explained to the viewer, even if incorrect (should be plausible). Work does not necessarily need to be all correct, but it should be mostly (~80%) correct.

Other formative practice comes via autograded online homework with multiple attempts. The online homework doesn't count in the final grade, but serves to "unlock" revisions of supplementary standards and video assignments.

How does the final grade work? Veazey uses the familiar grade table. This class involves many types of assignments, and so there are many categories. Table 7.3 shows some examples, although the full table includes a row for every possible grade.

TABLE 7.3
A Portion of the Final Grade Table for Joshua Veazey's Engineering Physics Class

	Core Standards at E (8)	Core Standards at S or E (8)	Waypoint Marks (7)	Preclass Prep at S (22)	Labs at S (13)	Video Solutions at S (13)
A	8	8	6	18	12	12
A–	7	8	6	18	12	12
B+	6	8	5	14	11	11
C	0	7	4	10	10	9
D	0	4	2	5	8	5

There is a final exam that covers all core standards: Each problem on the final exam is graded with the ESPI rubric and counts toward completing the core standards as needed. The exam also acts as a modifier on the final grade. Final grades are increased by one row in the table if a student earned at least two E's on the final, and all other standards on the final were "Satisfactory." The grade drops by a row if more than one of the final problems earned a "Progressing" mark, or any problem earned an "Incomplete."

Veazey sees many benefits from this assessment system:

> There was a marked shift in the types of conversations I was having with students. Conversations are now richer and deeper. They are focused on understanding and growth. . . . I have students eager to spend time with me in office hours going over a core learning target . . . really digging deep and being reflective about their thought process during the assessment.

He also saw better attendance, even though attendance isn't counted anywhere in the final grade: "Although I don't know if it is fully attributable to the grading system, it does seem like students are intrinsically motivated to remain fully active with the course."

Veazey teaches this Engineering Physics course regularly and converted it to this system over several years. He began with the labs, developing a specifications system and adding in a simple reassessment system, while keeping the rest of the course point-based. Over the following years, he added core standards, flipped the class, and then added the remaining standards-based aspects. Veazey's advice for instructors looking at a similarly complex class is to follow this iterative path: "The hybrid specs-based/points-based model and multiyear transition allowed me to spread the labor over a few years. It was helpful for me to learn a bit more each year . . . so that I could digest that information in smaller chunks." We agree: Start simple and iterate.

Portfolios

The fourth pillar of alternative grading, reassessment without penalty, represents a critical idea: It takes time for people to learn new ideas. Our case studies demonstrate ways to structure reassessments during the semester. However, a different way to embrace reassessments is to have students build a final portfolio.

Portfolios are common in art classes. Students select work that they have completed throughout the semester and submit it to the instructor, to demonstrate both their best work and how they have improved. Portfolios are also common assessments for capstone classes and other classes in which the goal is for students to reflect on their learning over a long period of time.

However, a portfolio can be used in any type of class, either as the primary means of summative assessment or as an ingredient in a standards- or specifications-based system.

If you want to use a portfolio, here are some general guidelines:

- A portfolio should include both "artifacts" (examples of student work) *and* reflection on what that work shows. Provide students with prompts and specific topics to address in these reflections. Also note that you can choose to allow artifacts that aren't traditional written work, such as video recordings or a podcast.
- Provide a clear description of the portfolio in the syllabus and mention it frequently in class. This way, students know what types of work they should be assembling throughout the semester. You can often link specific portfolio requirements to standards or course-level learning objectives (e.g., "Include an artifact that demonstrates your understanding of [a standard]").
- Portfolios, as final assessments, can't be reassessed after submission. Rather, portfolios work well with drafts, which can be thought of as preassessments. Provide "check-in" meetings or assignments throughout the semester, in which students submit a draft of part of their portfolio for additional feedback. This has two advantages: It helps keep students on track (rather than waiting until the last minute to start assembling the portfolio), and it lets you give feedback and direction to students. For students who are unfamiliar with portfolios, they can be stressful: "What is the instructor looking for?" Check-in meetings can help align your goals.

Portfolios can count in the final grade in several ways. Most commonly, the portfolio is treated as a type of project. It is graded holistically, earning "Satisfactory" or "Not Yet" based on whether it meets the specifications laid out in the syllabus. Completing the portfolio satisfactorily can be one of the requirements for earning an A or B. If doing this, consider what should happen if a student does excellent work during the semester but fails only to assemble and submit it in the final portfolio.

Alternatively—and most in line with the "ungrading" ethos—a portfolio could be the only "graded" assessment in the class. In this case, students receive only feedback (with no marks or grades) during the semester. Students revise their work before submitting a selection of it in their portfolio, using feedback as a guide. You can also allow students to make an argument in favor of a specific grade (typically based on criteria that you provide). This can be quite liberating for students, but it can also be stressful and confusing. Judge your situation appropriately and provide lots of support.

David often uses portfolios in upper-level proof writing classes. Here are some examples of the artifact requirements and reflective prompts that he uses. This is a reflective prompt that could be paired with an artifact that addresses it:

> Growth as a mathematician (two or three paragraphs)—Describe how you've improved as a mathematician and student of geometry this semester. Don't just tell me what you learned—focus on one or two important and specific ways that you have changed or grown over the course of this semester. Include at least one artifact in your portfolio that best illustrates your growth area. Explain in the essay how this artifact shows growth in the way you've described.

Another example of a prompt, which addresses specific content from the class:

> Parallels and Non-Euclidean Geometries (two or three paragraphs)—Identify a theorem whose proof relies on the Euclidean Parallel Postulate, directly or indirectly. Include this theorem in your portfolio and name it in this essay. Clearly explain why the proof requires the EPP, and identify the specific parts of the argument that rely on the EPP. Then include a picture of a counterexample to this theorem constructed in either the Spherical or Hyperbolic geometries. Explain why this picture shows a counterexample, and how you know that the hypotheses of the theorem are satisfied but conclusions are not.

You can also ask general questions, and may be surprised at what students tell you. For example, "Include an example of work from this semester that you are especially proud of. Explain why you included it, and what it shows about your work in this class." Frances Su, a mathematician at Harvey Mudd college, famously wrote "7 Exam Questions for a Pandemic (or Any Other Time)" that includes many such questions that could be used in nearly any course, not just math.[2] There are many more examples of how to use portfolios in *Ungrading* by Susan D. Blum.[3]

Key Ideas

"Hybrid" classes use elements of SBG, specifications grading, and ungrading. There's no need to commit solely to one approach. The elements that best fit a given context may tend toward SBG, specs, a mix, or may incorporate other approaches as well.

Key choices tend to involve discrete skills versus holistically graded assignments. Discrete skills tend to be best represented by standards, and assessed with SBG on quizzes, exams, or problem sets. Assignments whose purpose is to show synthesis and integration of multiple ideas, including communication, are better suited for specifications grading. These include essays, longer projects, and detailed writing such as labs or proofs.

Reassessments also depend on the type of assessment. Discrete skills can often be reassessed with a new problem on a future assignment, or a new problem given during office hours. Essays, proofs, labs, and similar assignments benefit from revision.

Final grades are typically assigned using a "grade table" that gives a list of requirements, phrased both in terms of standards, specifications, and any other requirements. If it is essential to include work that is inherently points-based (such as a common final exam or online homework), a requirement phrased in terms of points earned on that assignment can be included in the grade table. Other assignments, such as those focused on practicing skills, can be used to unlock revision or reassessment attempts, rather than counting directly in the grade.

Finally, don't forget to *keep it simple!* Hybrid systems are prone to the "everything but the kitchen sink" effect: Instructors try to include assessments and special rules or grade requirements to get a "perfect" view of student learning. The more complicated your system, the harder it will be for students to understand, and the fewer benefits you'll see. Start out simple, and add complexity—if needed—as you gain experience. Even more examples are in the notes.[4]

Notes

1. The EMRF rubric was first described in Stutzman & Race, 2004.
2. Su, 2020.
3. Blum, 2020.
4. Many published articles use elements from multiple systems. Some especially useful examples from math include Carlisle, 2020; Cooper, 2020 (here called "Techniques Grading," using a portfolio as well); Weir, 2020.

8

LARGE CLASSES

In this chapter we focus on how to implement alternative grading in large classes. For our purposes, *large* can mean either a single section with a lot of students in it or a coordinated course with many sections. We will see examples of both in this chapter. There are also some related case studies in other chapters. Renée Link's case study in chapter 9 shows how to coordinate a large multisection lab class that uses specifications grading. Chris Creighton's case study in chapter 10 shows how the instructor of one section of a highly coordinated course can partially convert it to use alternative grading, while staying within the requirements of the coordination.

Streamlined SBG in an Introductory Biology Course

Jennifer Momsen is a professor of biological sciences at North Dakota State University, a large doctoral-granting university with very high research expectations. She regularly teaches General Biology II, a survey course "focused on biological information flow, exchange, and storage." It is taken by biology majors as well as other life science majors and is a prerequisite for most upper-level biology courses.

General Biology II typically has about 135 students in each section. Momsen teaches it in a highly structured, activity-based format. She has two or three learning assistants who provide students with feedback during class activities.

Momsen's course is entirely standards-based, using 15 standards that are grouped into related categories. For example:

1. Explain how genetic information is stored in living systems.
   a. Use a model or series of models to illustrate the structures of DNA and RNA.
   b. Create a model to illustrate the relationships among DNA, chromosome, gene, and allele.

7. Explain how biological information is communicated using chemical, electrical, and/or behavioral signals to elicit biological responses within and between individuals.

   a. Construct a model based on evidence to explain how living systems use communication to acquire and exchange information about their environment.

   b. Use evidence to produce a model or series of models that illustrate the core components of communication (signal/reception/feedback) and how these components of communication impact biological function at different biological levels (within an individual, within and between species).

In these examples, statements 1a, 1b, 7a, and 7b are the standards that are assessed. Momsen developed these standards, as well as the example activity and assessment that follows, along with her Biology Department colleague Tim Greives. Momsen emphasizes that figuring out a good list of standards is hard, and she recommends asking colleagues and others in your discipline for support when first creating a list of standards. Standards written by professional societies can be a good starting point.

Momsen describes her overall goal for assessing her standards this way:

> [M]y focus was on creating opportunities for failure followed by success. This meant really coupling formative assessment with feedback. In addition, I incorporated many ways for students to retest each standard, whether in writing or verbally during office hours.

Students complete in-class activities in small groups. On each activity, students submit a single group paper for formative feedback (but no grade). These formative activities provide students with their first opportunity to practice with new ideas. Momsen notes that using group submissions makes giving feedback manageable: "I can give feedback on 45 papers from one class period to the next, but I can't do that for 135 individual students." Students have time in class to review their group's feedback, and Momsen also gives overall feedback to the whole class. The groups are kept together for the entire semester and become another form of support for students in and out of class.

Here's an example of one part of an in-class activity that addresses standard 7a, which we saw previously. After a preclass video lecture about biological information and feedback systems, students read a specific example related to chin coloration in one species of lizard.

Activity 2. Building a Model of Communication

Create a model that describes how biological information within a male lizard is communicated to melanin-producing cells.

In this case:

- What cell is the emitter/sender?
- What cell is the receiver? What is the receptor?
- What is the signal?
- What biological change is induced by the receiver cell?

Use your responses to the above questions to create a model.

This is followed up with additional activities that extend the model and use it to make predictions.

Students also have purely formative weekly homework that is posted on an LMS, taking the form of a short quiz or extended-response items. Momsen provides a rubric or answer key so that students can self-assess after completing the homework. After attempting homework, students fill out a short reflection form that is checked only for completion. Momsen uses these reflections for whole-class feedback, which also saves her grading time.

Momsen's only summative assessments are four or five take-home "problem sets," assigned every few weeks. There are no traditional in-class exams or quizzes. Each problem is aligned with one standard, and each standard is graded for proficiency: "Met" or "Not Yet Met." Most problem sets cover four standards, with a mix of new and repeated standards. As newer standards are added to problem sets, older ones "fall off."

Students need to demonstrate proficiency with a standard only once in order to "meet" the standard. Since each question is detailed and thorough, one demonstration is sufficient; one demonstration per standard also keeps the grading load manageable.

Here is an example of a question from a problem set that assesses standard 7a. The question is similar to, but in a different context from, the in-class activity. The overall goal is to provide a deep and authentic assessment of the standard, and so the question is detailed and involves each part of the standard. (Earlier in the problem set, students were provided background information about the *FOXP2* gene and animal vocalizations.)

Rodents can make vocalizations that humans can hear, such as a squeal. But they also can communicate during social interactions using ultrasonic vocalizations—vocalizations at a frequency higher than the human ear is capable of hearing. Sex differences in vocal communication, similar to observations in songbirds, are observed in rats, with adult male rats eliciting a typical type of ultrasonic vocalizations not observed in females.

As noted elsewhere in this problem set, *FOXP2* is involved in the development and neural control of vocalizations in a broad spectrum of species, including rodents. In humans it is linked to human speech and language disorders. In rats, *FOXP2* has been related to sex-specific vocalizations, like the male-typical ultrasonic vocalizations. *FOXP2* expression in neurons in the brain is greater in males than females. Further, recent research demonstrated that *FOXP2* is a target of activated androgen receptors (i.e., specialized receptors that bind androgens such as testosterone and di-hydrotestoterone)

Create a model that describes how biological information within a male rat contributes to the development and production of the behavioral phenotype of male-typical ultrasonic vocalizations.

As you work through the model, be aware of the following:

- What cell is the emitter/sender?
- What cell is the receiver? What is the receptor?
- What is the signal?
- What biological response is induced by the receiver cell?

How does this biological response contribute to the development and production of male-typical ultrasonic vocalizations?

Problem sets only have "suggested deadlines," rather than hard due dates. Momsen guarantees feedback only if students hand problem sets in on time, and she has found that students generally use this ability wisely.

Momsen also makes the first problem set small, covering just one or two standards, and assigns it within the first few weeks of the semester, to help students get used to SBG and build habits for success in the class.

There are two options for reassessments. One is the usual form for SBG: Subsequent problem sets include new assessments of previous standards. Students only need to attempt problems covering standards that they have not yet met. Momsen limits the number of standards on each problem set in order to keep grading manageable. There is one final comprehensive problem set, offering a new opportunity on every standard.

The other reassessment option is an office hour meeting. Office reassessments are only available during those weeks in which no problem set is due and no problem set is being returned. Students can sign up for a 10-minute meeting to reassess one or two standards. When they sign up, students must also fill out a "prereflection" with three prompts in which they reflect on:

- what you got wrong or omitted or were unclear about in your response on [the problem set]
- which class weeks correspond to this material
- how you would change your answer

The prompts help students prepare for the reassessment and ensure that students know which material to review. At the reassessment, Momsen provides a new problem that the student attempts "live." Momsen determines a new mark based on the office hour work and the prereflection. Most students choose to attempt new problems on a subsequent problem set, which keeps office hour reassessments from taking up too much time.

Momsen's 15th standard is a bit different from the others: It has to do with taking part in the key activities that enable students to learn and succeed in the class:

> Contribute to classroom *community development*. We are a learning community, focused on living systems. This community works when we are all prepared to explore new ideas, apply our knowledge, and learn from mistakes. Meeting this standard involves *both*:
>
> - *Individual accountability*. Reading text, watching videos, and successfully completing knowledge checks prior to class meetings.
> - *Group accountability*. Engaging in class meetings by contributing ideas, critically thinking, and responding to feedback.

This standard is met when a student completes a total of at least 80% of the otherwise ungraded assignments, including class attendance, homework, and group activities. By combining many different forms of participation, students have a variety of ways to meet this standard, along with some cushion. Final grades are based solely on the number of standards met by the end of the semester:

F: 0 standards met
D: 1–3 standards met
C: 4–7 standards met
B: 8–11 standards met
A: 12–15 standards met

Notice that this final grading scale does not set 60% performance as a failing grade. Momsen does this intentionally, inspired by Joe Feldman's *Grading for Equity*.[1] As she says: "An F is not doing anything at all," but beyond that the scale is focused on representing what students *have* accomplished. (North Dakota State University only assigns whole letter grades, so there is no policy for plus or minus modifiers.)

Momsen acknowledges that some students have a negative initial reaction to her system because it is "very novel." But she also notes that this response "quickly fades as they realize no single test or test question is going to tank their grade." She emphasizes that her system puts students in charge of their own learning. Students know what is required of them, and they can make informed decisions based on their own circumstances:

> Students appreciated this flexibility—they said outright that they didn't study or even turn in a problem set because they just didn't have time, but they felt safe doing so knowing they could pick it all up on the next problem set.

In other words, they take much greater responsibility for their own learning. One student wrote, "I found myself learning more since I felt free to make mistakes and did not have to worry about penalties from them." Students even reported that they *liked* coming to class.

The group tasks, homework reflections, and flexible deadlines all help Momsen identify students who are struggling or falling behind, which lets her reach out with specific advice and encouragement.

With problem sets taken home and submitted online, there could be plenty of opportunities for academic dishonesty. But Momsen hasn't had trouble with this. Indeed, she notes that since she grades one problem at a time, copied or overly similar solutions would stick out. She notes that her system has actually helped with academic honesty:

> Informal feedback from students underscored their feeling of less pressure, less worry about losing points. They trusted in me and the new system, and responded in kind. I do think that the alignment of class activities to the problem sets also helped. Students knew that what they did in class was what they would do for the problem set, just in a new context. They could use those class resources, too—the notes, the assignments, all of it.

Momsen's most important advice for new alternative graders is to "know your limits." Keep it simple, and do what you can, in your situation, to make a difference. She is especially grateful to her colleagues and others in the field who supported her, gave feedback on her list of standards, and helped her prepare her standards-based class.

Specifications Grading in a General Education Art History Class

Gretchen Bender is a senior lecturer in the History of Art and Architecture Department at the University of Pittsburgh, a large research-intensive university. Bender has taught at Pitt for over 20 years in the "appointment stream," a permanent nontenure-track stream, and has won multiple teaching awards in that time.

Bender regularly teaches a 200-student class, Introduction to World Art. This introductory course meets general education requirements as well as requirements for engineering, business, and other majors. Bender describes the course as "an 'antisurvey' which introduces students to the significant diversity of cultural production across the world and interrogates the term *Art*." Bender typically has support from two graduate teaching assistants and, sometimes, undergraduate learning assistants.

In the past, Bender used a very common assessment structure: two exams, a final paper, and nothing more. Bender's specifications-based assessment system now asks students to engage with course ideas on a weekly basis. She finds that this regular engagement drives student growth and learning, while also reducing her grading load.

Bender first used specifications grading in this course in spring 2021. The timing wasn't accidental, as she describes in her syllabus: "In 2020, during the pandemic and protests for Black lives and calls for social and environmental justice, [...] I significantly reevaluated my teaching practice." Summarizing a podcast by Laurie Santos,[2] Bender writes:

> When grades are the primary focus of both students and teachers, the goal is not to learn more or discover something new or find inspiration or make connections between different kinds of classes or disciplines, or between school and life, but simply to demonstrate content knowledge (following the quickest route possible) and get the A. You're not doing it for the love of learning.

Bender puts this philosophy into operation by using specifications grading with a distinctly ungrading flair. In all assessments, Bender emphasizes growth, engagement, and connection to each student's individual life.

Assessments come in four types: "Assessment check" quizzes covering comprehension of weekly material, class attendance and participation in discussions, skill-building worksheets completed during museum field trips, and a final essay. All of these are graded "Satisfactory" or "Not Satisfactory" based on meeting specifications. Bender emphasizes that grading on a two-level scale was "far less time consuming for me than when I was parsing points and percentages."

Each assessment is graded using specifications. Bender bases many specifications on the general course goals listed in the syllabus, such as the following:

- Make precise, accurate, and comprehensive observations about an image, object, or space that supports an interpretation.
- Develop terminology to describe and analyze works of art in various media.
- Identify specific makers and patrons and consider how their situated circumstance, living in a particular place and time, determines the form and function of art.

Each week a new "module" (a package of related activities) is posted on the LMS, containing short recorded lectures, readings, and links to other relevant items such as web pages or images. Students are expected to use these resources as needed to familiarize themselves with the week's topics before attending class, but they are also available for use after class and on assessments.

Each module includes an "assessment check," a short LMS-based quiz, containing questions that test comprehension of the basic content of the module. Students are allowed to use all resources in the module and can take the assessment check multiple times. Bender encourages students to use the quiz as a guide while working through the module, as a way to highlight the most important ideas. Assessment checks are considered "Satisfactory" for grade purposes if eight of 10 questions are correct.

Here's an example of a question from an assessment check:

In the first lecture, focus was given to what appears on the bottom of the Terra-cotta soldier's shoe because (select all that apply):

- The sculpture was also meant to "face" the earth.
- This degree of detail provides the project with a sense of intimacy despite its epic scale and ambition.
- The remarkable detail on the bottom of the shoe can help us think about visibility (why do this if the work was never to be seen).
- Decorative designs that signal good luck were imprinted there.
- It demonstrates the exceptional (almost obsessive) attention that was given to recreate the soldier in full and minute detail.

And an example of a question addressing art history interpretive methods:

Which of the following would be considered through a diachronic approach to the Mosque at Cordoba? (Select all that apply)

- the use of spolia
- the 1523 addition of a Catholic church

- the double-arches with red brick and white stone voussoirs
- the Visigoth church of San Vicente
- the elaborate rib-work of the dome over the maqsura

Class meetings come in two types: a "discussion section" that meets weekly and periodic "art lab" field trips.

Discussion sections are the standard weekly meeting for the class. Lecture is replaced by videos and other resources in the weekly module. Discussion sections instead involve "discussion, looking at works of art together to build analytical skills, wrestling with questions the material raises, and engaging in activities that enable [students] to connect with others."

Bender and her graduate teaching assistants (TAs) record attendance and participation in discussions, but students can also demonstrate participation via an asynchronous discussion board prompt included in the weekly module. These discussions are graded for participation by successfully engaging with the prompts. Bender says that "these posts often require detailed responses and are akin to brief essays or low-stakes writing exercises." Students engage deeply with these prompts: "Students are far more adventurous in these as they aren't afraid of posting a 'wrong' answer."

Here is an example of a discussion prompt aimed at connecting class topics with a student's individual experiences:

> Is there a sacred site or structure that's meaningful to you or your family? Or one you have visited that made an impression? Can you post a photo or photos? Describe and analyze it, thinking about the key questions we applied to the sacred sites we've been studying:
>
> - How does the building relate to the site in which it's located? How is it experienced by viewers who approach and enter it?
> - What are the component parts and features of the site and how are they organized?
> - How does this sacred space function?
> - What religious practices take place and how does the architecture accommodate, shape, and enable this practice?
> - What is the experience of the observer on the inside of the structure and how is this related to religious or ritual needs?

The dual options for participation let students choose either type of participation based on their preferences.

The other regular class meetings involve a significant on-the-ground component: the "art lab." These are field trips to the University Art Gallery and Carnegie Museums of Pittsburgh in small (25-person) recitation sections, in which students engage directly with works of art and cultural artifacts as case studies. The purpose of art labs is to "develop more acute visual and material analysis skills—how to build their visual acumen in a highly visual world."

In a typical semester, there are eight art lab field trips, each managed by Bender and two graduate TAs. Students work in small groups to complete a structured "activity packet" related to one or more specific works of art. Bender describes the activity packets as "purposefully scaffolded, helping students move from basic description to the consideration of contextual information as they work toward interpretation." If a student is unable to attend, Bender posts the activity and asks students to visit the gallery and complete and submit the activities when they are able to do so.

The activity is meant to be completed while in the presence of the work, so we only provide short excerpts from the questions involved. Here are some questions from the very beginning of one activity packet:

Pope.L, *Position Paper*, 2018–2019

Do not look at the label. Read the questions, answering each one before reading the next one.

> Think about material and facture. What materials are used to make this work of art? Try to list as many of them as you can.
> How was this work made or assembled?
> What meanings do you think might be conveyed by these items or materials?
> Think about the role paint plays in the work. Where does it appear? What colors do you see? How was the paint applied to the surface of the work?

The second page instructs students to view several other works by Pope.L and includes some background information about the artist. The second page includes these prompts:

> Does seeing these earlier works by Pope.L help you see *Position Paper* in a new or different way? Do you recognize similarities between these earlier works and the work you are studying today? Differences?
> What might be some of the narratives or messages conveyed by *Position Paper*? If you were to write an explanatory wall label for this work, what do you think would be important to include?

The subsequent pages ask students to engage with different pieces of art, and especially focus on questions of form, material composition, and how other pieces of work by the same artist can help put one piece of their work in context.

Activity packets are marked "Satisfactory" or "Not Satisfactory," using specifications in a feedback guide that emphasizes building "slow and close looking" at works of art. A one-page summary of these specifications is provided to students (see Figure 8.1).

Figure 8.1. Feedback guide and specifications for activity packets.

STUDENT:

Description					
Student Observes and Considers:	Accurate, Thorough, and Precise Observations Evident	Careful Observations Evident, Still Developing (Could Be More Precise or Thorough)	Vague or Minimally Evident	Not Yet Evident	N/A
Material and Condition					
Materials used to make work					
Process of making/facture					
Signs of age, use, or wear					
Recognition of Formal Elements					
Format or overall shape of work itself					
Scale					
Color					
Light and shadow					
A sense of movement (how eye is "led" or directed)					
Shapes					
Texture					
Organization of space					
How constituent parts relate to the whole or are arranged and composed					
Perspective and/or viewing position					
Handling or technical manipulation of material					

(Continues)

Figure 8.1. (*Continued*)

Description					
Student observes and considers:	Accurate, thorough and precise observations evident	Careful observations evident, still developing (could be more precise or thorough)	Vague or minimally evident	Not yet evident	N/A
Contextual Thinking					
Their viewing experience if encountering work in person					
Intended audience and/or first spaces of use					
The maker's decision-making process					

Interpretation			
Student . . .	Yes	Developing	Not yet
Applies concepts or terms learned in class materials to work			
Uses descriptive language evocatively (e.g., adjectives or adverbs) to help reader imagine the work or see it in a new way			
Considers and discusses work's mood, affect, or impact on viewer			
Recognizes what is unknown or not evident and how this impacts the analysis			
Analysis develops productively as new information or evidence is revealed or becomes known OR student builds a logical argument			
Effectively moves from description to interpretation (moves from what one sees or notices to what one wonders or assumes about the work)			
Fully engages reader with an analysis or interpretation that is compelling			

Bender describes the feedback guide as a way to help students understand "where their strengths and weaknesses are so they can improve for the next submission." The instructors base "Satisfactory" marks on conscientious effort and students exhibiting growth over time, rather than meeting a specific number of specifications or reaching a certain "level" in each row.

If an assignment is not "Satisfactory," Bender uses the feedback guide to provide concrete feedback on the areas in which the student needs to improve. Students can reassess their work based on the feedback, either through an optional office hour discussion or a written revision and resubmission.

The last type of assessment is a final essay, related to the art lab field trips. At the end of the semester, students are

> asked to select and write about a work of art without using one of [the art lab worksheets], generating their own analysis and interpretation based on the skills they've developed and their familiarity with the types of questions that we have applied to works of art throughout the term.

The essay is assessed using the same specifications as the art lab activity packets. As with art lab activities, instructors focus on student growth over time: "Because students enter the course on different starting lines/baselines, we look for conscientious effort and improvement and endeavor to show students where and how they've improved."

Bender uses a grade table to incorporate the assessments into a final grade (see Table 8.1). Students must complete all requirements in a column in order to earn that grade. Note that the table includes "plus" and "minus" grades (such as A– and B+).

For support, Bender typically has two graduate TAs. Bender is the primary instructor and runs two of the art lab recitation sections; each graduate TA runs three other art lab recitations. Each instructor grades assignments and records attendance for students in their own sections. There are sometimes undergraduate learning assistants as well, who may hold office hours to discuss course topics with students or circulate to help during art lab sessions. The entire instructional team meets weekly and jointly develops the art lab worksheets.

Bender notes that her students are used to high-stakes exams whose grades are determined by comparing students through "curves," which in turn lead to inequitable results. The specifications address this:

> I do think these teaching practices are connected to issues of equity and inclusivity. . . . In a traditionally graded class, Those who enter the class with less experience, less skill, and/or those who have not benefited from

TABLE 8.1
Final Grade Table for Gretchen Bender's Introduction to World Art Class

	Assignments	D Grade: Minimally passing	C–	C Grade: Satisfactory engagement / S GRADE if taking the class S/NC	C+	B–	B Grade: Commendable engagement	B+	A–	A Grade: Exemplary engagement
Content Knowledge	Module assessment checks completed (scoring 80% or higher)	8	9	9	10	10	11	11	12	12
Critical Engagement and Skill	Discussion board posts or in-class discussion participation	5	6	7	7	8	8	9	9	10
Development	Art lab worksheets	3	3	3	3	4	4	5	5	6
	Final essay	No	No	No	No	Yes	Yes	Yes	Yes	Yes

well-resourced K–12 institutions, or those who learn in different ways, or are first-generation students are often inherently disadvantaged. So we are perpetuating an exclusionary cycle. . . . All students in my class have an opportunity to earn an A. And if they all complete the requirements for that A, then all of them will get an A. That should be what we are aiming for as teachers—to generate enthusiasm, competency, skill development, critical thinking and growth for all students. When students know this, it removes competition from [the] class environment and students begin learning together, the class becoming a mutually supportive community.

Bender's students are enthusiastic about the grading system:

- "It encourages students to work hard for the sake of knowledge rather than for a high grade on an exam. . . . This class allowed me to focus intently on the material. It allowed me to move at my own pace; therefore, I could more comprehensively understand the material rather than rush to memorize key terms before an exam."
- "I am a student who can easily become concerned about grades to the point where I am solely focused on doing good on the next test rather than actually trying to embrace the course material. This course didn't do that to me and I couldn't be more grateful for that."
- "Allowing students to determine the grade they wish to earn makes them much more accountable for their work, especially when they know exactly what has to be completed in order to be successful."

Nearly three quarters of students reached the requirements for an A (or "S" for students who chose to take the class "Satisfactory"/"Not Satisfactory"). Each student who earned an A met *all* of the requirements and specifications found in the assignments through documented, authentic work. As Bender points out, with regular weekly engagement and less grade pressure, students exhibited significant growth and became more creative, engaging, and compelling in their analysis of art.

While there is time and labor needed to reimagine a grading system, Bender says that the benefits far outweigh the costs:

Students are far more engaged and the time you used to devote to point tabulation, configuring curves, addressing student concerns about points lost and grade disputes can now be devoted to engaging students on matters of greater substance, and enjoying work that is more creative and intellectually stimulating when the weight and pressure of the grade is alleviated.

Big picture thinking for students and instructors replaces the micromanagement of grade computation and explanation.

SBG in a Coordinated, Multisection Calculus Class

Hilary Freeman is a full-time nontenure-track teaching faculty member in Colorado State University's Mathematics Department, where she coordinates and teaches a large multisection Calculus course. Most of the rest of the instructors are graduate TAs that Freeman trains. There are typically around eight sections, with sizes ranging from 36 students (typically taught by graduate TAs) up to 85–120 students (typically taught by nontenure-track faculty).

In the past, the course was assessed using three midterm exams (each held in the evening), one cumulative final, and weekly written and auto-graded online homework. Freeman redesigned the class using SBG in fall 2020, when large evening exams couldn't be held due to the COVID-19 pandemic.

Freeman's course is based around 28 content standards, provided on a list that also includes a complete list of assessments for each standard. Students must demonstrate understanding of each standard multiple times, with the exact number of demonstrations varying between standards. Requiring multiple demonstrations ensures that students show their continuing ability to complete the relevant tasks over time. Table 8.2 is an excerpt from the list of standards and assessments.

TABLE 8.2
Sample of Content Standards and Assessments in
Hilary Freeman's Calculus Course

Derivatives:

D1: I can explain the purpose of each symbol in the limit definition of derivative. I can illustrate each part of the definition graphically and explain the role of the limit.

Assessments: ☐ Module 5 HW ☐ Module 6 HW ☐ Module 7 HW
Revisions: ☐ Module 5 ☐ Module 6 ☐ Module 7 ☐ Module 8 (Bonus)
BYOF/Special Revision: ☐
Once you have checked at least *two* boxes above, you can fill in a box on the front page.

D2: I can interpret the meaning of a derivative in context.
Assessments: ☐ Module 5 HW ☐ Module 6 HW ☐ Module 8 Q
Revisions: ☐ Module 5 ☐ Module 6 ☐ Module 8 ☐ Module 10 (Bonus)
BYOF/Special Revision: ☐
Once you have checked at least *three* boxes above, you can fill in a box on the front page.

The course is organized into "modules," about one per week. Each module covers multiple standards, and standards may appear in more than one module. Freeman shares modules and assessments with instructors via a course shell in the LMS, used as a template for each section. Thus, each instructor receives a "ready-to-go" set of assessments.

The assessments that appear in most modules include the following:

- Quizzes, given every other week. These are completed in class and on paper, although in some semesters they have been offered online using the LMS. There is also one midterm exam, which Freeman describes as a "glorified quiz," offering a larger than usual number of standards and reassessment opportunities.
- Homework, on alternate weeks from the quizzes. This homework includes questions that address both computational fluency and conceptual understanding.
- Two "live assessments," which are assigned to groups of four students ahead of a meeting with an instructor. The students individually submit work before their meeting, then meet with the instructor as a group to verbally address the questions, focusing on their reasoning, as well as follow-up extensions from the instructor.

When grading, instructors assign one of three marks on each standard: "Meets Expectations," "In Progress," or "Not Gradable." Instructors also give detailed feedback along with the mark. When a student earns "Meets Expectations," they can check off the corresponding box in the syllabus. Once they have checked the required number of boxes, the standard is considered "complete."

Freeman's class also includes automatically graded online assignments that primarily assess procedural or computational skills. Students have unlimited attempts, and only their final percentage is used in final grade determination. Student participation and attendance is recorded by each instructor using various methods, such as completing an exit ticket or participating in an online chat system. Finally, modules include ungraded interactive online activities that students can use for practice.

There is also a "build your own final" exam ("BYOF"). Students can choose up to four standards that they still need to complete, and are then given access to individual short quizzes (one per standard) on the course LMS. This is the entire final exam. Freeman has used this system both with online classes and face-to-face, in which case students brought laptops to class to complete the final. Those who needed computer access could take the final in a reserved computer lab.

Reassessments, which Freeman calls *revisions*, are actually new problems covering previous standards. To avoid logistical issues, only selected standards are eligible for revision in any given week. These are visible to students in the course syllabus.

Revisions take place in two ways. The primary form of revision is through regularly scheduled assessments. Each module includes optional new attempts at past standards, either via a quiz, homework, or live assessment, and can be completed by students who earned any mark.

The second form of revision occurs outside of class, using the "Calculus Center," a tutoring center that is available to all students and works with Freeman to support her Calculus class. She explains:

> Students receiving a grade of "In Progress" can download a revision guide which has some common errors students made, references to class materials where the topic was taught, and sample problems for them to practice. Students [then] visit the Calculus Center and have a conversation with a tutor about the metacognitive piece (what the mistake was, how to not make it in the future) as well as demonstrating [their] ability to handle a new question. After a successful demonstration of competency, the tutor will assign a revision quiz in Canvas [the institution's LMS] and the student will be graded on their performance on that quiz. These quizzes are usually automatically graded so the instructor can just look at the grade book and then update [it].

Freeman used to require written reflections, but "switching to a conversation with a live person helped reduce grading workload and improved the quality and success of the revisions." Metacognitive questions and review help students understand past errors, while completing a revision quiz ensures that they can complete a new problem fully correctly. The strictly scheduled options for reassessment help limit additional workload on tutors.

Figure 8.2 shows part of a "revision guide" that Freeman creates for each standard. This guide is for standard L7: "I can compute average rates of change and find slopes of secant lines." An earlier part of the guide states this standard, as well as where the standard was first addressed (in this case, Section 2.1 of the textbook, and a specific online activity).

The next page of the revision guide includes sample problems that tutors may ask students to complete and discuss before attempting a new problem for credit. Revision guides also give students some prompts to prepare for the metacognitive conversation, such as "I used to think ___, but now I think ___ because I learned ___."

Figure 8.2. Revision guide for standard L7.

My Favorite Mistakes:

The common mistakes I saw were more about following directions or paying attention to notation.

1. Notation: the data given to you was with x as a function of t, so if you used notation in your work, you should have matched with x as the output and t as the input. (Pro tip: "as a function of" is a pointer to the input value, so x as a function of t is telling you that x is the output and t is the input.)

2. Function notation: $f(a)$ means plug a in for the input variable into the rule f. In other words f is a set of directions for what to do with a. This notation here does NOT mean multiplication (I'm sorry for this notation meaning multiple things—I can totally see why this would be confusing.) If you have ANY questions about this, please ask at the Calculus Center ASAP as we will be using this notation all semester!

3. The most common 'not following directions' mistake was not computing the AROC on parts b and c.

Examples

1. Compute the average rate of change between $x = 4$ and $x = 7$. Then find two inputs where the AROC will be positive.

x	3	4	5	6	7	8
$f(x)$	3.7	4.6	5.2	8.7	3.8	2.7

$$\frac{f(7) - f(4)}{7 - 4} = \frac{3.8 - 4.6}{3} = \frac{-0.8}{3}$$

AROC is positive between $x = 5$ and $x = 6$.

2. Compute the average rate of change if $f(x) = \sin(x)$ over the interval $[0, \pi/4]$.

$$\frac{\sin(b) - \sin(a)}{b - a} = \frac{\sin(\pi/4) - \sin(0)}{\pi/4 - 0} = \frac{\sqrt{2}/2}{\pi/4}$$

3. Compute the slope of the secant line if $f(x) = e^x$, and $a = 1$ and $\Delta x = 0.2$.

$$\frac{f(a + h) - f(a)}{h} = \frac{e^{(1+0.2)} - e^1}{0.2} = \frac{e^{1.2} - e}{0.2}$$

These revision guides provide clarity about expectations for meeting standards and develop metacognition about a student's work. The guides also organize and structure the revision process.

Freeman allows submissions with no penalty until grading actually begins (typically 2–3 days after the stated deadline). Because there are multiple opportunities on each standard, a student who misses an assignment can simply try again in a later module.

Course grades are assigned using Table 8.3. Students must complete *all* requirements across three categories in order to earn a grade.

TABLE 8.3
Final Grade Table for Hilary Freeman's Calculus Class

Grade	Web Work (Online Homework)	Participation (of 70)	Standards Completed (of 28)
A	90–100%	≥ 60 points	≥ 25
B	80–89%	≥ 50 points	≥ 22
C	70–79%	≥ 40 points	≥ 19
D	60–69%	no requirement	≥ 17
F	Have not *fully* completed any other row.		

In general, students in Calculus will only earn a "whole" letter grade as shown in the table. Colorado State does include some partial grades (e.g. A–, B+, etc., but not C– or D+). Instructors meet together at the end of the semester to make decisions about assigning partial grades to borderline cases. Changes are only made that will benefit students.

To keep track of their progress, students can see the individual components of the final grade, including online homework and participation, in the LMS gradebook. Progress on standards is also recorded in the LMS gradebook by indicating which assignments students have successfully completed. However, this information can be hard for students to interpret since the LMS doesn't indicate which letter grade they have reached.

Freeman provides two places for students to keep track of their own progress. The first is the list of standards from the syllabus, which we saw previously, which acts as a fill-in-the-blank page that students can use. The second, on the front of the standards sheet, is a list of boxes that can be checked when a standard is fully complete (see Figure 8.3). This second page shows progress toward earning a grade.

Asking students to track their progress in this way is helpful for several reasons. First, it helps students become more comfortable with how the alternative grading system works. Second, the explicit list of assessment opportunities helps students plan ahead.

Freeman's students love being able to dig into ideas deeply and use revisions to show their understanding. The combination of smaller quizzes and revisions means that students have less test anxiety. As Freeman notes:

> The main benefit I experienced was the ability to say yes to students with requests for extensions or having missed assignments. Also, for students with documented disabilities, I had fewer accommodations to provide specifically for them because the entire class was already meeting most of their accommodations. Previously exam weeks involved handling alternate exam requests, judging which students got approved and which didn't, and organizing make-up exams. . . . I felt like I was no longer punishing students for having a life. (Really made me reflect on how punitive the "traditional" system is—ouch!)

Freeman has also noticed more students earning A's. Because of the SBG system, those A's aren't inflation: They mean that students have fully met the key course objectives.

Freeman notes that many of the keys to making her SBG setup function smoothly are the same as they would be in any coordinated class, using SBG or not: planning ahead with a clear schedule of topics and assessments, making assessments available to all instructors, and managing the logistics of proctoring. More specific to SBG, partnering with the Calculus Center and

Figure 8.3. Boxes for recording completed standards.

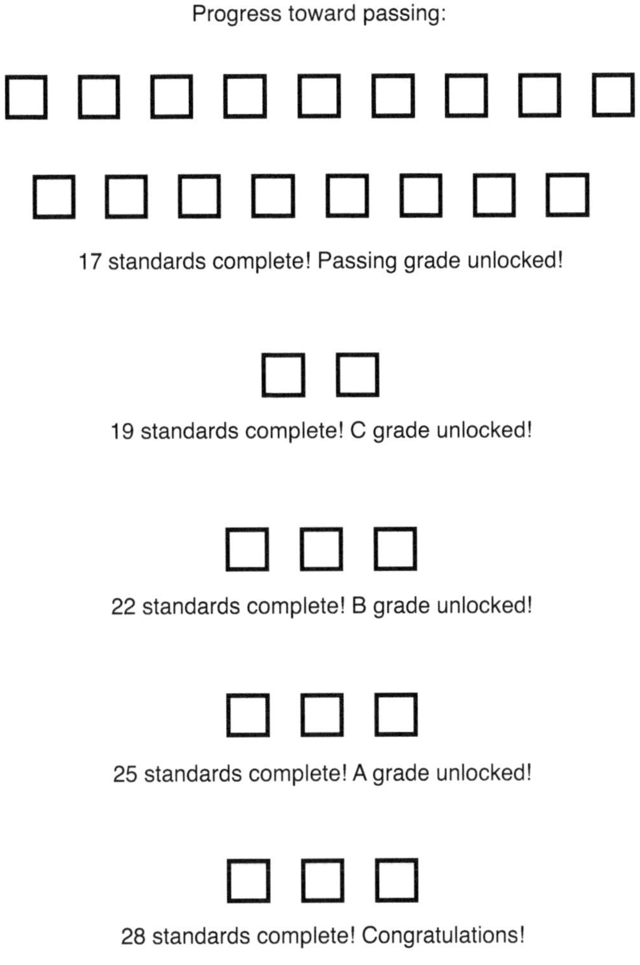

Progress toward passing:

☐ ☐ ☐ ☐ ☐ ☐ ☐ ☐ ☐

☐ ☐ ☐ ☐ ☐ ☐ ☐ ☐

17 standards complete! Passing grade unlocked!

☐ ☐

19 standards complete! C grade unlocked!

☐ ☐ ☐

22 standards complete! B grade unlocked!

☐ ☐ ☐

25 standards complete! A grade unlocked!

☐ ☐ ☐

28 standards complete! Congratulations!

having clear revision guides is critical to making out-of-class reassessments work. In addition, keeping in touch with students who aren't making appropriate progress is a challenge. Freeman has explored automated ways to send a "progress report" to every student at regular intervals, for example through a combination of a spreadsheet and mail merge.

Freeman mentions that it can also be challenging to train new graduate TAs and other instructors about SBG, since it is often an unfamiliar system. In addition to providing a clear syllabus and complete set of course materials, she begins with a presemester meeting to discuss the course and SBG. Another way that she trains graders is through common grading on the midterm exam. Besides developing norms for grading standards, this "grading party" also helps build community among the instructors. We will see more examples of how to support a large group of instructors in the next case study.

Supporting Instructors in Multisection SBG Statistics

Silvia Heubach and Sharona Krinsky are cocoordinators for a multisection general education introductory statistics course. Both teach at California State University–Los Angeles, a large urban university. Their course consists of many sections—typically around 80—each with at most 25 students. There are about 20 instructors teaching these sections. Here we will focus on how they support this group of instructors in using alternative grading.[3]

In this SBG course, all standards are assessed using the same rubric, as shown in Table 8.4. This rubric includes descriptions for students and "interpretation" notes aimed at instructors. Rubrics help instructors make consistent grading decisions. Students must earn two ✓ or ✓+ marks in order to earn credit for a standard.

Heubach and Krinsky engage in "group norming" discussions with the instructors. After students complete each major assessment, the instructors gather on a video call to discuss how each standard will be graded. Meeting online makes it easier for all instructors to attend, especially those who are adjuncts teaching at multiple institutions. To begin this process, the coordinators collect several anonymized examples of student work (often proposed by instructors), focusing on examples likely to be on the borderline of "Meets Expectations."

Focusing on one example at a time, each instructor first uses the rubric individually to decide on a mark. All instructors reveal their decisions simultaneously and discuss their reasoning and come to consensus. All of the agreements, notes, grading rubrics, and similar materials are posted in a central repository on the LMS, to which only instructors have access.

Instructors then grade their own sections' work based on this consensus. The coordinators perform spot-checks on the grading. However, in several years of teaching with this system, only once have these spot-checks found a significant deviation from the agreed norm.

Krinsky and Heubach noted that they have benefited greatly from a core group of instructors who teach sections of the course most semesters. As these instructors have "bought in" to the SBG system, they also help train new instructors and provide support and encouragement.

TABLE 8.4
Rubric for All Assessments in Heubach and Krinsky's Statistics Course

Mark	Formal Meaning	Informal Meaning	Interpretation
✓+	Exceeds Expectations—exceptional understanding	I own this! I can explain how to do this task and why it works to someone else. I can complete the task in both familiar and unfamiliar situations—I could teach it.	Student demonstrates complete understanding of the relevant concepts and solution methods. • Problems are solved correctly and completely. • Concepts are applied and explained correctly. • Arguments are complete, convincing, and clear.
✓	Meets Expectations—solid understanding	I know how to do this task. I can do problems independently, but I am not quite sure why it works. I can complete this task in familiar situations with good accuracy and few mistakes.	Student demonstrates understanding of the relevant concepts and solution methods. • Solution of problems may include some algebraic or conceptual errors, but they are minor. • Arguments are mostly complete, but may have some omissions of details.
◯	Needs More Work—partial understanding	I do not quite understand how to do this task and need to look at examples to complete the problem. I can complete the basics of this task in familiar situations only.	Student demonstrates partial understanding of the relevant concepts and solution methods. • Problem solutions contain a fundamental error, conceptual misunderstanding, or the solution is incomplete. • Arguments are only partially correct or are unclear.
X	Insufficient Evidence to assess	I have no idea what you are talking about and can't write enough down to make sense of!	Insufficient work was shown to determine the level of understanding of this standard.

Key Ideas

We can isolate some key principles for implementing alternative grading in large classes:

- *Plan ahead.* Make a thorough schedule of what will be assessed, when, and how, for the entire semester, including reassessments. A clear schedule helps everyone keep track of what's coming next. Keep graded assignments on a regular and predictable schedule.
- *Build in simple, automated flexibility for due dates.* The sheer number of students guarantees you will encounter the need for many due date accommodations. Find a way to build in flexibility that requires little, if any, intervention from you, and advertise it clearly to students.
- *Keep reassessments limited.* You don't need to allow students to reassess every standard on every problem set or exam. Allow one reassessment in a subsequent assessment, then let that standard "drop off" until later in the semester.
- *Use as much support as you can get.* There are many sources of support: TAs, graders, classroom or learning assistants, even your institution's tutoring services. Find out what those sources are and don't be afraid to use them.
- *Keep it simple.* Every one of our interviewees stressed that a streamlined grading system is essential to navigate the scaled-up requirements of large classes. The more complexity you add, the more opportunities there are for confusion. For example, try to limit the number of graded assessments, and check only for effort and completion when possible. Likewise, a short but focused list of standards can keep your assessments from becoming overwhelming. If in doubt, pick just one or two pillars to focus on: You will still see benefits.

Other examples of large courses, both one-section and multisection, can be found in the notes.[4]

Notes

1. Feldman, 2018.
2. "Making the Grade," *The Happiness Lab podcast*, November 19, 2019. https://www.pushkin.fm/podcasts/the-happiness-lab-with-dr-laurie-santos/making-the-grade

3. Full details can be read in their article about this course: Heubach & Krinsky, 2020.

4. Examples of large single-section classes include Boesdorfer et al., 2018 (chemistry) and Chen et al., 2022 (computer science). See Zimmerman, 2020, for details of a multisection math course.

9

LAB CLASSES

L aboratory-based classes pose unique challenges for alternative grading. They come in a nearly unlimited range of formats. "Studio lab" classes integrate the lab portion with lecture sections, while others have these separate. Some classes have the same instructor for both lecture and lab, while others have different instructors. Additionally, they have many of the challenges we've seen in other kinds of courses, including large class sizes. How does one begin to implement alternative grading in these courses?

The case studies in this chapter will give some insights on how to address these issues. They are organized based on the degree to which the lab and lecture components are independent of each other. As we will see, courses where the lab and lecture are integrated benefit from different approaches than those in which the two parts are taught separately.

Specifications Grading in Large Multisection Labs

Renée Link is a professor of teaching at the University of California–Irvine, a large research-intensive public university. Link is the coordinator for Chem 51LC: Organic Chemistry Laboratory. This is the second organic chemistry lab course in a three-course sequence, but it is the final organic lab that most students are required to take. There is an associated lecture course (called Chem 51C) in which students must enroll simultaneously, but the lectures are run independently from the labs, and students earn a separate grade for the lab course.

UC-Irvine's academic calendar uses quarters, making each course about 10 weeks long, plus a final exam week. While our focus here is on the lab aspects of this course, this case study also demonstrates that alternative grading can be done successfully in quarters or other short terms.

Chem 51LC is a truly enormous course, typically enrolling between 1,000 and 1,200 students, and is organized into lab sections of 16–20 students (so between 50 and 75 sections). Link's lab instructors are graduate student teaching assistants (TAs). The labs themselves are held for 4 hours, one time per week. In addition to the lab sections, Chem 51LC students also enroll in one of four 50-minute "lab lecture" sections taught by Link each week. Lab lecture sections, which are separate from the main "lecture course," include up to 400 students. Lab lectures may focus on developing conceptual understanding of the week's experiment or technique, analyzing sample data, critiquing sample lab assignments, or other topics as needed. Depending on their schedules, a student's lab meeting may occur before or after the lab lecture. As a result, all required prelab material is covered asynchronously via readings or videos.

Link uses specifications grading in these labs. She explains how lab courses have special requirements when it comes to alternative grading:

> Lab courses can be very different from other types of courses (oddly, they are actually more similar to writing courses in many ways) in that we don't have a large number of objectives. Rather, we have a small number of objectives that each appear in most, if not all, experiments throughout the course. Rather than build letter grade bundles based on meeting a certain number of objectives, I build the grade bundles on students being able to show me they can meet the objectives more times and at higher levels of difficulty.

Link uses three main types of assessments:

- *Lab notebooks.* These are a combination of prelab assignments, asynchronous prelab material, and in-lab experimental record keeping. They ask students to describe prelab preparation, safety, and experimental procedures before their lab section and to record data and observations during their lab section.
- *Postlab reports.* A detailed written lab report including methods, results, analysis, and conclusions. Since this is the second quarter of the course, students are expected to write lab reports with less scaffolding than in earlier courses.
- *Hands-on technique videos.* Students record a video of themselves demonstrating a specific technique (a partner can help record the video). This is recorded either during a regular lab period or during a designated week set aside for the purpose.

Each of these assessments includes a clear list of specifications. To earn a mark of "Satisfactory" on the assignment, students must complete a certain number of these specifications, indicated on the assignment. For example, passing a lab report may require meeting five out of seven specifications. On some items, such as technique videos, certain specifications are marked as required and must be completed in order to pass the assignment. If students don't meet the specifications, they earn a mark of "Needs Revision."

To illustrate how specifications work in Link's labs, we'll focus on one type of assignment: the hands-on technique videos. Students receive a complete set of instructions that covers both the technique to be demonstrated and general instructions for the videos. The specifications are included on the same sheet as the instructions. In the following example, five out of the six specifications must be met in order to earn "Satisfactory." Those five must include the four labeled "(required)."

Recrystallization (Mixed or Single Solvent) Hands-On Technique Video

To help guide your clips and the explanations you add later, here's what we are looking for when grading:

- Recrystallization setup: (1) Chooses appropriate glassware for recrystallization and solvents, (2) chooses appropriate solvents to recrystallize with, and (3) hot plate is set to appropriate temperature, and glassware and solvents are safely handled.
- First addition of solvent (required): (1) Appropriate amount of correct solvent is added, (2) solvent is at appropriate temperature, and (3) explains when and why to stop adding first solvent.
- Second addition of solvent (required): (1) Appropriate amount of correct solvent is added, (2) solvent is at appropriate temperature, and (3) explains when and why to stop adding second solvent. OR Explain why the addition of a second solvent is not necessary.
- Final addition of solvent (required): (1) Appropriate amount of correct solvent is added, (2) solvent is at appropriate temperature, and (3) explains when and why to stop adding second solvent. OR Explain why the addition of a second portion of solvent is not necessary.
- Steps to isolate crystals (required): (1) Correctly prepares glassware for cooling process(es), and (2) correctly isolates, rinses, and dries crystals using appropriate glassware and solvent(s).
- Percent recovery: Explains how percent recovery is determined.

Lab notebook and postlab report assignments also contain lists of specifications, and the requirements for these vary depending on the type of assignment. For example, specifications for the lab notebook assignments (which are completed before and during lab) focus more on completion and effort than on correctness. Here is what Link writes about these assignments in her syllabus:

> IT IS OK TO BE WRONG BEFORE LAB! Give the reactions, mechanisms, hypotheses, calculations, etc. your best effort. Fill out the tables completely. If you get to the lab section and find out you did something incorrectly or decide to change a piece of glassware or equipment, that's ok. Just make the change in your [notebook].

In addition to these main assignments, there are two different "final" exams: a multiple-choice "knowledge and safety check" (required for passing the course with a C or better) and an open-ended "proficiency exam" (required for earning an A or B). There are also smaller assignments that include prelab video quizzes, online homework, and participation in lab lectures. These are used to modify the final grade with a "+" or "−."

The final proficiency exam consists of six questions that are each graded on a three-level scale: 0, 0.5, or 1 point each. These correspond roughly to major errors or inappropriate work, a significant error but with relevant progress, and correct with at most minor errors. The "grade" for the final exam is the sum of the scores on each problem, leading to a number from 0 to 6. Because this exam is high stakes and can't be reassessed, Link sets B level at 1.5 points and A level at 3 points. She also allows students to make minor adjustments to this exam's grade using tokens, which we describe next.

All reassessments are organized around tokens. Link manages reassessments in a highly structured way that still leaves a great deal of flexibility. We'll go into some detail about these reassessments, because (as Link says), "I really think tokens are essential to doing this type of grading in a course this large." Link's reassessment system also demonstrates how to make reassessments manageable in a huge class with many TAs.

Students begin the quarter by completing a metacognitive assignment and earn their first four tokens for passing it. They can earn additional tokens by completing other special assignments throughout the quarter. Link records each student's current token total in the course LMS, where it appears as the "grade" for the metacognitive assignment and is updated by TAs as tokens are used. Link points out that limiting the number of tokens (eight at most) is important for keeping workload manageable for instructors.

Students can use a token to submit a revised lab notebook or postlab report. These must be submitted within 72 hours of receiving the "Needs Revision" mark, although students can use additional tokens to extend this revision deadline by 24 hours each. Link says, "This time limit is necessary to manage the grading workload on the TAs and to keep students from digging themselves into a hole with too many assignments that they need to resubmit."

Technique videos, on the other hand, may need to be rerecorded. Instead of a 72-hour window, there is one hard deadline for technique video revisions at the end of the quarter. Link sets aside a week during which students can rerecord videos in the labs. There are only three techniques video assignments in total, which helps make this reassessment approach manageable.

Smaller assignments also benefit from tokens. For example, students can use two tokens to reopen an online homework assignment for 48 hours, and one token can substitute for missing a lab lecture. Link posts a complete list of ways that tokens can be used on the course's LMS page.

To use a token for any of these purposes, students submit a short Google form that indicates which assignment the token will be used on. No instructor permission is required: The form is just for record keeping.[1] Separately, either Link or one of her head TAs updates the student's token total in the course gradebook and leaves a comment on the appropriate assignment indicating that a token was used. She finds that this is a quick and easy process.

If a student misses a lab entirely, they can instead use three tokens to make up the missed lab. This is a heavy price, but also allows students to make up a lab with no excuse required. Link has special policies for unusual circumstances, such as health issues, that cause students to miss multiple labs.

The "knowledge and safety check" final exam (which is required to pass the class) can be reassessed by taking a new version of the exam at a designated time. This retake does not require a token, but is only available to students who don't earn "Satisfactory." This exam is multiple-choice, so it can be autograded, making this retake feasible. If a student doesn't pass on the second attempt, Link uses an element of ungrading: She asks them to suggest an appropriate grade with supporting reasoning. She finds that students almost always suggest an appropriate grade, and are sometimes too hard on themselves.

The proficiency final exam (which is only required to earn an A or B) has open-ended questions, and so must be graded by hand. This means that reassessments of the exam aren't possible at the end of the quarter. Instead, Link allows students to use two tokens to adjust their score upward by 0.5 points, although this can only be done once. This allows students to move upward

TABLE 9.1
Final Grade Table for Renée Link's Organic Chemistry Lab

	Lab Notebooks (7)	Postlab Reports (5)	Technique Videos (3)	Knowledge/ Safety Check Exam	Proficiency Exam (6 pts)
A	6 Satisfactory	4 Satisfactory	3 Satisfactory	Satisfactory	3 pts
B	5 Satisfactory	3 Satisfactory	2 Satisfactory	Satisfactory	1.5 pts
C	4 Satisfactory	1 Satisfactory	1 Satisfactory	Satisfactory	Not required
D	3 Satisfactory	Not required	Not required	Not required	Not required

into the next grade category if they are almost there. For example, a student who earns 1.0 points can move up to 1.5, which is required to earn a B.

Table 9.1 shows how all of these elements work together to give a final "base" grade (A, B, C, or D). Link presents these grades as a list of requirements, with the instruction that "Your grade is the highest category for which you meet all criteria."

Students earn a "+" or "−" on this base grade based on their performance on the prelab video quizzes and online homework (which are both points-based) as well as participation in lab lectures (which is measured by being present to answer "clicker" poll questions). For example, to add a "+" onto their base grade, students must do *all* of the following:

- at least 90% average for online homework
- at least 90% average on prelab video quizzes
- credit for at least seven of eight lab lectures

On the other hand, students drop to a "−" if *any* of these occur:

- less than 60% average for online homework
- less than 60% average on prelab video quizzes
- credit for less than three lab lectures

Link also sets a "B− safety net": Students who have met all other requirements for an A or B, but who score below the B-level requirement on the proficiency exam, will earn at least a B−. This is another way that Link addresses the high-stakes nature of the exam.

The biggest benefit Link sees in this system is the flexibility that is built into it both for her as well as for students. The tokens incentivize revisions and make the process simple for students. Link finds that as a result, she gets fewer requests from students for deadline extensions, grade bumps, and so on. In addition, "When we hit pandemic teaching, it was easy to modify the grade bundle requirements [when] we had to work out how to do lab online."

Most students like the system: "I have students emailing me to specifically thank me for the grading system because it made them feel like it was ok to make mistakes and learn from them and that they can recover from an assignment where they don't do well." In addition, final grades have increased under this specifications system: "I set clear grade requirements and they met them, so I'm ok with the grades being higher." In particular, Link no longer needs to worry about "normalizing" or "curving" grades, as is often done in multisection courses: "Now I know what the grades are coming from. . . . It's much clearer to all of us now."

This isn't to imply that Link's specifications system is without difficulties. As many instructors have noticed, students aren't used to alternative grading, and this brings up different issues than in a traditionally graded class. "You have to sell it to them in the beginning and then keep talking about it and reminding them of how it works throughout the course."

One way Link has addressed this issue is with a midquarter grade-check assignment. In it, students compare their current progress to the grade requirements listed in the syllabus, list what they need to do to earn their desired grade, and make a plan to accomplish these items. This process helps students engage with the grade system and make concrete plans. It also earns them an extra token. However, "No matter how well and how often you explain and give examples of the grading system, in a class this large you have to assume 5–10% of students *and* TAs will be confused at any given time. You just have to accept that and keep answering the same questions and pointing to the same course documents explaining all of this over and over."

Because the lab course has so many students, in addition to teaching multiple lab sections and lab lectures, Link has the additional responsibility of overseeing a "small army of TAs" and ensuring they understand her grading system. She uses regular staff meetings, held weekly with all lab instructors, to discuss both practical and philosophical aspects of grading (in addition to discussions about lab details and safety issues). For example:

> In our first TA meeting of the quarter I talk about the grading system, why I use it, and what they are supposed to be doing. I keep a bullet point version of these talking points on our weekly meeting notes document so that it appears on their TA notes every single week.

Here are the key "talking points" from the meeting notes:

How Coursework Is Graded

1. Course grading scheme is specifications grading.
   a. Grade requirements are clearly defined.
   b. Most assignments are "Satisfactory"/"Needs Revision." No partial credit.
      i. This means that each individual rubric item will either get 0 points or 1 point. No decimals, no fractions.
      ii. "Needs Revision" ≠ fail
   c. If students meet all requirements to get a grade, they get the grade. There is no curve.
      i. It is up to you (the TA) to check the passing requirements for each assignment. For example (passing thresholds change):
         1. In-lab assignment A has seven possible rubric items. Five are needed to pass.
         2. If a student gets five or more rubric items, give them a ["Satisfactory" mark] on the whole assignment.
         3. If a student gets four or fewer rubric items, give them [a "Needs Revision" mark] on the whole assignment.

Why This Grading Scheme?

   d. High grades are not scarce resources and should not be treated as such. All students who meet A requirements earn A.
   e. Learning should be collaborative, not competitive.
   f. Students should be allowed to make choices—about their target grade, when to revise and resubmit, and so on.
   g. System provides much needed flexibility.

At this first meeting, Link emphasizes the importance of using the rubrics that she provides for grading; the amount of time that grading should take (10 hours per week, with a turnaround time of at most 1 week); and the fact that it is okay if students select a desired grade and therefore decide not to submit certain assignments. Link finds that having clear rubrics in particular helps her TAs use this specifications-based system.

A Physics Class With Instructor-Run Labs and Specifications Grading

In chapter 7, we discussed Joshua Veazey's Engineering Physics class. Here we provide a brief review of how Veazey runs the lab that is attached to his course.

Veazey's class has several lab sections, all of which he teaches. Labs are part of the final course grade, and Veazey has complete control over these labs. Topics covered are electricity, magnetism, and optics.

Each lab is structured with a guided worksheet, which has prompts for both data collection and analysis. Veazey grades these worksheets using three general specifications:

1. *Clarity.* All work is clear and legible. Physical reasoning is explained where appropriate.
2. *Plausibility.* Experimental data are plausible, or there is an explanation for why they are not plausible, specifically what went wrong.
3. *Mostly correct.* Most of the work is fully correct. Depending on the lab, "most" may be as low as 70% or as high as 100%. (This is described in more detail on each set of lab instructions.)

Labs earn a mark of "Satisfactory," "Progressing," or "Incomplete." A lab earns a mark of "Satisfactory" only if it meets all three specifications, "Progressing" if two specifications are met, and "Incomplete" if at least one question is unfinished or the student has not made a good-faith attempt.

Students can revise labs one time each. Revisions are due the week after the lab is returned. How a revision is done depends on which specifications weren't met. For example, a lab that isn't "mostly correct" can be corrected by reanalyzing data and resubmitting the lab worksheet. Students can revise a lab with implausible data by writing a reflection that suggests a reason why the implausible data were collected, supported by evidence from their lab notes.

Notice that, in general, revisions don't involve reattempting the lab, thereby avoiding the logistical problems of setting up and reattempting previous labs.

An example of the course's grade table, including details of how labs are counted, appears in chapter 7. Veazey notes that the lab was the first part of the course that he reworked to use specifications, and that this has motivated quality work.

Studio Lab With Specifications and Cross-Cutting Standards

Gloria Ramos is a professor in the Department of Physics at Citrus College, a community college near Los Angeles, California. Ramos teaches "studio"-style lab courses, in which lab and lecture time are integrated. We will focus here on her Electromagnetism and Thermodynamics course, which is the second semester of a required physics sequence and typically has 25 to 30 students per section.

Ramos's approach to assessment straddles the line between SBG and specifications grading. Ramos's standards (which she calls "outcomes") are much broader than the standards we have seen in other case studies. These outcomes are assessed in a wide variety of ways and in multiple contexts (such as labs, class activities, and written work), and final grades are based primarily on meeting outcomes. To help students understand what is expected, Ramos provides specifications describing what it means to "meet" each outcome. Different outcomes have different specifications.

Outcomes are divided into two major categories: physics content and cross-cutting scientific skills. These two types of outcomes have different requirements and are assessed differently. Ramos developed her outcomes based on curriculum guides created by the American Association of Physics Teachers.

Physics content outcomes are assessed on exams, as we have seen in several other SBG examples. These outcomes are divided into two categories that show the balance of topics in the class: "Electromagnetism" (16 outcomes) and "Thermodynamics" (four outcomes). Students must meet each content outcome once in order to earn credit for it in their final grade. Ramos observes students practicing with each outcome quite often during class, which gives her confidence in requiring only one demonstration of content outcomes on exams.

Examples of "Electromagnetism" outcomes include the following:

- EM 03: I can calculate the electric field due to multiple point charges.
- EM 04: I can apply the Energy Model to predict, analyze or explain charge interactions both qualitatively and quantitatively.
- EM 05: I can calculate the electric potential of a simple system of source charges such as point charges and linear charge distributions.
- EM 06: I can translate between multiple representations of the electric potential and the electric field associated with it.

The four Thermodynamics outcomes are the following:

- TD 01: I can predict, analyze, or explain any thermodynamic process of a gas as depicted on a PV [Pressure-Volume] diagram.
- TD 02: I can predict, analyze, or explain the behavior of a basic thermodynamic device.
- TD 03: I can predict, analyze, or explain any thermodynamic process of a gas as depicted on a TS [Temperature-Entropy] diagram.
- TD 04: I can predict, analyze, or explain thermal interactions resulting in phase changes and/or temperature changes.

Cross-cutting skill outcomes, called "Best Practices," cover a wide mix of scientific, community-building, and critical thinking practices, as well as completion of specific assignments.

Because these outcomes are broad, students practice with them in multiple contexts. Some examples include the following:

- I will actively participate in group discussions and treat colleagues with professional courtesy.
- I will prepare for class and actively practice doing physics.
- I can compose a scientific argument articulating my claim, evidence, and reasoning and/or doing problem analysis.
- I can keep an accurate lab notebook following course protocols, be respectful of our equipment, and follow lab equipment and lab safety protocols.
- I can write a lab report following standard IMRD [Introduction, Methods, Results, and Data] structure.

The goal of Best Practices outcomes is to help students learn what it means to do science. They are key to the integration of theory and practice in a studio lab course. These outcomes are assessed frequently, and the number of demonstrations required varies.

The Best Practices outcomes are quite varied, and so are the types of assessments that Ramos uses for them. We give a few examples here. To assess these outcomes, Ramos needs to observe some sort of action taken by students, but those observations don't always happen on traditional paper-and-pencil assignments. Some are observed directly during class time. For example, "I will actively participate in group discussions and treat colleagues with professional courtesy" can be practiced during class time with instructor feedback, and later assessed through instructor observation during class time. Ramos keeps a gradebook in which she can briefly record demonstrations of appropriate skills during class.

On the other hand, "I will prepare for class and actively practice doing physics" is assessed by completing at least 80% of practice assignments. *Prepare* here means preclass preparation assignments, while *practice* includes in-class activities (which are checked only for completion and effort) and "Skill Builder" assignments, which involve practicing writing parts of a lab report and will be described later.

Students have frequent opportunities for practice with feedback in Ramos's class. Indeed, most of class time is focused on practicing and being given feedback on outcomes, with only completion grades assigned for in-class work.

Regardless of how they are assessed, students earn one of three marks for most outcomes: "Successful," "Partial Understanding," or "Insufficient/ No Evidence." Ramos provides specifications for each of these marks in each assessment context, much as we saw in Joshua Veazey's hybrid class (see chapter 7, or the brief summary in this chapter). For example, for content outcomes that are assessed on exams, Ramos defines the marks using the "S, P, N" rubric in Table 9.2.

A few Best Practices outcomes are assessed in different ways. We'll focus on one example: "I can compose a scientific argument articulating my claim, evidence, and reasoning and/or doing problem analysis." This outcome ties together content and scientific methods. Students practice this outcome through in-class work and practice lab reports, which are checked only for completion and receive formative feedback. The outcome is formally assessed on exams by considering the problem-solving methods used across all relevant problems. Each content outcome is assessed independently from this Best Practices outcome, leaving room for a student to succeed on one outcome but not the other.

One particular argumentation method that students practice in class, "If-Then-Because," is an example of a method covered by this outcome. Students use "If-Then-Because" for making predictions or writing hypotheses. Ramos provides a template for students to use:

If the manipulated (independent) variable is changed in some specific way, *then* the responding (dependent) variable is affected in some specific way *because* of this reason supported by physics principles.

TABLE 9.2
Rubric for Outcomes Assessed on Exams

Mark	What It Means
Successful (S) (You got this!)	Proficiency in the outcome is evident through correct work and clear, audience-appropriate explanations. No significant gaps or errors are present. No additional instruction on the outcome is needed.
Partial Understanding (P) (Almost there!)	Partial proficiency of the outcome is evident, but there are significant gaps that remain. Needs further review/practice and evidence/ reassessment.
Insufficient/No Evidence (N) (Not yet!)	Not enough information is present in the work to determine whether there is proficiency of the outcome.

Ramos provides a special list of specifications for using If-Then-Because arguments on an exam question (see Table 9.3). Students must complete all parts of a row to earn that mark.

There are a number of other assignments and activities in the course, many of which contribute toward meeting specific outcomes. For example, lab reports and related assignments are assessed using specifications and ultimately contribute toward meeting the outcome "I can write a lab report following standard IMRD structure." Ramos explains how she helps students learn how to write lab reports in this style:

> I have students practice "building" a lab report in the order that they should be written. For the 1st and 2nd experiments, they only do [the] Methods section and the Data and Results section. For the 3rd experiment, they do methods, data and results, and introduction. I keep adding parts as we go. . . . This way they practice the hardest parts most often and can get detailed feedback over the first three or so labs.

TABLE 9.3
Rubric for Assessing If-Then-Because Arguments on Exams

Mark	If	Then	Because
Successful (S)	Clearly describes the manipulation of the (independent) variable.	Clearly describes the *specific*, expected effect on the responding (dependent) variable.	Provides reasoning components that support how the manipulation of (independent) variable will result in the predicted effect on the responding (dependent) variable.
Redo (R)	Manipulation of (independent) variable is vague.	Makes a general statement regarding expected effect on the responding (dependent) variable, but does not include specific details.	Repeats description of manipulation of (independent) variable and effect on the responding (dependent) variable, but does not explain how the one results in the other.
Insufficient/No Evidence (N)	Does not describe the manipulation of (independent) variable or description is inaccurate.	Does not provide expected effect on the responding (dependent) variable.	Does not provide reasoning, or only provides inappropriate reasoning.

Thus, students "build up" to writing full lab reports over the course of the semester. Ramos provides a detailed set of specifications for each part of a lab report.

When students practice individual parts of a lab report early in the semester, Ramos calls these "Skill Builder" assignments. Students are assessed only on the parts of the report that they are currently practicing, and earn credit for the Skill Builder assignment if each of those parts meets the specifications. As we saw previously, earning credit for Skill Builders contributes toward meeting the Best Practices outcome "I will prepare for class and actively practice doing physics."

Here is an example of the specifications for one section of the lab report. These are inspired by the work of LabWrite.[2]

Data and Results

Data and Results section only reports and describes what you observed, collected, and analyzed during your experiment. (The Data and Results does not explain, discuss, or draw conclusions.)

- Opens with effective statement of summary of overall findings
- Presents visual representations of data (tables, graphs, or other figures) clearly and accurately
  - Uses separate paragraphs for each visual with
    - A sentence of overall finding of the visual
    - A sentence describing the key details from the visual
  - All measured and calculated quantities' uncertainties reported in an uncertainty budget
- Presents verbal findings clearly and with sufficient support
- Successfully integrates verbal and visual representations

There are also specifications for Methods, Discussion, Conclusion, Abstract, Title, and References, as well as general specifications for formatting.

Once students have practiced each part of a lab report (via Skill Builders), they graduate to summative assessment. For the remaining lab reports, Ramos assesses each section using specifications, and students earn credit for the entire lab if each section earns "Successful." Each lab completed in this way counts as meeting the Best Practices outcome "I can write a lab report following standard IMRD structure."

Finally, Ramos includes "challenge problems" on in-class exams. These are broad, general questions where the goal is to demonstrate understanding of physics concepts in novel scenarios that cut across outcomes. The problems include a list of specifications describing "Successful" work. These challenge problems do *not* count toward meeting outcomes, but instead are required for earning an A or B in the course.

Reassessments of outcomes are completed in office hours, either via a conversation or by working a new problem. Students can also petition to revise lab reports or other written assignments, but must first show evidence of improved understanding.

To earn an A, a student must do the following:

- earn an S on seven of the eight Best Practices outcomes
- earn an S on 14 of the 16 Electromagnetism content outcomes
- earn an S on three of the four Thermodynamics content outcomes
- earn an S on the end-of-semester project's lab report
- earn an S on 14 (of about 17) challenge problems on in-class exams

For a B, a student must do the following:

- earn an S on seven of the eight Best Practices outcomes
- earn an S on 13 of the 16 Electromagnetism content outcomes
- earn an S on two of the four Thermodynamics content outcomes
- earn an S on the end-of-semester project's lab report
- earn an S on seven (of about 17) challenge problems on in-class exams

To earn a C, a student must do the following:

- earn an S on seven of the eight Best Practices outcomes
- earn an S on 11 of the 16 Electromagnetism content outcomes
- earn an S on two of the four Thermodynamics content outcomes
- earn an S on the end-of-semester project's lab report

The end-of-semester project is a special lab report that is graded using the same specifications as other lab reports. If a student doesn't meet the requirements for a C, Ramos assigns a D or F based on how close they were to a C.

Ramos likes that "students' grades reflect what they actually have learned." Her students like the flexibility that the system offers, especially the opportunities to improve their grades. Ramos sees that the practice aspects of the class—such as preclass preparation, in-class activities, and Skill Builders—greatly benefit students. "Practice without penalty and learning from mistakes is OK. They are never surprised about what they are asked to do on a test for the content outcomes because I've told them what I expect them to be able to do."

Key Ideas

Our case studies in this chapter give three rather different examples of lab experiences, formats, and approaches, varying by their degree of connection between lab and lecture. Here are some key takeaways:

- Alternative grading practices can be used successfully in lab-focused courses of all shapes and sizes, including large lab courses and those where the lab is integrated with a lecture section.
- Specifications grading is a common feature in many lab courses, since specifications are ideal for describing the processes and procedures assessed in labs, as well as for higher-level learning outcomes involving evaluation and synthesis.
- Courses that feature a tight integration of lab and lecture, such as those in a "studio" format, can combine standards that address specific content objectives with standards that address the integration of theory and practice.

Notes

1. Students are automatically emailed a receipt from the form, which they then forward to their lab instructor. This lets the instructor know that they should look for and grade the revised assignment.

2. LabWrite, 2004.

10

PARTIAL CONVERSIONS

For many, the alternative grading concepts we've seen in this book are deeply appealing—and deeply problematic, thanks to constraints they encounter in their particular situations. For example, you might be teaching one section of a tightly coordinated course that is graded traditionally. Or you might be a contingent faculty member with limited creative freedom over your course. Or you might simply have too much on your plate right now to commit to a full transition to alternative grading.

This chapter is all about taking a partial step toward alternative grading, by converting only a few aspects of your course and focusing on just one or two of the four pillars.

Standards-Based Testing

One of the simplest ways to introduce the concepts of the four pillars into a class without completely redesigning the grading system is through standards-based testing, also called mastery-based testing. SBT is "characterized by three essential features: clear course concepts, credit only for mastery, and multiple attempts to display mastery."[1] SBT is distinct from SBG in that it applies these concepts *only* to a subset of assessments and not to the entire course. (The "T" part of SBT should not be taken too literally; while the idea applies to tests, it can also be applied to quizzes, homework sets, or other forms of assessment.)

A typical approach to using SBT is shown in the following:

- Course content is divided into a small number (say, 10–20) of main course concepts. These concepts are similar to standards in SBG, but broader, roughly equivalent to a single section of an introductory textbook.
- Each concept is assessed on an exam, with each exam problem (or page of problems) corresponding to one of the concepts.

- Students do not receive partial credit; their work either demonstrates understanding of the concepts or it does not. The instructor makes the call in this case; a useful yardstick is the question "Will this student benefit from studying this topic again?"[2]
- If the work on the exam problem is not satisfactory, the instructor gives helpful feedback to the student along with an opportunity to try again. (The exact system for reassessment can vary; see the Creighton case study later in the chapter.)

Specific examples of SBT are given by Collins et al.[3] The authors are nine mathematics faculty at nine different institutions, each teaching different courses using SBT.[4]

In the authors' courses, the standards used for SBT are 10–20 "concepts" that represent fairly broad topics. The first exam in these SBT classes has one page of problems for each concept covered so far, perhaps concepts 1 through 4. The second exam has a page for each new concept covered since the last exam (perhaps 5–8) plus new pages with new problems that address the previous concepts (1–4). This continues, until the last exam includes a page for each concept. Typically the final exam is simply one last chance to complete any remaining concepts.

On each exam, students earn one mark for each concept page, based on how well they've demonstrated their proficiency with that concept across all work on the page. These marks are typically "Meets Expectations" or "Not Yet."

The instructor gives detailed feedback, especially for students who earn "Not Yet," and students can try again without penalty on a subsequent exam. Only one "Meets Expectations" is needed for each concept, after which the student no longer needs to attempt questions on that concept. Reassessments are handled entirely by making new attempts on scheduled exams. The same approach can work for weekly quizzes, in which case the authors recommend including fewer concepts, and keeping concepts on only two or three quizzes in a row before they "fall off," to appear once more on the final exam.

The key benefit to SBT is that it can fit into an existing weighted-average grading system without any other changes. A student's exam percentage is calculated as

$$\frac{(\text{number of concepts completed})}{(\text{total number of concepts})} \times 100,$$

and this value can be used in whatever weighting formula the class requires. This lets an instructor smoothly "drop in" SBT into a class with traditionally weighted grades. There are many alternatives for how to calculate this exam percentage, for example by allowing students to miss one standard and still earn 100%.

The authors recommend setting aside a few "core" concepts, much as Bowman did in chapter 5 on SBG. You can require students to "recertify" those core concepts on a final exam, which in turn can either be graded with a traditional percentage or used to modify the final grade with a plus or minus.

The authors also recommend having brief "quizzes" that assess only one or two especially difficult concepts, in between regularly scheduled exams. This gives students a chance to focus exclusively on one harder concept, while also giving extra opportunities to complete it. Quizzes can also keep the exams from becoming overwhelming for students who need to complete many reassessments.

Finally, some instructors use a three-tiered rubric, adding a middle level of "Progressing" or "Revisable" that allows students to revise work with minor errors rather than making a new attempt.

The authors developed a survey about SBT and gave it to their classes at multiple institutions. Students strongly agreed that the tests fairly assessed their knowledge, helped them learn, deepened their understanding, and prepared them to solve a variety of problems. They also found evidence that students experienced lowered test anxiety in SBT classes. The authors quoted one student as saying:

> I feel that [SBT] alleviated a lot of the pressure brought upon me as a college student from exams normally, and also reinforced learning concepts I had difficulty mastering in a different way, helping to solidify knowledge of concepts that I did not understand as well.

SBT provides an excellent first step to converting a class, and allows a partial implementation of alternative grading within an existing system.

Reassessments in a Heavily Coordinated Class

Chris Creighton is a lecturer and STEM curriculum specialist at Colorado State University–Pueblo, a small, regional Hispanic-serving institution. He teaches an introductory "precollege algebra" class, Math 101, which is one of many coordinated sections. The class has a required common schedule and common final exam, plus a required grade calculation method. Within these constraints, Creighton works to find ways to add in support for students while not going too far out of the coordinated bounds.

The class is fairly traditional: 10 quizzes, three midterms, and a final, all completed in class. There is autograded online homework as well. Quiz questions are each graded out of 5 points (two questions per quiz) and exam questions out of 10 points (eight to 10 questions per exam), and each form of assessment uses partial credit. Within this structure, Creighton focuses on the second and fourth pillars: helpful feedback and reattempts without penalty.

Creighton's main change is adding the ability to reattempt up to two quiz or exam questions each week. To do this, he uses a token system. At the start of the semester, each student initially gets 12 tokens. One token lets a student retake a quiz question, two tokens allow a retake of an exam question, and one token can extend a homework deadline. The "retakes" involve several steps. Students must first redo the original question correctly, and then attempt new practice problems supplied by Creighton. Finally, students schedule a time to complete a retake during Creighton's office hours.

Creighton put this procedure in place to ensure that students make a genuine attempt on the original problems and complete relevant practice, rather than rushing to the reassessment. The retakes are done via online office hours (using videoconferencing software), which Creighton finds is especially convenient for his students. They tend to attend online office hours more regularly than in-person ones, possibly due to work and family commitments.

The "retakes" are new questions that target the same general outcomes; Creighton prepares several versions ahead of time. The new grade on each problem replaces the previous grade. He notes that this process lets him be less worried about assigning partial credit or low scores, since students can boost their grades whenever they want. In addition, "I encourage them to write 'I'm not sure' on their work so that I can reach out afterwards." Creighton says, "The biggest change [is] in the messaging as the tokens send the message that 'it's okay if you need to return to this problem.'"

Although his sample size is small, Creighton notes that underrepresented students are more likely to take advantage of reassessments. Students report that the system reduces their test anxiety, and test scores are generally higher than other sections.

Creighton intentionally uses reassessments rather than other common options such as dropping low scores, offering extra credit, or adding points to an exam. This is because these other options do not actively encourage student learning; instead, they apply a bandage to a grade after the fact. His goal is for students to "do the work." He views reassessments as a way to achieve a similar end, but in a way that lets him "systematically do that in a fair way."

Creighton makes one other small but potentially impactful change: He grades all work online (using a special tool, Gradescope) and leaves only feedback on the work. Numerical scores are uploaded later to the school's LMS. Thus, students see feedback first, and this feedback is actionable due to the reassessment system.

He notes that the changes didn't take much time to plan and can be adjusted quickly depending on the course requirements.

> As it is an add-on to a traditionally run course, it is more work than not doing it. But most of the time is (1) proctoring (but that can happen quickly during office hours) and (2) creation of new problems (but that depends on how quickly I can modify them, which is quick for this class).

Creighton's approach shows how instructors in even tightly restricted situations can make changes that benefit students.

Using a Partial Conversion to Help New Students Track Progress

Betsy Barre is the executive director of Wake Forest University's Center for the Advancement of Teaching. She's a comparative ethicist who also teaches in the Department for the Study of Religions.

Barre splits the grading system in her "Ethics of Intimacy" first-year seminar into two halves. One half is based on Dustin Locke's "Levels" system, which we described in chapter 6 on specifications grading. The other half is traditionally graded using points and percentages.

Barre previously used the full Levels system, but found that her first-year students were anxious to know their "current grade" throughout the semester. Traditional grading systems can produce a current grade at any point, and Barre's students wanted to know this to help them keep track of their progress.

So Barre developed a way to calculate a "current grade" that includes the Levels essays. In her class, a student's grade consists of 1,000 points: 500 points from Levels essays and 500 points from other assignments.

Levels essays are initially assessed without points, in the way Locke described: A student either earns "Complete" on a level or not (after which they must attempt a new essay at the same level). However, for grade calculation purposes, students earn up to 500 points based on the highest level they have successfully completed and their progress toward the next level (if any). For example, successfully completing a Level 4 essay is worth all 500 points, while completing Level 3 with good progress toward Level 4 is worth 450 points. Completing Level 3 with no further progress is worth 400 points.

The other assignments, which are graded with points, include reading quizzes (150 points), a group podcast (150 points), and a final essay that is separate from the Levels system (200 points).

Thus, a student can calculate, and Barre can report, a "current grade" at any point in the semester by averaging together the currently completed assignments. For the Levels essays, the grade can be calculated using the maximum possible progress so far. For example, if the furthest any student could have progressed is Level 3 (worth 400 points), then the Levels grade can be calculated out of 400 points.

Barre calls this "giving the students a signal": a concrete report on their current grade. She finds that this approach gives students some sense of familiarity in their grade, while also getting much of the benefit from the specifications-based Levels essays.

If this interests you, you may want to read more about the Levels system in chapter 6 on specifications grading. Also be sure to read about other ways to report midterm grades and progress checks in chapter 12.

Key Ideas

In this chapter, we looked at different ways to implement alternative grading in situations where a full conversion isn't possible or desirable. Each of these instructors found a way to bring at least one of the four pillars into their classes. We saw three approaches:

- SBT, which localizes the concepts of SBG to individual assessment types rather than an entire course, allowing SBG-like assessment to take place within a points-based system
- adding retakes of traditional tests and quizzes using a token system, allowing students the opportunity to engage in feedback loops without altering the surrounding grade system
- coupling the "Levels" approach to essays with points to build a system that enables helpful feedback while still giving students concrete numerical measures to estimate their current grades

Partial conversions of grading systems are limited only by your creativity. The main point you should take away from these case studies is that if addressing even just one of the four pillars is what you can manage, then you are still helping students in a significant way.[5]

Notes

1. Collins et al., 2019.
2. Collins et al., 2019, p. 451.
3. Collins et al., 2019.
4. SBT is especially prevalent in math. In addition to Collins et al., 2019, see also Barth & Higginbottom, 2021 (describing the use of only a "Gateway Exam"); Halperin, 2020; Harsy, 2020; Mangum, 2020; Stange, 2018 (although it is described as "standards-based grading," the system uses SBT principles). SBT is also used in chemistry: Ring, 2017, calls their system "Specifications" but uses SBT principles.
5. Another example of a partial conversion in a math class that uses points while focusing on several of the other pillars can be found in Fernandez, 2021.

PART THREE

MAKING ALTERNATIVE
GRADING WORK FOR YOU

II

A WORKBOOK FOR
ALTERNATIVE GRADING

This chapter has a different setup and intention from the rest: It's a workbook for you to use to build a prototype of an alternative grading system in a course of your choosing.

In this chapter, you'll put all of the information from the book into practice. The goal is to create a complete working version of your assessment plan and grading system. The result may still need work, but it will be something that could be given to real students or colleagues for feedback. However, we're not going to build the entire class or make lesson plans.

The Process

The process you'll use in this chapter has 10 steps:

0. Compile background information on your course and identify what's special about it.
1. Determine the course structure and specific learning outcomes.
2. Do a high-level outline of the class and its systems.
3. Make a prototype of the marking methods and what A and C grades represent.
4. Outline the core feedback loops.
5. Build one assessment and rehearse the feedback loop.
6. Finalize all the components and think about implementation.
7. Devise the course grade assignment system.
8. Look for details and unintended consequences.
9. Sleep on it, then make it simpler.

Most steps begin with a detailed description, and a "Now You Do It" portion where you're given specific tasks. You will get the most out of this chapter if you work through these steps actively. First skim through this chapter to get familiar with what's in it, then loop back to the beginning, notebook or laptop in hand, ready to get your hands dirty. Between the description and instructions, you'll find a running example that helps illustrate each step.

But while this is a workbook, it's not a cookbook. You can, and should, adjust our steps in order to find what works best for you. The case studies show just how much variety can result. Just like any form of learning, the process you'll use here will necessarily involve mistakes, backtracking, multiple attempts, and iteration. We've built some feedback loops into the workbook to support this process. In addition, chapter 12 gives direct advice on some day-to-day items we've left out of the workbook.

Before You Begin

Right now, choose one course whose grading system you are interested in redesigning. You'll work through the workbook with this course to get the hang of the process; you can start over with different ones in future semesters.

What course should you choose? We're of two minds on this; here's our reasoning, and you can choose for yourself.

David

Pick a class you've taught several times, one for which you already have a solid schedule made up, a good feel for the flow of the class, and know where the tough spots are for students. This will let you focus on just one big change: the new assessment and grading system. This sets you up for success since the fundamentals of the class are already solid.

Robert

Pick any class you want, as long as you feel passionate about using alternative grading in it. Even if you've never taught it before, you can learn the details; it's your own commitment to and enthusiasm for alternative grading that will win the day. Fortune favors the bold. But remember to communicate with and listen to your students, be ready to make changes, and make sure you have the capacity both to learn a new course *and* use alternative grading in it.

Second, you'll need time and space for the work ahead. We suggest dedicating one entire (6-hour, plus lunch and breaks) day to this process and putting strict time limits on each step to keep yourself moving. Clear your schedule and find a space free of distractions. These constraints inject a helpful dose of creativity to your work and can help you generate ideas that you might not have otherwise had.

It's easy to *think* about your grading system but not actually *build* anything until the last moment, or get caught in the weeds and never actually complete anything. We're asking you, in this chapter, to "move fast and make things." If there are tricky details or big concepts you want to take time to explore, make a note and come back to them later. Don't let the perfect be the enemy of the good.

Finally, and above all else, observe the prime directive: Keep it simple. You will want to do it all, adding in details and special cases. *Do not do it all.* When in doubt, make choices that are easy to understand and leave flexibility for both you and students. Examine your ideas through the lens of a student. If it feels overcomplicated, it probably is.

Ready? Let's go!

Step 0: Compile Background Information on Your Course and Identify What's Special About It

In this step, you will do a quick but thorough round of research on your course and create a repository of materials to use later.

To have a successful and satisfactory experience with alternative grading, it helps to start by getting familiar with your course. We'll use a framework called the five W's that centers on five questions: *who, what, when, where,* and *why*? These questions may not be directly about grading, but they surface information that will affect your process and philosophy when designing a grading system.

In the following, we elaborate on each of these five W's with many examples of specific questions for each W. You don't have to answer every one of these questions. Use them as inspiration and keep moving rather than getting stuck on answering every prompt. Even if you can address only a handful of these (especially the "why" questions), you will have a much better grasp on your course.

Who?

Start with the humans involved.

- *Who are the students in the class?* Who typically takes this class? How new or experienced are they likely to be, and what prior knowledge might they have? What are their majors? What might their life experiences and situations be like? What other activities and commitments might they have? What are their goals and their perceptions of the subject and your discipline?

- *Who are the other stakeholders of your class?* A "stakeholder" is a person or group with an interest in your course. Is your course a general education requirement? Is it a prerequisite for some other course? Other stakeholders might include graduate programs at other institutions, the community in which you live or your students work, the families of your students, and more.

- *Who are you?* You are one of the most important stakeholders in the course. Are you at a point in your career and your personal life where you feel confident trying something new in your teaching? What is your experience level with the course, with these students, with your professional surroundings? Do you have a support network?

What?

We also want to know about the course itself.

- *What is the course about?* What are students supposed to learn by taking the course? What are its main points, or the main body of knowledge the course teaches?
- *What special requirements or features does the course have?* Are there any required assessments, such as a common final exam? Must a certain portion of the grade come from an assessment or group of assessments?
- *What level of creative control do you have?* How much freedom do you have over the grading system in this course, and to what extent do you need to meet external requirements or expectations in grading? (These relate to your stakeholders, described previously.) For example, is your course part of a coordinated collection of sections?

By this point, it's likely that constraints are becoming clear, and they may tempt you to give up. If you realize that you have a common final exam that counts for 25% of the course grade, a part of your brain will say, "I can't do this." While you must take constraints into account, don't give up. Constraints aren't a "no" to your plans; they are a call for creative thinking (and simplicity). Review the case studies and find examples that apply to your situation, and make sure you are plugged into a supportive community of practice.[1]

When?

The timing of a class is a huge factor in how you assess student work.

- *What's the academic calendar?* On what date does the academic term begin? If that's the date the course must be 100% ready, then by what date should the initial version of your course be ready?
- *What's the schedule for course meetings?* How does grading fit into the course schedule? The process of giving helpful feedback will change if your class meets three times a week versus once per week versus not at all (such as an asynchronous online course). Likewise, the length of your semester or term will affect your assessment plans.

Where?

The space that a class occupies—physical, virtual, or a combination—affects how student work and assessment take place.

- *What is the modality of the course?* Is it in person, synchronous online, asynchronous online, hybrid, or something else? How might this affect the types of assessments you can give?
- *Where will the class meet?* Do the meetings happen in a lecture hall where student movement is restricted by the design of the room? Do they happen in a flexible active learning space? Or on a video call? The answers to these questions might affect how you implement assessments and reassessments.

Why?

This is the most important group of questions. Even though we are trying to move fast, take some time with these.

- *Why does the course exist?* Why is it offered at all? What is its relationship to the rest of the curriculum in that discipline, and beyond the discipline?
- *Why do students typically take the course?* (This is related to the "who" questions.) Is it required for everyone? For anyone? Is it a general education class, an introductory course in the major, an advanced course in the major, a completely free elective? Is it intended for students on a particular professional trajectory?
- *Why are you teaching the course?* What drew you to teaching this course? Did you have a choice? What role does it play in your teaching portfolio or your overall career? What do you hope to accomplish by teaching it, and especially by using an alternative grading system?

We suggest that you take your answers to these "why" questions and put them on a 3×5 index card or a digital note so that you can review them from time to time, to remind yourself of your purpose and to help ground you when things don't go according to plan.

Finally, create a space (online or physical) for class materials. Add course materials that you can refer to as you design the grading system. If you've taught the course before, include a few old syllabi and assessments for potential reuse later, or ask colleagues for copies of their materials. Include the textbook, if you're using one. Put a few useful items in there right now and have a dedicated space to add more later.

A Running Example: The First-Year Seminar Course

In most of the steps of this workbook, we'll present an example of how that step works out in practice, using a fictitious but reality-based example that most instructors will find familiar: the First-Year Seminar course.

While the format and content of these courses vary widely, most are similar in that they focus on helping new college students adjust to college life, connect with the campus community, and learn how to be a successful student. These courses cut across all academic disciplines, which makes them good places to see how an alternative grading system might work. In fact these courses are excellent test cases for alternative grading on your campus, if you're looking for a place to start.

The fictitious First-Year Seminar course we will feature in this chapter has the following course description:

FYS 101: First-Year Seminar. 2 credits.

Description: A discussion- and experience-oriented course for new students at the university, focusing on the development of life skills, strategies for academic success, policies, and opportunities at the university, and becoming a lifelong learner in a global context. Each section limited to 16 students. *Prerequisite*: Enrollment in the university.

Let's also assume that FYS 101 is a required course for all students, and that students have to take it in their first year at the university and typically do so in their first semester.

Let's meet this fictitious class's fictitious professor: Professor Alice is a faculty member in her fifth year in a tenure-track position. She is teaching one section of FYS 101 this fall. She taught the course last fall, so she is familiar with it and enjoyed teaching it, but she didn't like the points-based grading system she used. She's eager to change things up and has the freedom to do so.

So Professor Alice takes a Friday in June, clears off all appointments, and books a study room in the campus library for the day. She packs her notebook, a laptop, and a productivity playlist on her music service. And like you, she's ready to get to work.

Step 0 in the First-Year Seminar Course

At the library, Professor Alice is all set up with her tools, beverage of choice, and a clear schedule for the day. She sets a 30-minute timer on her phone and launches into Step 0. Here is a sample of some of the questions she asks and her answers.

- *Who.* The students in the class are in the first 30 credits of their college experience, and they come from a mix of majors (including undecided) and backgrounds. Around 45% of all students at my university are first-generation college students, and many of them will have perceptions of college that are very much works in progress. I'm up for tenure next year, so I need to be mindful of getting buy-in not only from students but also my department chair and the First-Year Seminar coordinator. I also have an 8-year-old kid in school, and I need to make sure to set things up so that I am not grading night and day.
- *What.* The course is part of a coordinated group, all using the same overall syllabus of record. While I have creative control over how we engage with the material and how I grade, all FYS 101 instructors need to be more or less on the same schedule, and we have regular check-in meetings during the semester to talk about how things are going.
- *When.* The class meets in person, Mondays and Wednesdays from 2:00 to 2:50 p.m. The semester starts in 2 months so I have about 1 month to get a prototype done.
- *Where.* We will meet in person in a standard classroom that seats about 32 people (even though the enrollment is capped at 16). There's technology in the room but just the basics—instructor computer, digital projector, and some whiteboards.
- *Why.* Students take the course primarily because it's a graduation requirement. First-generation college students might get a lot out of the course because of their unfamiliarity with college; other students might feel resentful having to take a course over stuff that (they feel) they already know. There is not a sense across campus that this is an important course for students to take. I'm teaching it because I enjoy it and it lets me help students acclimate and succeed, especially minoritized and first-generation college students. It's fulfilling for me,

even with a standard grading system, and I want to try an alternative system to make that meaning more apparent to students and take some stress off them.

After brainstorming for 20 minutes on these and other questions, Professor Alice reviews the required syllabus and add a few more items to her answer to "What":

All FYS 101 sections

- require completion of a research paper on a topic of the student's choice.
- require a field trip to the campus library for basic training from library staff.
- work together on a daylong community service project at the end of the semester, followed up with a two-page reflection paper from each student on their experience.

Alice has 5 minutes left on her timer. She sets up a Google Drive folder labeled *FYS 101 Fall semester*, puts her older materials into it as a subfolder, and shoots an email to some of her colleagues requesting some of their materials as well.

Now You Do It

Time estimate: 30 minutes

- Set a timer for 30 minutes.
- For 15–20 minutes, go through each of the five W's and briefly answer *some* of the questions under each heading. You do not need to answer every question, nor do the answers need to be detailed or thorough.
- For 10 more minutes, create the folder that you will use for storing reference materials. Put it in a place that's easy to access. Then collect any materials that might help later.
- When the 30-minute timer goes off: Stop and move on to Step 1.

Step 1: Determine the Course Structure and Specific Learning Objectives

In this step, you will draft the overall learning objectives for your course, determine the module structure of the course, and make a first pass at writing assessment-level objectives.

You are now clear on the high-level goals of your course. In this step, we'll come down a few thousand feet in altitude and think about specifics.

First, you will write out the overarching, course-level learning objectives. These are the high-level aspirational goals that spell out, in very general terms, what students should learn or acquire through the course. Some of these may be boilerplate from your department, university, or even your government, and you may have little or no input on them. Others you may write yourself. There is no need to be terribly concrete: "Students will understand the concept of hypothesis testing" or "Students will gain an appreciation of the historical importance of the United Nations" are acceptable styles for course-level objectives.

Second, you will determine how the course will be subdivided. Most courses move through distinct stages, which we'll refer to as "modules," as time passes. A module often corresponds to a unit of content, but it might also represent a phase of a major process that the course focuses on (such as a semester-long research project) or even parts of a general theme that is revisited throughout the semester.

Typically, each module will involve a similar assessment structure. That structure and consistency is important for students and for you: It lessens cognitive load and makes the course experience more predictable, so they (and you) can focus on learning and not the schedule.

How you set up your modules is up to you, but we recommend using around four to six modules in a 15-week semester. Too few (e.g., just two or three) defeats the purpose of subdividing the course. Too many (e.g., 20) makes each module so small that there will be too many assessments to manage.

The text, if you are using one, can suggest modules in the form of chapters; course materials can do the same. It helps to write out the overall theme of the module (e.g., "Graph algorithms" or "Sonnets") and then a short list of the items that will be learned in that module.

Third, you'll complete one of the most important and difficult steps in this entire process: making a first pass at assessment-level objectives. These are different from the high-level, aspirational course-level objectives you wrote out earlier. Here you'll identify units of knowledge or skill that students will acquire in your course and phrase them in a way that makes them assessable. In other words, at this point you are going to make a rough draft of your *clearly defined standards*. The high-level course objectives and module list you've just created will help you structure your thinking about these standards.

We're asking you to create these objectives even if you're not planning to use SBG. (In fact, you might have noticed that we haven't even talked about what kind of assessment system you're using yet.) So why write objectives now? It's because they will form the core of any assessment system. If, for example, you're going to use specifications grading, these objectives will guide and focus the process of writing the specs for each assignment. If you're going to use ungrading, you and your students still need to know what things matter in your course. And if you're planning to focus on SBG, these objectives will be exactly what you assess.

This is both an important process and one that many instructors find challenging. So let's take a time-out from course design to think about how to write good standards.

How to Write Good Standards

A *standard* is a clear and observable action that a learner can take to demonstrate their learning of some important topic or concept. Let's look at each part of that definition:

- *A standard is an action.* It is a concrete action that a learner performs, described by an action verb. Unlike high-level course objectives, standards should avoid abstract dispositions or states of mind, such as *know*, *understand*, or *appreciate*. While we value these, we cannot assess them reliably.

- *The action should be clear and observable.* We mean "clear" from the learner's point of view: Students should be able to read and understand the standard after taking part in class. Actions must also be "observable," which lets you determine what information about learning the results convey. This lets you give good feedback. Note: *Observable* does not necessarily mean "quantifiable." Not everything that is worth assessing can be measured with a number, but it cannot be assessed unless you can see or otherwise observe a result.

- *The action should result in evidence of learning.* The purpose of the action is to give instructors direct information about whether a student has learned what they need to learn. Some actions are concrete and observable but don't tell us anything about student learning. Consider attendance: It's easy to observe a student's attendance, but attendance in itself conveys no information about what (if anything) a student has learned.

- *Each standard is tied to at least one specific and important concept.* The hard part here is making sure the concept is important enough to assess. There will be some topics in your course that you personally find important or beautiful, or which you may feel pressure to assess. But you can't assess everything. So at some point, you will need to cut or consolidate topics. This is where "keeping it simple" begins.

A question you might ask at this point is: Do I really need to write standards for my course at all? Can't we just all come together and have a great learning experience without making some huge checklist of topics?

It's not so much that you "need" standards, but that you already have them. Whenever you assess student work, you have some idea of what is "good enough" and what isn't. Those ideas are your standards. It benefits your students to be clear and transparent about those standards, because it shows them what matters and clarifies the evaluation process. It benefits you, too, because it makes your decisions fairer and will make your grading go faster. Make no mistake; nearly every person we interviewed for our case studies mentioned how difficult it was to write their standards. But they also emphasized how useful it was to clarify their thoughts.

Now that you know what a standard is and why you should write them out, how *do* you write them?

The course-level objectives we saw earlier are typically too general to be assessable. At the other extreme, when planning an individual lesson, you might write out every minute detail a student could learn. This is useful, but gives far too many standards to assess.

There's a layer of objectives in between course-level objectives and lesson-level objectives that we'll call "assessment-level objectives," and these are the "standards" we're after (see Figure 11.1).

Figure 11.1. Levels of objectives.

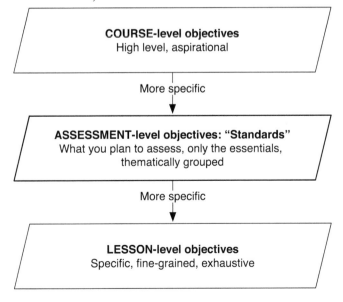

There are likely topics that students encounter in your course that aren't worth assessing individually. However, they make sense as part of a thematically related group of concepts, and you could assess the group. Such a group will be one of your standards: not so fine-grained as to be overwhelming but also not so broad as to be unassessable.

There's no magic formula for writing standards at the right level, but we have suggestions:

- Go through your course module by module and brainstorm the topics and concepts you'd like students to learn at as low of a level as you feel comfortable thinking about. If you are familiar with the course, this could be an exhaustive list of lesson-level objectives. If you are less familiar with the course, or if you are making significant changes to it, you might start with the course-level objectives and break these down into specific topics or concepts that students will encounter.
- Then go through that list and remove anything that isn't truly essential, and consolidate thematically similar topics into single objectives. (Keep it simple!)
- For each of the items remaining, identify a concrete action students could perform that would provide useful evidence of learning. Reframe the item as a task, using a concrete action verb.

We recommend the following template for writing standards:

I can \<action verb> . . . \<conditions>.

Here the "conditions" limit or qualify the action. For example, "I can create a model that illustrates the relationships among DNA, chromosomes, genes, and alleles" was a standard from Jennifer Momsen's biology course we saw in chapter 8. The main action is *creating a model,* and the list of objects to appear in the model are the conditions. Other examples include "I can compare differing views on the causes of World War I" or "I can write working Python code to implement a variety of sorting algorithms."[2]

Bloom's taxonomy provides a good source of action verbs (see Figure 11.2).

For example, if you phrase a standard as "Students will know each part of the definition of the definite integral," the action isn't clear yet. What will a student *do* to indicate that they "know" each part of the definition? The answer to that question is the standard we want. There can be many answers: Perhaps we want to see if students can remember the different parts of the definition. In that case, we might phrase the standard as:

I can state the definition of the definite integral.

Figure 11.2. Bloom's taxonomy.

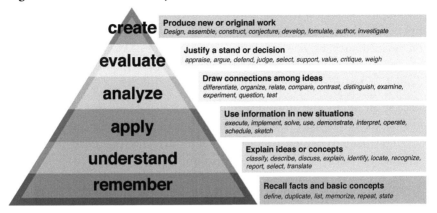

Note. Used under CC-BY license. Created by Vanderbilt University Center for Teaching.

Maybe what we want isn't just recall but to check whether students understand what the definition means. Accordingly, we might look at the verbs attached to the "Understanding" level of Bloom's taxonomy:

> I can explain the meaning of each part of the
> definition of the definite integral.

Or maybe what we *really* mean is that we want students to be able to apply this definition in a new situation. Looking at the "Apply" level, we could phrase the standard as:

> I can write the definition of a definite integral for a
> given function and limits of integration.

These are just a few possibilities. In each case, we've taken a general idea of what students should learn and sharpened it into an assessable action that is clear and observable.

We mentioned previously that it can be helpful to consolidate some standards by grouping them together if they are thematically similar. If you do, beware of creating "double-barreled" standards that ask for two different actions that are not similar enough to belong together. For example, in a music class, "I can identify the notes in a major chord" and "I can identify an example of a major chord in a piece of music" are likely to be similar and small enough to group together and assess all at once ("I can identify the notes in a major chord and identify an example of a major chord in a piece of music."). But consolidating the first of these with "I can perform musical compositions using a variety of chord changes" leads to a double-barreled standard, because this new second standard is quite different in nature from the first. A student might have learned how to identify notes in a chord and chords in a piece of music, and yet needs more work on performance, or vice versa.

Step 1 in the First-Year Seminar Course

Back at the library, the timer for Part 0 has ended, and Professor Alice has taken a quick walk to have a break. She returns to her space and digs into Step 1.

The first part of Step 1 is made easier for her since the course-level objectives are provided for her by the institution:

Following the completion of FYS 101, students will:[3]

- understand the differences between secondary school and college-level work and expectations;
- set personal and career goals, and manage time effectively;
- articulate the value of the liberal arts in a university education and in career preparation;
- use library resources to retrieve, evaluate, interpret, and use information;
- demonstrate skill in fundamental academic activities including writing, test preparation, critical thinking, and collaboration;
- make connections with peers, faculty, university services, and the surrounding community; and
- identify, analyze, and evaluate ethical issues, with attention to students' own values and those of diverse perspectives.

Using this list and from the course materials Professor Alice has assembled from Step 0, she generates a list of modules:

- *Module 1: Introduction to university life.* Topics include college versus high school expectations, setting personal and career goals, the importance of the liberal arts, time management, wellness, and academic integrity.
- *Module 2: Academic success strategies.* Topics include critical thinking, study skills, test preparation skills, research and library skills, oral presentation and writing skills, and technology usage.
- *Module 3: Making connections.* Topics include academic services, campus resources and policies, faculty and peer interaction, campus activities, off-campus activities, and engagement with the community.
- *Module 4: Becoming a global learner.* Topics include ethics, leadership, citizenship, diversity and inclusion, and global perspectives.

She notes that the required research paper and library training fit into Module 2. The big community service project makes more sense as part of Module 3, but it would not happen until the end of Module 4, assuming these modules happen one at a time in this order. Is this a problem? Should she flip Modules 3 and 4? She's not sure, but she makes a note to come back to this later because that's a detail that isn't important for now.

Finally, she goes module by module and writes down specific learning objectives at as low of a level as she feels comfortable writing. Here is a sample of the objectives she writes for Module 1:

- I can explain why time management is important for success as a college student.
- I can identify specific ways that I can improve my time management.
- I can list specific ways that procrastination can adversely affect my success as a student.
- I can use time-blocking strategies to schedule my week on a calendar.
- I can use the Pomodoro technique to manage my time within a time block.
- I can use digital and analog tools to track my commitments and manage my tasks.

Note, these are learning objectives for only *one part* of Module 1, on the topic of time management. They are quite low level. By the time Alice has completed this process for the entire course, she looks at her list and notices that she's generated around 100 learning objectives. Assessment-level objectives should be assessed, and there is no way that she can assess all these without grading day and night, nor does every single one of these objectives rise to the level of importance that it needs to be assessed individually. In other words, this list is at the "lesson level" in our earlier language. Alice needs to turn this into a much shorter list of assessment-level objectives by both combining related objectives and by cutting some objectives from her wish list of topics.

After looking at the six objectives, Alice realizes that the first three items are thematically related; they are all about articulating key concepts of time management and analyzing one's own practices. So are the last three, which are about using specific tools and strategies. She groups these into two consolidated, assessable standards:

- I can explain the value of time management and identify specific ways to improve my time management habits.
- I can use specific tools and strategies to manage time, tasks, and commitments.

Professor Alice will still introduce specific items from the original list in an individual lesson; for example, she will introduce the Pomodoro technique during class. That's why that objective is considered lesson-level. Alice wonders if the first standard is double-barreled; for now, she thinks that *explain* and *identify* work together as a single unit, but she might think some more about this later.

This process takes time. But in the end, if Alice keeps reducing lesson-level objectives into assessment-level objectives at a similar rate, her list of standards will have shrunk from around 100 to around 35. With some judicious (possibly ruthless) additional cutting of inessential topics, she can get this list into the 25–30 range.

Now You Do It

Time estimate: 60–90 minutes. As with Step 0 and all the remaining steps, we recommend that you set a timer for each part in the following and observe the time limit. This will keep you moving and prevent you from overthinking the process.

1. Take 5–8 minutes to write out the high-level, aspirational course-level objectives. Don't wordsmith; just get your unedited thoughts into your notes.
2. For 8–10 more minutes, draft the module structure you think the course will have. This isn't final; you can come back and modify it later.
3. For 45–60 minutes, the hard/fun part: Go module by module and write out learning objectives, at the lowest level you are comfortable with. Don't dwell for long on any one topic: Work fast, and remember this is a draft. Then go back through your list with an eye toward grouping lesson-level objectives into thematically related groups and otherwise consolidate, cut, and simplify.

Step 2: Do a High-Level Outline of the Class and Its Systems

In this step, you will decide on the overall focus of the course and start planning assessments and your overall approach to grading.

We've used the word *system* a lot to refer to the assessment and grading setup in a course, and that's intentional. To build a cohesive course plan we must make sure the assessments we give and the methods by which we evaluate student work are in tune with the overall focus of the class.

By the "focus" of the class, we mean the general kinds of learning students will do. This isn't the same as subject matter. Some mathematics courses, for example, focus on building computational skill and applying it to basic real-world problems; other mathematics courses focus on high-level abstraction, analysis, and writing, with relatively little focus on "skills." Both courses will be filed under "Math," but they require very different approaches to assessment and grading.

We can identify two main areas of focus, for just about any course:

- courses that are primarily focused on content and discrete skills
- courses that are primarily focused on concepts and general processes

"General processes" refers to activities and competencies that professionals use in a discipline: broad categories of work as opposed to specific tasks. For example, organizing and writing a significant research paper is a general process. So are representing data in the form of useful maps, writing lesson plans, and using a database to investigate government regulations. By contrast, writing a single thesis statement, factoring a polynomial, and describing the structure and purpose of DNA are all discrete skills.

Most courses have some focus on content/skills and some focus on concepts/processes. For example, an introductory Spanish class for non–Spanish speakers might sometimes focus on vocabulary and grammar, but at other times highlight overarching concepts of language and culture. Likewise, an upper-level Spanish class might focus mostly on culture and history, but it will occasionally need to delve into specific items of vocabulary or grammar.

The question to answer in this step is whether your course has a primary focus on one of these, and if so, which one. The learning objectives you drafted in Step 1 can give you a good sense of the primary focus:

- If the learning objectives tend toward the lower half of Bloom's taxonomy, then the course is probably a content/skills-focused course.
- If the tendency is to the upper half, then it's more of a concepts/processes-focused course.
- If it's an even mix, then . . . it's an even mix, and that's fine as well.

Content/skills courses tend to happen earlier in the curriculum than concept/process courses—and "even mix" courses may happen in the middle—but this is not an ironclad rule. There is no scientific way to determine the focus; use your judgment along with notes from Steps 0 and 1.

The primary focus of the course will guide you toward the types of assessments and the grading system. We'll develop a general outline of the assessments and grading system now and build these further in later steps. There are two questions to ask, which can be addressed in either order:

- *What general kinds of assessments might I give in the course?* Give only high-level descriptions. For example, "weekly in-class quizzes," "one essay for each major theme," or "two major projects with multiple steps."
- *What general kind of grading system might be a good fit for the course?* Look back through this book, your notes, and your experiences and think about grading approaches that have resonated with you and fit the facts of your course.

Base your answers on the course's structure and focus and your notes from Steps 0 and 1. While there's no deterministic way to decide on a specific grading approach, generally speaking:

- Content/skills-focused courses tend to work well with standards-based grading, where there is an emphasis on demonstrations of skill on fine-grained specific tasks that accumulate over time.
- Concept/process-focused courses tend to work well with specifications grading or ungrading where there is less emphasis on discrete skills and more on the holistic qualities of work, creativity, and cross-cutting general processes.

Often, you'll find that your course is a hybrid: Some parts of the course are more skills-based and are best graded using SBG, while others focus on processes and are better addressed using specifications grading or ungrading. You can pick different approaches for different types of assessments (and it's much better to choose appropriate approaches than to shoehorn an important assessment into an inappropriate grading system). None of these is "better than" the other.

You do not need to make a final choice about your grading system yet. Instead, make a preliminary sketch of the general approach you might want to take. Consider your own curiosity and excitement level, too. You're more likely to succeed with a system you are interested in than by limiting yourself to a copy of somebody else's system.

As you consider your overall grading system, also note *how* and *whether* each assessment needs to be graded at all. Categorize each assessment:[4]

- The instructor (or possibly a TA) must evaluate and give feedback.
- Peers could give feedback.

- It could be automatically graded.
- It needs to be checked only for completion and/or effort.

Not all student work needs to be graded in the first place, nor does it need extensive evaluation, and even if it does, you don't necessarily need to be the one grading it. This makes a big difference in Step 3, when you'll think about how to mark each assessment.

Before moving on to the next step, simplify the list of assessments you just made. Ask the following questions about each item:

- Does it align with the primary focus of the course?
- Does it align with the learning objectives?
- Is it worth the time and effort of reassessment?
- Does it demand too much from students in or out of class time?
- Does this item need to be assessed at all? (Perhaps it can become a class activity, or simply doesn't need to exist.)

If any of the answers is "no"—or if the answer is "yes" but you're tentative about it—then reconsider that assessment. Modify it or, perhaps better, cut it entirely.

Step 2 in the First-Year Seminar Course

Professor Alice is feeling very productive. She has spent the last 2 hours gathering information on her course and clarifying what she wants to do with it, as well as building a coherent (but unfinished) list of learning objectives for each module. She puts all this information in front of her and dives into Step 2.

What is the primary focus of the course? Looking at the entire picture of FYS 101 and her list of learning objectives, Alice notices that while there are several low-level objectives about factual knowledge and skills, the work in the course is tending toward the middle and upper one third of Bloom's taxonomy—for example, her two standards from the time management part of the class:

- I can explain the value of time management and identify specific ways to improve my time management habits.
- I can use specific tools and strategies to manage time, tasks, and commitments.

These are largely about *evaluating* and *applying* techniques. Thinking more about these standards and others, she realizes that although this is a class for beginning college students, it's not about content but about concepts: how to succeed in college and find your place in the community. The skill-based details of these concepts are still present, but are not the main focus.

What general kinds of assessments might I give in the course? Alice chooses to think about this first, partly because some assessments in FYS 101 are pre-determined: the research paper, the field trip to the library and basic library training, and the community service project and its follow-up reflection paper are required for all sections. (The second item is technically an *activity*, not an assessment, but presumably some record of its completion must be recorded, which makes it part of the assessment scheme overall.) Since these assessments are part of the landscape of the course regardless of what she does, Alice figures that's a good place to start.

Apart from the required items, Alice makes a list of some types of assessments that might fit well with the overall scope and focus of the course:

- Each module in the course is quite different from the others, so it might make sense to develop an assessment package that's unique to each module. For example, Module 2 ("Academic success strategies") could involve the library visit and training; doing some brief oral and written communication demonstrations (like a 3-minute speech to the class or a video); completing some self-paced training on specific tech tools; and some assessments on critical thinking, study skills, and test preparation. Then Module 3 ("Making connections") would consist of a package of assessments of a different nature, where students connect with various people and offices and report on what they learned. This makes each module into a "bundle" in specs grading language, and perhaps the course grade can be based on completing these bundles at different levels of attainment. Come back to this later.

- At the same time, some cross-cutting assessments that happen the same way in each module might help provide consistency and structure. For example, weekly readings or video viewings would be useful to set up activities in the class; maybe prepare a package of these each week, and have students read or view before the Monday meeting along with completing an online form where they answer some basic factual questions about them and give brief responses to open-ended prompts.

- Maybe some low-stakes quizzes on the course LMS can be done at the end of each week, to bookend the beginning-of-week readings and viewings.

- We should split up the research paper into stages and have each stage be an item that is drafted, given feedback, revised, and reassessed separately.

- "Participation" seems like an obvious thing to include because this is a "seminar" course. But what do I mean by that? Just showing up, or contributing something to a conversation, or something else? Or would this put students in a position where something nonacademic is contributing to their course grades? Maybe I want something other than just "participation," but what? Completing an exit ticket each day to certify that the student was present and active? Or some daily quiz? Or nothing? I need to think some more about this.

Once the ideas start flowing, they're hard to stop. But Alice also realizes that students have lives just like she does, so not all these ideas will make it into the final version of the class.

Next, Alice considers: *What general kind of grading system might be a good fit for the course?* Based on everything in the preceding, Alice is learning toward specifications grading built around the four modules, conceived as "bundles" in the course, while also including completion of the recurring weekly assessments in the system. She also has ungrading in mind for the research paper's stages. The precise grading structure comes later.

Now You Do It

Time estimate: 40 minutes.

1. Get your notes from Steps 0 and 1. Take 5 minutes to review and add further thoughts.
2. Take at most 5 more minutes to decide on the primary focus of the course: content/skills, concepts/processes, or a mix. The assessment-level learning objectives should be your primary guide, but use your professional judgment. (This should be a fairly quick decision, having done all that research in Steps 0 and 1.)

Now do the next two steps in whatever order makes sense for you, or bounce back and forth between them. Observe a total 20-minute time limit on these. Keep moving and don't overthink.

3. 10 minutes: Ideate a list of types of assessments you might give in the course. It's okay if this list is way too long to be practical; you'll cut it down later. Just get your ideas out of your head for now, and make sure they align with Step 0, Step 1, and the primary focus of the course.
4. 10 minutes: Decide on the general approach to the grading system. Which models or case studies resonate with you? Would assessments be graded in different ways?

Finally:

5. Take 10 minutes to simplify your list of assessments.

Step 3: Make a Prototype of the Marking Methods and What A and C Grades Represent

In this step, you will think about the marks (if any) that you will use on each assessment and write a high-level description of what minimal passing looks like (a grade of C) and what excellence looks like (a grade of A) in your course. Then, you'll refine your assessment plan in light of these choices.

In the previous step, you outlined your vision for how students will experience your course as a whole, especially course assessments. Now, using that list, you'll be doing a couple of grade-related tasks, one at the assessment level and one at the course level.

First let's zoom down to the level of individual assessments and how to mark them. For now, you're just deciding what the marks will be, not the specifications or rubrics by which you will assign them (that comes later).

The goal is to identify your marks that indicate progress. You might do one of the following:

- *Give only feedback with no marks (i.e., use ungrading).* Ungrading, as we've seen, works well for assessments where you want students to focus only on feedback and not on any extrinsic motivator (which marks frequently are). You can use ungrading selectively as part of a hybrid system, for example by focusing only on feedback for steps in a project, while using SBG for quizzes.
- *Use a two-level scale.* "Satisfactory"/"Not Yet" is the default option for specifications grading and can be a good fit elsewhere. We highly recommend *not* using the word *Fail* here (as in "Pass/Fail"). There are many examples of different label names in the case studies.
- *Use a three- or four-level scale,* such as the EMRF or EMPX rubric (see chapter 7). This is useful if the assessment has more nuance to its outcomes. For example, if you want to distinguish work that is "outstanding" from work that is "good enough," then you might use a three-level scale like "Excellent"/"Meets Standards"/"Revisable." Or you may wish to distinguish work that can be revised from work that must be restarted from scratch.

We do not recommend using more than four levels of marks. Doing so does not yield better information about student learning and begins to make consistent, fair grading decisions harder.

As you review the individual assessments, you might discover that some of them don't fit with your standards or should be combined or rearranged. Thinking about the marks you'll use may even cause you to change your mind about grading them at all. Feel free to make modifications, or even remove assessments entirely, as you complete this step.

Now zoom back out to the level of the entire course. Your completed grading system will need to translate marks into a letter grade for the course. Right now, it's helpful to draft some criteria for just two grades: C and A (we will get into letter grades in detail in Step 7).

These two letter grades are useful bookends for passing student work in a course. Write a short narrative description or bullet point list that answers these questions:

- What characterizes student work that is minimally passing (i.e., "C-level")? What does it look like to an outsider, examining that student's body of work? Focus heavily on the *minimal* part here: Include only the bare essentials needed to pass.
- What characterizes student work that is exemplary (i.e., "A-level")?

Write these without being too fine-grained, but detailed enough to be meaningful. We're looking for a narrative description, not a table of requirements. Aim to create something you could hand to a colleague to see if they agree without needing to know the inner workings of your course.

Modify our advice as needed if your context requires different meanings for some grades. If your institution views D as the minimum required for a prerequisite course, begin by writing a description for D instead of C. Likewise, your students may need to earn a B– or higher to be eligible for admission into a future program; focus on setting B– requirements first.

This process will be helpful later in several ways. First and foremost, making decisions about what a C includes will help clarify your thinking about what matters in your course. It may even make you want to delete or change some assignments or objectives. Second, you can use these descriptions later to reality check the finalized grading system in your syllabus, making sure they represent what really matters. Third, once we have an idea of what a C and A mean, it will be easier to determine how to earn a B or D.

Step 3 in the First-Year Seminar Course

Professor Alice knows that there are some assessments in FYS 101 that must be included: the research paper, the library training and field trip, and the community service project and reflection paper. She can't cut or modify those, but she does have creative control over how they are marked. She decides:

- The research paper will be split up into stages: identifying the topic, gathering sources, organizing notes and making an outline, writing the

first draft, editing and writing a second draft, and then producing the
final paper. She will later write up detailed specifications for each and put
deadlines on each stage, and mark each stage as "Successful"/"Revise."
She'll need to think about the feedback loops and revision process for
each one (in a later step). She considered ungrading these parts, but given
the makeup of the students (all new to college, many first generation,
etc.) she feels that having no marks would remove structure that can help
students succeed. But she may come back to that decision later.

- The library provides its own assessment for the basic training in the
  form of a 20-item multiple-choice quiz available on the LMS. Professor
  Alice decides to mark that quiz as "Pass"/"No Pass" with "Pass" being
  a score of 17 out of 20 or more. As for the field trip itself, the simplest
  thing is to just mark it as "Done"/"Not Done" (i.e., a checkbox) on the
  basis of attendance. (She'd consider not recording attendance at all and
  only focusing on the quiz, except the college requires a record that each
  student attended the training session.)
- Similarly, participation in the community service project is "Done"/"Not
  Done" based on participation, and the reflection paper will be marked
  "Successful"/"Revise" like the stages of the research paper, except using
  different specifications (which will amount to just completeness and
  effort, since this is not as significant a product as the research paper).

On the subject of "participation," Alice knows that simply showing up for
events can be problematic for some students, for example those who help
take care of their families or who have jobs outside of school. So she'll need
to be careful in defining what "participation" in the service project will mean,
how she will assess it, and whether there are alternatives for those who cannot
"participate."

As for the other assessments, Alice goes through her wish lists and starts
questioning the value of each one. Some of them make the cut, but others
don't. For example:

- Initially, she wanted to have multiple assessments involving "making connections" (Module 3) with campus services and the community. Having
  several of these seemed like a good idea at the time, but now that the
  specifics of the course are coming to light, having just one or two of these
  seems like a better idea. The main goal (getting students connected with
  the community) will still happen, but doing this with a few assessments
  is better than overloading students and herself. So perhaps each student
  will do two "connections" assignments as part of Module 3—one on
  campus, one off campus.

- And perhaps she can "double dip" with those assignments by having students make short videos of their experiences. This would use the same assignment for two different purposes: to make connections and to provide practice with oral presentations (Module 2). Then the assignment can be marked "Successful"/"Revise" based on specifications that include completeness, effort, and the quality of the presentation.
- She also put "self-paced training on technological tools" on her wish list. Looking back at her notes so far, this doesn't seem to fit with any of the assessment-level learning objectives. It's part of Module 2, but she decides that this is covered by the library training. So she happily cuts "self-paced training on technological tools" from the course.
- As for attendance, she decides that attendance will be tracked, but not graded. She'll use attendance data as a basis for reaching out to students who show patterns of absences, but otherwise the attendance data don't seem to add anything to the course.

In the end, in addition to the required assessments, Alice has the following assessments that cut across all modules:

- Weekly quizzes due each Monday over the week's readings and videos. These will be marked "Pass"/"No Pass" on the basis of completeness and effort only.
- Friday reflections over the week's activities. These will also be marked "Pass"/"No Pass" on the basis of completeness and effort only.

And that's all. To complement those, each module will have some assessments that are particular to that module, like the video presentations listed previously. She puts those in a separate list, both the assessments themselves and how they will be marked.

Finally, Alice writes a narrative description of what she thinks C and A work would look like:

- A student who earns a grade of C has picked up novice-level skills needed for future success in college. They've shown that they know, basically, how to use the campus library. They have done some very simple research on a topic of interest and have done an okay job with both the research and with writing about it. They've made some simple connections with the campus and community, and they've completed at least half of the weekly assignments. Essentially, they have a lot of room for improvement, but they have picked up the skills that will make them happy and successful while they are at the university.

- A student who earns a grade of A has all the characteristics of a C student, but their research is much more thorough and their writing more polished. They've shown they can communicate their ideas well in oral and written formats. They've shown not just competency but strong skill in nearly all the topics of the course, and they've completed almost all of the weekly assignments with only one or two exceptions.

Again, none of this is final; Alice can and probably will alter these answers as the course planning progresses.

Now You Do It

Time estimate: 20 minutes.

1. For 10 minutes: Go to each assessment and decide on which marks you'll use (if any). You're not aligning standards or specifications yet; just identify the marks themselves. Feel free to rearrange or even cut assessments from your previous list.
2. For 10 minutes: Write a narrative description or bullet point list of what is required to minimally pass a class (usually at a C level), and another description for excellent work (usually A). Your audience for these narratives is yourself, or a colleague who knows the subject matter but not the details of your course. Keep it short, but detailed enough to elicit good feedback.

Step 4: Outline the Core Feedback Loops

In this step, you will decide how feedback and reassessment will take place for each of your assessments. The assessments in your course will give students things to do that will help them learn. But in order to unlock the real power of alternative grading and focus your course on growth, you'll need to decide how to activate a feedback loop. We want to be intentional about setting up these structures, so that feedback loops are first-class citizens in the course and not something bolted on after the fact.

A feedback loop needs two things: a plan for giving feedback and a mechanism for reassessments. As always, we are not aiming for a completed system yet, but rather a general idea of how the feedback loop will operate. If you have ideas about the details of implementation, it's fine to make notes on those. For each general type of assessment you've identified, do two things.

First, identify the means of giving feedback: Will you be writing on paper? Leaving comments on a PDF or via your LMS's grading software? Having individual meetings with students?

Next, identify the form of reassessment. Two fundamental options are new attempts or revisions of previous attempts. New attempts are often paired with skills and standards. They could be done in class, in office hours, online, or with many other methods. Revisions, on the other hand, make sense for processes and specifications. Think about what makes the most sense for your situation and what you want students to get out of the reassessment process.

Whatever you decide, remember that every assessment should include a feedback loop unless there is a compelling reason not to have one. This means that for nearly every assessment you give, you should plan on giving not just a mark (if you plan on giving one at all) but also helpful feedback, and students should be allowed to reattempt without penalty. There are some cases where a full feedback loop isn't feasible, or where it will need to look a bit different:

- *Preclass work.* If students complete work as preparation for a class session or activity, redoing the work once the event is over might not make sense. You can still give feedback on the work. But instead of a reattempt, consider making the assessment more mistake-tolerant—for example, by grading it on completeness and effort only.
- *End-of-term projects or essays.* Items that occur at the very end of an academic term are difficult if not impossible to reattempt. For items like projects and papers, you can have students turn in drafts earlier in the term, allowing you to "preassess."
- *Final exams.* Final exams suffer even more from end-of-term limits. There are many examples of how to handle final exams in the case studies, and even more details in chapter 12.

As you think through the feedback loops for your assessments, also keep in mind that while we want students to have reattempts without penalty, this doesn't mean there should be no limits. It's okay to place reasonable restrictions on how reassessments will work. (Imagine yourself in the last week of the semester. How much are you willing to do when the reassessments are piled up?) A token system, like we saw in the case studies, is a common way to regulate reassessments. See chapter 6 for details of tokens and chapter 12 for other advice about keeping reassessments reasonable. Don't skip this: Being overwhelmed by reassessments is one of the places where new alternative graders have the most trouble.

At this point, begin to keep an eye on the overall student workload in your class. Reassessments should be treated as a normal and expected part of a student's workload. We usually estimate that reassessments will take half as much time as the original assignment. Trust your gut: If you begin to think that an assignment plus its reassessments will be too much work or take too much time, consider reducing or cutting out assignments entirely.

Step 4 in the First-Year Seminar Course

Alice thinks carefully not only about the assessments she has lined up so far but also about how the feedback loops will be experienced by students and by herself. She is trying hard to balance the students' need for feedback and reattempts with her own desire to have nights and weekends free from grading. In her notebook, she takes a blank page and makes the chart shown in Table 11.1.

TABLE 11.1
Professor Alice's Feedback Loop Plans

Assessment	Basic Feedback Loop
Research paper	Sequence of deadlines for student work on each stage. Once a stage is submitted, put feedback on it (via the course LMS) and a "Successful"/"Revise" mark. Students get two chances to revise each stage to get it to "Successful" and have to wait at least 2 days in between revisions.
Library training	Set up the LMS quiz over library training so that students get up to five attempts to get to the 17/20 "Pass" level. I can enter feedback to be given automatically in case of incorrect responses.
Service project + reflection	The project itself cannot be redone; you either participated or you didn't. The reflection paper is a pretty light affair, so make the initial attempt and give students one opportunity to revise before the end of the semester.
Weekly preclass work	Build in time on Mondays to address big questions that came up in the preclass work, to provide feedback. No reattempts possible here, but it's graded only on completeness/effort and students are allowed to collaborate with each other freely.
End-of-week reflections	Have students submit via the LMS and leave feedback there. These are just graded on completeness/effort, so no revision "should" be necessary, but if someone turns in something without good-faith effort or not at all, give a 24-hour grace period to get it done.

She continues through her module-specific assessments in the same vein. She notes that there are some holes and "gotchas" in her plans in some places. For example, what happens if a student never makes it to "Successful" on the first stage of the project—should they be allowed to continue on to the next stage, or should they be given extra revision opportunities but with a penalty attached, or what? It's an important detail to figure out, but not now.

Now You Do It

Time estimate: 30 minutes.

Go through each assessment in your plan and answer the following questions. Keep answers brief but detailed enough to elicit good feedback from a colleague.

- How will you give feedback on that assessment?
- How will reassessment work?
- What limitations on reassessments might be helpful?
- How much time will reassessments add to this assessment? Do you need to reduce or even eliminate an assessment to avoid overworking students?

Some assessments will have easy answers to these questions, while you might need to spend more time on others. Set a timer and observe the time limit. You can (and will) come back to this later to finalize.

Step 5: Build One Assessment and Rehearse the Feedback Loop

In this step, you will create a working version of one of your assessments, and practice the process of assessing it, giving feedback, and handling reassessments.

So far, you've been outlining and drafting all kinds of items for your course. In this step, you're going to zoom in on one assessment by building a prototype and practicing the feedback loop process with it. A "prototype" of an assessment is not a final or perfect version, but something that has just enough features to be usable by real people.

If you're converting a class that you've previously taught, you likely already have assignments from the last time you taught the course. We encourage you to reimagine one of those as a new assessment and follow the steps we've listed here to generate it anew. This helps you think about how your assessments align with your new grading system.

Your prototype should include the following:

- *A mock-up of the assessment.* Ideally this should be in whatever format the final version will have: a PDF, a quiz on your LMS, or a printed sheet of paper.
- *The specifications or standards used to evaluate student work.* Write a full set of specifications or standards in a form you will share with students. Use your work from Step 1.
- *The workflow for how students will turn in their work.* For example, will students turn in their work on paper, type and submit it electronically, or scan and submit paper to an LMS or via email? Write this out for yourself and add detailed instructions.
- *The workflow for how you will grade and give feedback on the work.* How and where will you indicate marks? How will you give feedback?
- *The workflow for how you will return marks (if any) and feedback, and how students will access it.* There can be significant technical issues here. For example, if you are marking work as "Satisfactory"/"Not Yet," then how will you get your LMS to display those marks, rather than points? Do you need to add a list of standards to the assignment, or a checklist of specifications?

As you build this prototype, use the narrative for A and C grades, where you wrote out what "minimally passing" and "outstanding" work look like, to help yourself and your students understand why the assessment exists and what's important about it. Once you build the assessment, ask yourself: *How does this help determine if a student minimally passes the course? How is it used to determine if a student has done truly outstanding work? Why is this assessment significant in the course?* Develop good answers to these questions, because students will probably ask them. And if you're having trouble answering them, it might be a sign to rethink whether that assessment should be given at all.

Next, rehearse the feedback loops you outlined in the previous step. Think through how the process of reassessments will unfold. If you're using new attempts, when will they happen and how will you show which problems are new and which are reattempts? If using revisions, how, where, and when will students submit them, and when will you grade them? In all cases, how will you communicate the results?

Finally, "stress test" the standards and specifications. How would you mark and give feedback on submissions with common misconceptions, errors, or omissions large and small? If you've taught the course before, use that experience to identify typical examples of student work and how you would manage them. Are there likely "borderline" cases? Does something important get missed, or something unimportant cause trouble? Can you clarify the specifications or standards to address these issues?

Step 5 in the First-Year Seminar Course

Although the research paper is a required component of every section of FYS 101, individual professors have the freedom to structure the paper as they see fit. As we saw in Step 3, Professor Alice is electing to break the research paper into six parts throughout the semester. This is a big assessment in more ways than one. So she decided to make a prototype of it first.

As she's worked, Professor Alice has decided to consolidate two of these parts: the part where students pick a topic and the part where they gather sources. Although there are pros and cons to doing these two parts separately, in the end she decided it was better to simplify and do them together.

She creates a handout to give to students that introduces the research paper. Here are some snippets from it:

> *Introduction.* The purpose of this assignment is to give you a chance to explore a topic of your own interest by doing real research on it.
>
> *What you will do.* In this first stage of your research paper, you will decide on the topic of your paper and do some initial background research on it.

After writing some details such as deadlines and how to submit the work, Alice includes a clear list of specifications.

Requirements for This Stage

Your work on this stage (and all future stages of the paper) will be marked "Successful" or "Revise." To earn a "Successful" mark, your work must include:

- A good research question. The subject of the question is open for you to explore, but in order to be "good" it must have no simple answer, be answerable using accessible facts and data, and be interesting to your target audience (classmates).
- Between three and five legitimate, scholarly resources that address the research question. These must be found in peer-reviewed journals or published books (not magazine articles, blogs, preprints, podcasts, etc.), and cited in APA format (we will discuss this in class).
- One or two complete sentences for each source explaining how the source addresses the research question.

Submissions that meet all of these criteria will earn "Successful." Otherwise, they will earn "Revise" and you will get feedback and the opportunity to try again.

You can revise this stage up to two times by simply uploading a new version of the work to the assignment folder on the LMS. If your work has not reached "Successful" after two revisions, I may meet with you to individually discuss your submission.

Alice ends with some additional details, such as encouragement to reach out with questions before submitting the first stage.

Professor Alice thought through some of the details of this assessment while writing the handout. For example, she decided to have students type up their work and submit it to the LMS, which she will use for managing the versions, the marks, and the feedback. But this is not a final version of the assignment for at least a few reasons:

- Professor Alice intends to give some links to web resources at the end of the handout. But as she was writing up the handout, she realized that perhaps it would be more helpful to make up her own examples of good versus bad research questions, and perhaps a more detailed explanation of what a "legitimate scholarly resource" is. Maybe the library training, which will take place the week before, could be used as well. So while she'll still give resources to students, the details may change in the future.

- She's wondering, too, if there ought to be some limitations on the question topic. In the past, students have come up with questions that follow the letter of the guidelines, but which were so far out or hyperspecialized that she couldn't identify whether the questions were "good." So she's wondering if there should be a topical area that *all* students in her section should research, which would keep things focused (and provide a common set of interests and debate topics for her class).

Still, this document is a viable prototype that she could give to friends or former students to get their thoughts on it. Before doing anything else, she sends a copy of it to her department colleague, Professor Bob, to see what he thinks.

With this prototype, she now practices the feedback loops. She runs through different scenarios in her mind about how giving feedback will work. Ideally, students upload documents to the LMS, she opens them and types in feedback in the LMS, then adds the mark and hits "Submit." Then students access the feedback by opening their submission on the LMS. (Students at her university get training on this and lots of practice in their other courses.) She does encounter a few issues, however:

- She accesses one of her old courses on the LMS to set up a mock-up assignment folder and realizes that the LMS only recognizes numerical points. An important technical issue, but not something to solve right now; she makes a note to email the LMS administrator about it.
- Some "what if" scenarios come to mind: What if a student fails to turn in their submission and doesn't ask for an extension? What if a student turns in the work but it's on paper or in a file format the LMS can't read? Again, these are important issues; they need to be addressed before this assessment goes live. But right now, we're working on the feedback loops, not exceptions to the instructions. So she assumes that students follow directions, and presses on.
- One potential issue emerges that perhaps does need to be addressed right now: She can imagine a student fabricating their sources or citing a book or journal that is less than legitimate. Should she check each source and give the student feedback on their choice of sources? After some thought, although she doesn't like the amount of work it will add, she decides checking sources will help avoid issues later in the project. To make this easier to implement, she edits her prototype document:

> Additionally, each source must include a link back to the original document so that the quality of your source can be validated. You can include the URL where you found the source, or the source's "digital object identifier" (DOI). If the source has no link, please contact me.

This way, she will just have to click on a link to check the source. If there's no link given and the student doesn't contact her about it, she'll mark the work with "Revise" and ask the student to provide the link.

The rest of the feedback loop is simple: If students need to revise, they will just write up a new or edited version of the previous submission and submit it to the LMS the same way, and so on until it's "Successful."

It's likely that more such issues will emerge before this is all over. But for now she has a working prototype for this assessment that, apart from finishing touches, is ready to go.

Now You Do It

Time estimate: 60 minutes.

Pick one of the assessments from Step 3, something that's not too easy to prototype but also not too large or difficult. If you're converting a class you've taught before, consider reimagining an existing assessment. Then:

- Make a mock-up version of the assessment, using the same format and language as you intend to use in the final version if possible.
- Write the specifications or identify the standards you will use to evaluate the work. Base these on your assessment-level objectives from Step 1. Write these on the assignment using the same language that you intend to use in the end.
- Plan workflows for how students will submit their work, how you will evaluate and mark it, how students will access the feedback, and how students will do revisions. Make notes on technical issues or "what-if" scenarios.
- Practice the process of receiving work and giving feedback on it. Use the marking system you identified in Step 3. Also practice the process of receiving and marking reassessments. Again, if any issues emerge that require immediate attention, go ahead and deal with them; otherwise write them down to address later.
- "Stress test" your standards or specifications by identifying common issues you may see in student work and identify the mark they would earn. Revise standards or specifications as necessary.

You can keep going in this step and do as many assessment prototypes as you want, but realize that you do not have to prototype all your assessments right now; this step is just getting you used to the prototyping process.

Step 6: Finalize All the Components and Think About Implementation

In this step, you will go back through the results of Steps 1–5 and deal with any issues, what-if scenarios, unanswered questions, and so on. You'll arrive at a nearly final version of the basic components of the grading system, and you'll also think concretely about how to implement these items with the tools at your disposal.

Throughout this process, we've urged you to move fast and make things, to avoid dwelling on the "weeds" of the grading system and instead make notes on any issues that arise so you can deal with them "later." We're happy to inform you that "later" has arrived.

In this step, look back over all those postponed items from the following components:

- *Your standards/learning objectives.* Are there any that don't make sense to include anymore, now that you've built more of the system? Are there any you can eliminate or consolidate? Do you need to add any more? (We highly recommend not adding things, but if it's critical then go ahead.) How will they be posted and communicated to students?
- *Your overall assessment plan and workload.* Is there anything in your list of assessments that no longer makes sense to include? Estimate how much time your students will need to complete assessments, both in and out of class, and make sure it fits within the course expectations. Include reassessments; we advise estimating that they take half as long as the original assessment. Is your plan overly full? Can you cut back on the number of assessments or eliminate some entirely?
- *Your marking system.* Are you happy with how you plan on marking those assessments, including any plans to use ungrading? How do you feel about the names and meanings of your marks, assuming you are giving any? How will you record these marks (if any) in your LMS? How will you help students keep track of their own progress?
- *The feedback loops.* Are you satisfied with your plans for feedback and reassessment? Are the feedback loops simple? Can you make them simpler?

The last two sentences are well worth repeating: *Keep it simple.* Is your prototype as simple as possible? If not, what can you do about it? This is not your last chance to simplify your system, but simplification will be harder to do after Step 7.

If you run into significant issues, consider looking ahead to chapter 12, where we give direct advice on many topics you may encounter.

Note that while the previous items will now be "finalized" (although you can keep editing if needed), we are not finalizing the assessments themselves. Unless you intend to post assessments quite far in advance, your assessments won't be in their final form until they are assigned. However, you can continue to work through Step 5 with additional assessments, getting closer to final versions in each. When you do begin to finalize each assessment, here are some things to think about:

- Along with finalizing an assessment, how will you provide examples of different levels of student work?
- If offering reassessments through new attempts, make a plan to prewrite new attempts to save yourself time in the future.

Step 6 in the First-Year Seminar course

Professor Alice takes another walk around campus to clear her head. Upon returning to the library, she looks over all the items in this step to handle any unresolved questions:

- *Standards/learning objectives.* A look through her list of assessment-level objectives revealed one standard that was double-barreled: *I can explain the value of the liberal arts to my career and set good career goals.* Earlier in the day, she wrote this thinking of it as a single objective about careers. Now, it looks like two objectives, so she breaks them up: *I can articulate the value of the liberal arts,* and *I can set good personal and professional goals.*

- *Assessment plan.* Overall, she is feeling good about the general plan for assessments: The research paper, library training, and service project augmented by weekly readings and Friday reflections, along with occasional assessments within modules for one-time learning tasks. She found a few of the latter than she could live without and cut them from the course.

- *Marking system.* Alice realized that she was using three different nomenclatures for two-level rubrics: "Done"/"Not Done," "Successful"/ "Revise," and "Pass"/"No Pass." That might get confusing. So she simplifies by using a common pair of words for all of these: "Pass"/ "Not Yet." She realizes that because the weekly readings assignment cannot be redone, giving a mark of "Not Yet" is a little misleading. But she can mitigate the risk of confusion by being clear in her syllabus, and the potential for confusion is offset by the gain in simplicity.

- *Feedback loops.* She's still waiting on a reply from the LMS administrator about nonstandard grades on the LMS. In the meanwhile, a few what-if questions came up in the prototyping of Stage 1 of the research paper that Alice wants to handle now. First, if someone fails to turn in Stage 1, then rather than invalidate their work on the whole project, Alice decides she'll reach out to the student first; if they persist in not turning in the work, it will have serious consequences (which she'll encode in Step 7: Devise the course grade assignment system). If the student turns in the work but it's in the wrong format, then she will mark it "Revise"—sorry, "Not Yet"—and explain the situation; to make this clear, she adds a requirement about the format to the list of items needed for a "Pass" mark. Finally, if a student doesn't earn "Pass" even after two revisions, she will handle it on a case-by-case basis as she would someone not turning in the work.

Now You Do It

Time estimate: 30 minutes.

Look through all the basic components of your system so far other than assessments themselves:

- the standards and learning objectives
- the plan for assessments
- the marking system
- the feedback loops

Answer the previous questions, and any related ones that surface, until you are happy with the results and confident that you can work with them on a day-in/day-out basis. And make sure that the whole thing is as simple as possible: Cut, consolidate, and make clearer anything you can before moving on. Trust your gut: If it feels too complicated, it is.

Step 7: Devise the Course Grade Assignment System

In this step, you will determine the method for translating student work into a course grade, including plus/minus modifiers. We'll determine how all the feedback and marks in your prototype system will come together to determine a course grade.

Start with the narrative description, developed in Step 3, of C (or whatever letter is "minimal passing" at your institution). Now that you have more definite plans, how might you encode this description in concrete terms? Begin to write a grade table or bulleted list of requirements that will eventually become part of your syllabus. Be specific, and write these requirements in terms of the items you've developed in the previous steps (standards, assignments, marks, completed assignments, etc.).

There is no formula for how to create this table or list, but it should focus on two things: being minimal and representing passing. By this we mean that you should include items that any student wanting to pass the course *must* do, and *only* those items. Ask yourself if each item is absolutely critical to passing, and if not, leave it for a higher grade (or remove it entirely). Use the case studies for inspiration, and avoid requiring perfection.

If you are working in a partially converted course, or with required grade bands, this is where you will consider how to make your grades fit into a traditional system. That typically means converting the requirements you've written here into percentages; see chapter 10 for examples.

Once you've made a table or list of accomplishments that would indicate a C, follow the same process for determining an A. Generally speaking, an A requires everything a C requires along with either more hurdles or higher hurdles, selected from items that aren't essential for passing. Again, use the case studies for inspiration.

For both C and A grades, the requirements for the grades should faithfully reflect your narrative description of what those grades mean. For example, if you cannot honestly say that the list of requirements for an A represents truly excellent work—or if excellent work could be indicated with fewer requirements—then adjust your requirements.

Once you have determined the requirements for a C and for an A, the remaining letter grades can be formulated quickly:

- Requirements for a B should be somewhere between those for a C and for an A. Not necessarily halfway between, although that is one simple way to do it.
- Requirements for a D should be fewer than for a C but should still indicate the student has given a good-faith effort to engage with the class. Anything less should indicate nearly complete disengagement from the course.
- There are no "requirements" for an F grade; this grade is given if the requirements for a D aren't met.

You can find many examples in the case studies.

The previous suggestions apply to ungrading too, with modifications. Students in a partly or wholly ungraded course still benefit from concrete descriptions of work that constitutes different letter grades. But ungraded courses are typically less prescriptive. You could create a list of qualities describing work at the level of a C, B, and A, and then students would be responsible for making the case, using a portfolio of work, that they have met those requirements. These qualities are your standards, and you should be as clear as possible about them.

If your institution does not give "partial" grades, then you're done. Otherwise, you'll need to determine how those modifiers are assigned. There are several examples in the case studies and a summary of options in chapter 12.

Finally, think about how you will help students understand partial progress in the course, for example midterm grades, periodic progress checks, or if a student-athlete needs a weekly checkup. Examples and advice can be found in chapter 12.

Step 7 in the First-Year Seminar Course

Looking back over the FYS 101 design so far and looking at her narrative descriptions from Step 3, Alice knows that the "must-haves" in her class are completion of the research project, the library training, and the service project. Therefore "Pass" marks on these are required for a C as indicated by the university. In addition, she believes a student earning a C should also show good-faith effort at engaging in the course, which she will interpret as modest completion rates of the weekly readings and Friday reflections. Finally, each of the four modules will have a collection of module-specific assessments, and a C should indicate successful completion of at least half of those. An A requires everything a C does, as well as a high level of engagement with the course and with the modules.

Looking at the academic calendar she studied in Step 0 and comparing it with a standard calendar, she sees that after factoring in holidays, she will be giving 14 weekly reading assignments and 14 Friday reflections. That's enough for her to create the following that will eventually go in a syllabus:

To earn a C or higher in the class, you must earn "pass" on:

- all five stages of the research paper project;
- the library training unit;
- the community service project;
- at least 7 weekly readings;
- at least 7 Friday reflections; and
- at least two bundle modules.

Using this list along with her narrative description of an A grade from earlier in the process, she creates a similar list for what an A grade requires. Then she makes a list for what a B and D require. Once those lists are made, she reorganizes them into the chart shown in Table 11.2. A grade of F is given if not all of the requirements for a D are met, including the research paper, library training, and community service project.

Finally, Professor Alice is required by her institution to offer plus/minus grades. She isn't interested in adding any more "stuff" into the course (e.g., a final exam) and although she eventually went the route of specifications grading, she still has ungrading on her mind from earlier in the day. So she writes the following to add to the system.

Plus/Minus Grades

Generally, a "plus" grade on a letter grade means that you satisfied all the requirements for a letter grade but did work that was above and beyond those requirements, and a "minus" means that you almost met the requirements for a letter grade but fell a little bit short. If you believe that your basic letter grade should be modified with a plus or minus at the end of the semester, you will have the chance as part of your community service project reflection paper to make a case for yourself. Details will be provided later, but it will involve adding at least one page to your reflection paper in which you present concrete evidence of learning that shows you've earned a "plus" or an explanation for why you should have a "minus."

As it says, she will write up the details a few weeks from now. She decides now, however, that if a student asks for a minus but their work is better than that, she'll just assign a higher grade and talk with them about it.

And yes, students do sometimes assign themselves minus grades. Sometimes when this happens, it is because the student legitimately fell short of the requirements of a grade and is being honest. At other times, though, the student may be downplaying actual achievement. Be on the lookout for the reasons behind the minus.

Now You Do It

Time estimate: 60 minutes.

- 5 minutes: Review your narrative description of what constitutes C-level work and what constitutes A-level work.
- 20 minutes: Using your assessments and marking system, decide in concrete terms what a student would need to accomplish to earn a C. Review it, to see if it's a good fit with your narrative description. Keep it minimal. Repeat for the grade of A.
- 5 minutes: Similarly, create the requirements for grades of B and D.

TABLE 11.2
Final Grade Table for Professor Alice's First-Year Seminar Course

Grade	Stages of Research Project "Pass" (5)	Library Training "Pass"	Community Service Project "Pass"	Weekly Readings "Pass" (14)	Friday Reflections "Pass" (14)	Completed Bundle Modules (4)
A	All five	Yes	Yes	12	12	4
B	All five	Yes	Yes	10	10	3
C	All five	Yes	Yes	7	7	2
D	At least three	Not required	Not required	3	3	1

- If you are ungrading: Modify the previous steps to allow for student choice in how they will advocate for a given grade. But give concrete examples of things they might do to construct a good argument for a grade.
- 10 minutes: If you must give "partial" grades, determine how this will be done.
- 20 minutes: Make a plan for helping students understand partial progress.

In all cases, see the case studies and chapter 12 for help.

Step 8: Look for Details and Unintended Consequences

In this step, you will stress test the entire grading system, especially the course grade assignment methods from Step 7, to look for any undetected issues or unintended consequences.

At this point, all the pieces are coming together and it's looking like a system. Congratulations! But there's a crucial step to be done next: Find as many places as possible where the system could fail.

A particular focus in this step is the course grade assignment method from Step 7. It's the newest addition to your system, and without examining it now, you run the risk of having a first encounter with potentially serious problems at the very end of the term when it's too late. The following issues illustrate some questions you might ask about your plan:

- *Does it handle edge cases and false negatives?* What happens if a student meets all the requirements for a grade except for one? For example, consider a student who has met all the requirements for an A except for one, but the one they missed doesn't even rise to a D level. Do they really get an F in the class? Work out your plan for handling such cases now, not later.
- *How likely are false positives?* This is when a student earns a grade that is higher than their evidence of learning would suggest. False positives plague traditional grading, but alternative methods aren't immune. Have you set the bar high enough for a grade of A (or B, etc.) that only truly excellent work in a course meets it?
- *What is your plan to handle disagreements about course grades?* This is especially critical if using ungrading, but it applies to all grading systems. If a student argues that they deserve an A because of how hard they worked, but the actual results of their work are not really A level, how will you respond? Conversely, what happens if a student has done work that merits an A but they argue for a B?

There are other potential pain points in your system:

- *How likely is "grading jail"?* Could student submissions, particularly at the end of the semester, pile up so badly that the grading load becomes unmanageable? Do you need to limit the frequency of reassessments or initial submissions to mitigate this?
- *How will you communicate and build trust with students?* Think about how you will introduce the new grading ideas to students. Will this be too much for students to handle in terms of workload and attention? Is the system so complex that it takes lots of effort just to understand what it says? See chapter 12 for more on building trust with students.
- *Do students have enough opportunities to demonstrate evidence of learning, especially at the end of the term?* If there is a standard or assignment that doesn't appear until near the end of the course, do students have enough chances to engage in a feedback loop? Could there be alternative methods of demonstrating skill?

You'll likely think of more questions as you do this step; make the time to address them.

Step 8 in the First-Year Seminar Course

Alice had been hard at work at her system all day, and it's really taking shape. After another walk around campus (breaks have to come more frequently for her near the end of the afternoon), she comes back to her study room and looks over all she's done.

For the most part, it feels like a good system, one that is doable and simple. But she's bothered by something in her grading assignment table (see Table 11.2): To earn an A in the course, students have to successfully complete all four of the "module bundles" (her term for the collection of all the module-specific assessments in a module). This seems appropriate, but there's a potential issue if a student, for whatever reason, doesn't manage to complete one of the modules. Is she prepared to give a B to a person who meets all the requirements for an A except for one item that would cause them not to pass one module? It's an edge case that isn't handled by her system.

Professor Alice debates several ways to handle this better. In the end, she decides to require only three module bundles for an A, and increases the requirements for weekly readings and Friday reflections by one each. She keeps the rest of the grading table in its current form. Therefore the only difference between a B and an A is more engagement with the course through the weekly assignments, and Alice decides that's a good solution. "Perfection" is no longer required on the module bundles for an A, but an A still means excellent work.

Now You Do It

Time estimate: 30 minutes.

- Think about your course grade assignment method, or hand it off to someone you trust for feedback. What could go wrong with what you've created?
- Also think through all the other components of the system: the learning objectives, assessments, feedback loops. What could go wrong? Especially, are there any unintended consequences for the workload for you or for your students?
- Make changes as necessary, remembering to *Keep It Simple*.

Step 9: Sleep on It, Then Make It Simpler

In this step, you will put all of your work away for at least 12 hours while you get a good night's sleep, then come back when you are rested and find any places where the system could be made simpler.

After a long day of single-minded focus on building a prototype of your grading system, you need a break. Save your files, close the computer, erase the whiteboard, and go home and do something else, including sleep so you can have a clear head the next day.

Having slept on it, there is one more task to complete before the prototype is done: Read through everything and find ways to simplify it.

We have stressed simplicity throughout this book because simplicity is, in our experience, perhaps the most important part of any grading system, especially one that is different from what students are used to. Grades, for better or worse, are important to students, and making major modifications to how they are earned might be viewed as a threat. Your enthusiasm about alternative grading and the clarity of your explanations are important. But it's even more important that the system is easy to understand and easy to live with. Leonardo da Vinci said, "Simplicity is the ultimate sophistication"; it is also the ultimate broker of trust.

You may come to your prototype after a night of sleep and find that some parts of it don't make sense. You may find that the *parts* make sense but the system feels unclear or overcomplicated. After sleep, your brain is ready to find holes, glitches, and complexities that you couldn't see yesterday. Look with a critical eye over everything you've done and ask, over and over: *Can this be simplified?*

Epilogue: Professor Alice and the First-Year Seminar Course

Professor Alice had a *lot* of coffee during her work day, so her sleep wasn't as good as it could have been. But she still wakes up feeling like she accomplished something, and she is excited about the system she's built. She takes an hour in the morning to review her work and even start drafting some parts of her syllabus, using the prototype she built. During that hour, she makes a few more changes, including cutting some of the more ambitious and less important learning objectives and smoothing out some of the wording in her assessments.

What she is left with is not a final product. In fact, there's still work to be done, to flesh out the specifics of some of the system. But her draft is *done*—not complete or final, but she has a real, honest-to-goodness alternative grading system that she could give to her colleagues for feedback. She plans on doing just that, asking a colleague she trusts to review her work and find more ways to improve before the semester starts. But even her imperfect product represents a huge improvement, since it focuses student grades in the seminar course on student learning and gives students a chance to grow—which is exactly what they need.

What to Do Next

If you've followed our suggestions, you've spent a day of focused work about a month before the start of the term. In that remaining month:

- Distribute your prototype to others for feedback. It's not perfect or final, but it's a complete "minimum viable product" that you can use for learning. Use feedback from others to learn what's good and what needs additional work. Listen carefully and openly.
- Then revisit the system and create a second version, updated using the feedback you've received. Continue to engage in a feedback loop.
- Continue to execute Step 5 with different assessments, building up a library of prototypes for each type of assessment in your class.
- Before classes start, write up the final version of the grading system as part of the syllabus along with anything else you need for the first day of classes. In particular, begin to create a gradebook or learn to work with

your LMS (see chapter 12 for advice on this). As we mentioned earlier, it's not truly "final" since you can make changes to your syllabus after classes start . . . but it's hard to do so.

That's it. You've created a prototype of an alternatively graded class that is uniquely your own. *You* understand it deeply; once the semester begins, you'll see how it works in action. The next chapters are all about what happens after that: how to run your system on a day-to-day basis, things to expect during the semester, and where you can go in the future.[5]

Notes

1. See chapter 12 for some specific advice on getting support from colleagues and others.

2. A common formulation for standards is "*Students will be able to . . .*" We prefer the "*I can . . .*" template, because the first-person active-voice phrasing frames students as the true owners of a skill. We've found this template to be useful for student self-evaluation as well.

3. This list was adapted, with permission, from the first-year seminar learning objectives at Kutztown University: https://www.kutztown.edu/academics/general-education/first-year-seminar-at-kutztown-university/first-year-seminar-learning-objectives.html

4. Credit goes to Renée Link, professor of teaching in the Chemistry Department at University of California–Irvine for this idea and the categories that are listed.

5. Another example of an alternative grading-focused syllabus workbook can be found in Cilli-Turner et al., 2020. Focused on math, it provides a summary of common choices at each step.

12

HOW TO DO IT

Between the case studies and workbook, you've made a plan to set up your own class to use alternative grading. In this chapter, we'll look at how to make alternative grading work on a day-to-day basis. We'll address common on-the-ground issues and give some direct advice to help make your class succeed.

You can read the sections in this chapter in any order. We envision most readers flipping to different sections as the need arises, while they are planning an alternatively graded course or as the semester progresses.

To begin, here's some advice about what to do, and not do, in an alternatively graded course that applies to everyone:

- *Focus on student learning.* As you go through the semester, you will undoubtedly encounter unexpected issues. As a rule, resolve them with student learning as the highest priority and not by setting arbitrary policies and expecting compliance. Ask yourself: *What resolution to this issue will make it easier for students to demonstrate what they have learned?* But at the same time . . .
- *Set boundaries.* In particular, limit reassessments, which are the major place where a new practitioner can become overwhelmed. See our advice in this chapter for details.
- *Work ahead.* If you're expecting students to need multiple attempts to complete a standard, prewrite three or four assessments for each standard *before the semester begins.* Although writing a single reassessment isn't terribly time-consuming, many instructors become overwhelmed by having to write several of them at once during the semester; you can save yourself some stress by doing this beforehand.
- *Get connected.* Find a colleague to convert a class with you, or find an online community. It helps to have people to talk with, and to provide advice and support when you need it.

Finally, enjoy! You'll see benefits for both students and yourself, and you may never want to go back to traditional grading methods again.

How to Decide If Work Meets a Standard

Deciding whether a student has met a standard or specifications can be quite different from adding or deducting points. It's harder than it seems, and it's one of the places where new alternative graders can get hung up. On the other hand, deciding if student work has met a standard is something that, with practice and experience, will become much quicker and easier than allocating points.

Here's one way to think about what "meeting a standard" means: *A student has met a standard if they consistently demonstrate relevant evidence of learning without important errors.* Let's analyze that sentence in reverse order:

Important Errors Matter

An "important" error is one that's central to the standard you're assessing. For example, in "I can explain the causes of the American Civil War," the causes and explanation are what's important. However, spelling and grammar are not important for meeting this standard, as long as the student's ideas are understandable, and so an error on those grounds shouldn't be seen as reason not to meet the standard. On the other hand, if you have specifications for writing a professional-quality essay about the causes of the American Civil War, then spelling, grammar, and attention to detail are absolutely important issues. Of course, those elements should be clearly stated in the specifications.

"Important" is not the same as "big" or "small." Leaving off a negative sign in a calculation is "small" but may surface an important misunderstanding. Conversely, a student who copies a problem incorrectly (in a way that doesn't oversimplify the problem) and completes it correctly might have made a huge typographical mistake, but their understanding of the underlying ideas is still sound, and therefore they have met the standard.

Most importantly, *never require perfection*. Perfection, by definition, makes everything into an important issue, down to the finest detail. Perfection turns students into perfectionists (if they weren't already) by making them focus on details that are not truly important, and they become unclear on what matters and what they need to do in order to learn. That's not growth.

Evidence Must Be Relevant to the Standard

The evidence a student provides on an assessment should not just be correct, but related to that specific standard. Students sometimes answer a question in a way that avoids the key issue, for example by applying a different method than asked for or using technology to automate a process that the standard asks the student to demonstrate. That work isn't relevant, even if the result is correct, so it's not a trustworthy source of information about what the student knows about that standard.

Students Must Consistently Demonstrate Evidence of Learning

Students need to show consistent work relevant to a standard. If a student responds in a way that shows some agreement with the standard in one part of a question or assessment, but then displays an important error or omission on another, then they haven't shown consistent evidence of learning. They're clearly getting there, but not quite enough.

Standards describe actions, so a student must positively demonstrate that they can do that action. For example, if you are assessing a process, and a student leaves out a critical step, then the work does not demonstrate enough to meet the standard (you could call this "thoroughness"). Similarly, if a student's work is so unclear or filled with small errors that you can't be sure what they actually did, then they haven't demonstrated evidence.

If it looks like we're saying you should hold students to a high standard, we are! Not perfection, of course, but rather a high standard that is informed by a genuine inquiry into what a student has (or hasn't) learned.

Another way to think about whether student work has met a standard is to ask: *Will this student benefit from studying this topic again?*[1] If the answer is "yes," then the student hasn't met the standard (yet). Other descriptions might also help:

- Correct in all fundamentals.
- Any remaining difficulties the student has with this topic won't seriously hinder them in future work.
- Demonstrates a solid enough understanding to reteach the idea to themselves when needed in the future.

You may also want to see Linda Nilson's description of the level for "Satisfactory" in her book *Specifications Grading*.[2] There are also many example rubrics in our case studies.

How to Give Helpful Feedback

Helpful feedback is critical to effective learning. Here we'll look at what helpful feedback is and how to give effective feedback on student work.

What makes helpful feedback tricky isn't the "feedback" part but the "helpful" part. *Unhelpful* feedback is easy to give; being helpful requires work. A *Harvard Business Review* article by Cynthia Phoel gives a useful guide on providing helpful feedback.[3] Here's a summary in academic terms:

- *Focus on standards and growth.* Feedback isn't the same thing as "criticism." When framed in terms of clear and specific standards, feedback presents "an opportunity to solve a problem rather than criticize"[4] as Phoel puts it. So keep feedback *specific* and *focused* on the standards, rather than the person. Put the emphasis on problem-solving. For example, when grading an essay or logical argument, avoid a vague and pejorative comment like "Your argument doesn't make any sense" for the more specific and focused comment "This argument has unjustified assumptions."

- *Ask questions.* Phrasing feedback in the form of questions invites learners into a feedback loop, depersonalizes your comments, and helps learners take ownership of their growth. For example, suppose a learner sets out an argument with incorrect assumptions. Instead of just telling them what was wrong, such as "Your assumptions here are incorrect for this kind of argument," turn it into a question: "What assumptions should you be making for this kind of argument?"

- *Give feedback often.* You should definitely give feedback on assignments that figure into a student's grade. But don't save feedback *just* for the graded items. You can give feedback any time there's an opportunity: During a class activity, while waiting for class to begin, while class is ending, or during office hours, for example. As Phoel says, "Praise good performance right away. When negative feedback is required, talk with the [learner] within 24 hours."[5]

- *Keep your feedback data-driven.* This is an aspect of making feedback specific. Feedback about an issue that isn't supported by any particular form of evidence is unhelpful and easy to ignore. Instead, tie feedback to specific items in a student's work, and avoid generalizations like "You always . . ." or "You never . . . ," or referring to something that isn't present in the work the student has provided.

- *Don't assume that you're right.* Sometimes when grading, you know you're right. But as your assignments climb higher in Bloom's taxonomy, it's more likely that your evaluation of student work could miss something, and what looks like an "issue" in student work is more of a disagreement. So stay humble and helpful, realizing in such cases that you may not have the full picture. You can always talk with a student before assigning a mark, and this discussion can be enlightening.

Helpful feedback takes practice, just like any learning. Feedback loops are the "roof" that the four pillars support, so it's worth taking time to practice and improve your own feedback.

How to Keep Reassessments Reasonable

Reassessments without penalty are one of the pillars of alternative grading and key for engaging in feedback loops. Throughout the case studies, we've seen two main approaches to reassessments:

- *New attempts.* Students complete new questions that address the same standards. This can be done on a regular schedule (e.g., on the next exam) or by request (e.g., during an office hour). New attempts typically fit best with SBG and are used with quizzes, exams, or problem sets.
- *Revisions.* Students revise and resubmit previous work for a new mark. Revisions fit well with assignments that are graded holistically using specifications or ungraded using only feedback, such as projects or essays.

This is not an either/or choice: Many systems use revisions for minor errors and new assessments for major issues, or use different types of reassessments on different assignments.

Instructors need to consider the workload that reassessments will impose both on students and on themselves. Small changes in reassessment policies can be the difference between a successful semester and being buried under an avalanche of work.

Workload for Students

In every course, it's important for instructors to estimate the total workload on students. Reassessments are part of this workload. Avoid adding reassessments on top of an already full workload, which can overwhelm students. Instead, cut back on the regular workload to make room for reassessments. A good rule of thumb is that students will need half as much time to complete reassessments as on the original assessment.

This advice applies to in-class assessments too, where the combination of new attempts at "old" standards in addition to "new" standards effectively makes more work for students who didn't succeed on their first attempt. Again, adding reassessments on top of an already full exam or quiz is a recipe for demotivating and overwhelming students. Consider having more frequent (and therefore smaller) exams or quizzes, or offering a special one-question quiz covering an especially difficult standard.

Limit Reassessment Opportunities (With Flexibility)

Reassessments can overwhelm you with grading. It's important for your own sake to put reasonable but flexible limits on the amount of reassessment. For example:

- *Allow reassessments only on a predetermined schedule.* This works best with new attempts: Students may only reassess on a subsequent quiz (or exam) that contains new questions on previously assessed standards. Or set aside dedicated "reassessment days" dedicated to new attempts. This guarantees that you can predict when reattempts will need to be graded. This approach is a key part of SBT, described in chapter 10.
- *Limit the frequency of reassessments.* For example, students may only submit one reassessment per week, or three reassessments between exams.
- *Use tokens.* Tokens can limit the total number of reassessments but give students the power to choose what and when they reassess.

Help Students Engage the Feedback Loop Effectively

Reassessments work best when students take time to understand previous issues and work to correct them. If you don't encourage metacognition and careful study, some students may reassess with abandon, throwing ideas at the wall to see what sticks. This isn't helpful either for you or for the student. Here are some ways to help engage that feedback loop effectively:

- *"Unlock" new attempts via practice.* Before attempting a new problem, require students to show evidence of completing some concrete practice that will help improve their understanding. This could be done during office hours, via autograded online homework, with posted practice problems, or in a tutoring center. If a student is still struggling, an office hour reassessment can seamlessly turn into a discussion of the student's questions.
- *Have students fill out a reflective cover sheet.* The cover sheet is then attached to a submitted reassessment. Some example prompts: What did you do to improve your understanding before this revision? What resources did you use to study and prepare for this revision? What important mistakes were in the original, and how did you fix them?

Plan for Changing Reassessment Loads Throughout the Semester

It's likely that you will have few reassessments early in the semester, but you will probably see a significant uptick when the need for reassessments becomes more obvious. This often happens around the middle of the term, after a major assignment is returned, and especially near the end. Budget extra time during those periods for grading and office hours.

How to Manage Tokens and Add Flexibility

In chapter 6, we introduced tokens and gave a short definition: Tokens are a form of imaginary currency that students can spend to "buy" exceptions to course rules. Tokens are a common way to add flexibility into a course. In this section, we'll dig deeper into how to manage tokens, as well as looking at other options for adding flexibility.

Tokens add a layer of bookkeeping to a course that isn't effortless, but is easily managed. You can keep track of tokens in a spreadsheet, a custom LMS column, or a paper ledger.

When a student wants to spend a token, all they have to do is let you know via an email or verbally. However, the social cost of those interactions sometimes discourages students from using tokens. A good solution is an online form that students fill out to spend tokens. The form can simply ask for the student's name and have them select from a list of ways to use a token, asking for extra information as needed (such as which assignment they want to revise). Then link to the form on your course's main LMS page. Students fill out the form once per token they want to spend.

Many online forms can be set to send you an email whenever a student fills it out. We usually instruct students that as soon as they submit the form, they have made the "purchase" and can go ahead and do what they need to do: No need to wait for approval. We've noticed that some students are much more willing to use this sort of form than have a one-on-one interaction with the instructor.

Although tokens are a simple and easily managed way to let students bend any rules that you'd like, there are other options.

Special Purpose Tokens

One of the most common uses of tokens is to extend a deadline, and so some instructors use dedicated tokens just for deadline extensions. A "grace day" is a single-purpose token that can extend a deadline until the next class period (or 24 hours, or whatever makes sense). Other instructors give students separate types of tokens—one for extensions, another for revisions.

No Cost Flexibility

If you don't like the transactional aspects of tokens, another option is to allow essentially unlimited flexibility for deadlines, without tokens. To do this, require students to request the extension and suggest a new deadline via a form such as the one described previously for tokens. Students simply fill in their name, the assignment they need an extension on, and propose a new deadline.

Instructors often find that students use this power wisely, and they even suggest shorter extensions than the instructor might have been willing to grant. We want students to use these resources, and any way to lower barriers to their use is a good thing. As always, it's wise to make it clear that you will not be able to provide feedback as quickly for delayed assignments.

In all cases, know your students and what will work best for them. For example, are your students used to succeeding on the first try and possibly surprised at the high bar for assessments? Ensure they aren't delaying deadlines until it's too late to reassess. Likewise, we highly recommend keeping a clear set of deadlines in place, even if you plan to allow unlimited flexibility. Deadlines help students make plans and engage effectively with course content.

How to Assess Participation or Engagement

In chapter 4, we discussed how assessing participation enforces an instructor's expectations about what engagement looks like, which is highly subject to bias. However, many instructors are required to record attendance or want to incentivize students to do "enabling activities" that support learning. Here are some ways to "count" student engagement (in various forms) in a way that is more equitable.

Completion

Certain assignments are important to complete, but don't need a grade. For example, preclass assignments for flipped classes are critical preparation, but usually aren't meant to be "correct." The same idea applies to in-class activities and practice homework. In these cases, if it's necessary to record anything at all, then record only completion (perhaps looking for a minimal amount of good-faith effort). This checks that students have made a genuine attempt at the work, without penalizing their grade for initial mistakes.

Many Routes to Participation

An approach to flexibly incentivizing participation *and* attendance is illustrated by Sharona Krinsky, who we first met in chapter 8. She uses a separate grade category called "Preparation, Participation, and Practice" or PPP. Each letter grade requires a certain number of points in the PPP category. Students earn points toward PPP by completing items such as "reading the textbook and watching prep videos, participating in class, doing homework, attendance, and doing practice problems." These are all based only on completion, and the number of points required is deliberately set low compared to the number of options available. This allows students many paths to meeting the requirements and avoids penalizing them for occasional lapses or difficulties with one particular aspect of engagement.

Specifications for Participation

Our last approach to assessing participation combines the wisdom from two instructors: Amy Werman, who teaches social work at Columbia University, and another instructor who asked us not to use their name.

The core idea is to ask students to self-assess their participation. The first step is to clearly define what *participation* means, using specifications. For example, specifications for participation in class discussions could take the form of a detailed checklist, including items such as "Frequently uses readings/media/lecture to support one's argument."

Werman collaboratively constructs this type of list of specifications with students. Students fill in the prompt "I know I participated in class today because . . ." and submit it as part of an "introduction" to the class. She then combines the responses into a list, which she provides to students. Rather than reflecting the instructor's particular expectations about what engagement looks like—something that is prone to bias—a collaboratively constructed list gives students many options, including ones that the instructor might not have considered.

After defining *participation*, both instructors ask students to periodically review the participation specifications and write a brief reflection on their recent participation. The instructor can respond or give feedback as needed, leading to a conversation about participation that engages both parties. This is a very "ungrading" approach to participation: No grade is assigned yet, but students and the instructor come to an agreement, and students have a chance to adjust as necessary. At the end of the semester, students complete a final reflection, and only this contributes to their final participation grade. This approach also helps shine a light on the "invisible work" that instructors don't always see.

How to Maintain a Gradebook

When using an alternative grading system, you'll need to think carefully about how to record progress in your own gradebook and possibly in your

LMS. Here we provide general advice and describe common pitfalls. While detailed advice that applies to specific LMSs is beyond the scope of this book and will be quickly out of date, there are lots of people ready to help out on the internet. Reach out to colleagues and online communities and you will find concrete, hands-on help for your specific situation.

Reporting Progress in an LMS Gradebook

Most LMSs assume that you want to use points or percentages, and so reporting alternative grades via the LMS can be an exercise in frustration. Luckily, most LMSs let you create "custom" grade columns that you can enter manually. Create one column (or grade category) for each standard or specs-graded assignment. Enter only 1 or 0 to indicate whether the student has completed that standard or not. If your LMS allows it, change these to display words instead of numbers, such as "Complete" or "Not Yet."

If you have students upload assignments to your LMS, then the LMS will most likely create a gradebook column for that assignment as well. You can apply the principles described previously to this column. Avoid including points in these assignments at all costs, or limit them to just a 1 or 0 as described previously. LMSs are notorious for using points in inappropriate ways.

Help students track their progress by creating summary columns for each major grade category. For example, you may have a column indicating "Total Number of Standards Completed."

In every case, you'll most likely need to enter grades manually. Turn off any automatically calculated "total" or "weighted average" columns that your LMS may automatically display to students. LMSs have a bad habit of using anything that looks like a number to create a running total or percentage that is meaningless (and misleading). If that's not possible, as a last resort we have sometimes renamed those columns to "Ignore This Total. Grades Are Determined by the Table in the Syllabus."

Creating Your Own Gradebook

Most instructors keep a separate spreadsheet in addition to using their LMS gradebook. For SBG, each assignment now requires multiple columns: one for each standard on that assignment. If using specifications, you likely only need one column per assignment to record "Satisfactory" or not.

Contrary to what we recommended about communicating with students, we *do* recommend using numbers to enter marks in your own spreadsheet, since spreadsheets work best with numbers (and only instructors will see them anyhow). For example, you can enter a 1 or 0 to indicate a standard that was successfully completed (or not). To see overall progress, you can create "summary columns" that use spreadsheet calculations to determine a student's best (or most recent) work. However you structure your gradebook, think ahead about how you will use it, and organize it to make those tasks easier.[6]

Using a Student-Maintained Grade Record

It can be very helpful to provide a way for students to record their own progress in each grade category. This helps students get their heads into the system and understand it more deeply. One example of this can be found in Freeman's case study in chapter 8. Instructors shouldn't rely on students to record their own progress. Rather, student-maintained grade records help students track their progress in addition to other forms of communication.

How to Assign Midterm Grades and Give Progress Reports

Reporting midterm grades (and, similarly, progress reports for at-risk students and student-athletes) requires careful thought in an alternative grading system. You'll need to vary your approach depending on who requests the grade. This determines what information is actually needed, and how much leeway you have in reporting it.

Progress Reports for Students

It can be valuable to send regular progress reports to all students, without reporting a letter grade. This provides helpful feedback and aligns with what students typically want from a grade report: *Am I headed in the direction I want to go, and if not, what do I need to change?*

These progress reports should include actionable feedback to help steer the rest of their semester: What is a student doing successfully and what do they need to work on? Your records likely already have what you need to give useful progress feedback. You might include items such as the following:

- Has the student been meeting standards regularly?
- Has the student been taking advantage of reassessments, when needed?
- Is the student doing other, nongraded things that enable success, such as completing prep work, attending class, meeting with teams, and so on?

This feedback can be given via email, on the LMS, or through informal office hour meetings.

Midterm Grade Reports

Your institution might require you to report midterm grades or grades-in-progress at other times before the end of the term. Here are some options for when you must do so.

Give the Letter Grades Meaning

Just as you can write tables or narrative descriptions for final grades, do the same for midterm grades. We advise assigning only three midterm grades: A, C, and F. Write out specific definitions for each, such as the following:

- A: This student is making satisfactory progress and is taking advantage of reassessments as needed. I have no significant concerns about their progress.
- C: I have a significant concern about this student's progress for at least one reason, such as meeting very few objectives, not taking advantage of reassessments when needed, or not completing important ungraded work (such as preclass prep).
- F: This student has stopped coming to class, has missed a significant number of assignments, or is otherwise in a situation that suggests they will not pass the class.

You could define B's and D's too, but it is easier to make consistent decisions about a limited number of options. Share these definitions with students to help them understand their meaning.

Make a Projection Based on Current Progress

Suppose you have 20 standards, but students have only attempted 10 of them by midterm time. That's half of the standards, and so a student who has met seven standards now might be expected to complete about 14 by the end of the semester. You can use this with your final grade table to estimate a final grade. Just like in a traditional system, this is not truly a valid grade, but rather a "guess" with very large error bars.

Because of reassessments, things can change dramatically before final grades are due. So be very careful with projections. We recommend "fuzzing" the final grade criteria to give students the benefit of the doubt, or "round up" students who are making progress on standards but haven't earned full credit yet. In the end, none of these approaches are very satisfying, and we tend to avoid them.

Ask Students to Grade Themselves

This is an "ungrading" approach to midterm grades. Have students complete a structured midterm reflection or one-on-one meeting, in which they reflect on their progress and self-assign a current grade (perhaps based on narrative descriptions of letter grades, as described previously), along with providing evidence to support it. This can be a lot of work, but it is also enormously helpful to both students and instructors.

How to Give a Final Exam

Many institutions require instructors to have a final exam or "culminating experience" of some type. Others require a common final that may be points-based. Some instructors simply want to give one final assessment of student knowledge. Here are some ways to incorporate final exams into an alternatively graded class:

- *One last opportunity to meet standards.* The "final exam" is just one final attempt over all the standards in the course, or a limited selection announced in advance, and students attempt only the standards that they haven't met yet. This is the simplest approach to a final exam in an SBG class. Be ready for the possibility that some students may not need to (or want to) take the final exam at all, if they are happy with their current progress. Examples in the case studies include Veazey (chapter 7) and Freeman (chapter 8).
- *Required recertification of core standards.* Identify a few "core" standards and require students to complete another attempt on the final exam. This is a way to test if students have retained core knowledge, in a way that keeps it simple for the instructor. Be careful with what happens if students don't meet these core standards, considering that exams tend to be high stress and that students have no opportunity to reassess. Options include reducing the penalty for missing a standard or using the result to add a "plus" or "minus" to a grade. See Bowman (chapter 5) for an example.
- *Use something else (e.g., a final portfolio) or nothing at all.* There are many options beyond a final exam. If you don't have to have a final exam, leave it off. Final exams are high stress and rarely demonstrate a student's true learning. You could replace a final exam with a final project that synthesizes key ideas (graded with specifications), a portfolio of work that demonstrates student progress on various standards and gives students a final opportunity to show their growth, or a free-form final reflection such as Frances Su's *7 Exam Questions for a Pandemic (or Any Other Time).*[7]

If you must give a common, points-based final exam in your otherwise alternatively graded course, you still have options. A common practice is to include the final exam as a separate requirement in the course grade table or list; see Muchalski's case study (chapter 7) for an example. Or, if your situation allows it, you can use the final exam to modify the grade earned through the alternative system; for example, a student could earn a "plus" on their grade by scoring above an 80% on the final and a "minus" if they score below a 60%, and otherwise there is no change. It's helpful in this case to keep the ranges for each outcome wide, since final exams are high stress and there is no reassessment.

How to Assign Final Grades

Here are some common ways we've already seen to turn progress on standards or specifications into final grades:

- *Grade table.* Each row corresponds to a letter grade, and each column is a category in which students can make progress (e.g., "Number of Standards Met" or "Daily Prep Completed"). Students must meet *all* requirements in a row to earn that grade. Examples are found throughout the case studies, including items graded for completion, or using points or percentages.
- *List of requirements or "narrative."* Write out requirements for each grade in words. This can sometimes be simpler than a table, if the requirements for some items involve more than just numbers. Bowman (chapter 5) gives an example.
- *Number of standards.* In SBG, a grade might be based only on the number of standards completed. Momsen (chapter 8) demonstrates this.
- *Include standards in a weighted-average system.* See "Standards-Based Testing" in chapter 10 for an example.

Partial Grades (Plus, Minus, or AB)

Often, it's easiest to communicate how to earn "whole" letter grades (A, B, C, D) in a grade table or list. If your institution assigns partial grades, you'll need to clearly explain how these are determined. Here are a few options:

- *Modify a "whole" grade.* Whole letter grades are assigned using a table or list, and you provide general rules for how modifications happen. In the "near miss" approach, students earn a "plus" for completing all requirements for a letter grade and also some of the requirements for a higher grade. A "minus" comes from completing all but some of the requirements. Be clear about what *some* means. In the "extras" approach, identify a few activities that do not factor into the basic letter grade, but which could contribute to a plus grade. A minus may not be given at all, or it may be given for failure to complete any of the extras, or some combination of them. Alternatively, use the final exam to modify the final grade (see "How to Give a Final Exam" for details).

- *Include partial grades in the grade table or list.* This can make the table quite large, but allows fine-tuning. For examples, see Veazey (chapter 7) and Bender (chapter 8).
- *The "ungrading" approach.* Write a narrative description of what a plus or minus means in general and let students make a case for themselves, based on concrete examples from their work, that they should earn (or not) one of these modifiers.

One way to help students understand modifications is to visualize their grade on a "scale," like in Figure 12.1.

Adjustments can be phrased in terms of taking a "step" one block to the right or left. For example, "Take one step right if you complete at least 90% of Beginning Activities."

How to Build Trust and Promote Buy-In With Students

When you've created a new grading system from the ground up, you know it better than anyone else. It is very easy to forget how alien this system can seem to your students. It is sadly true that many students expect their instructors to try for the "gotcha" or to implement harshly punitive rules. Having a strong plan to build trust will help you work against a culture of mistrust and confusion, and encourage students to take advantage of the benefits of your system sooner.[8]

Most Importantly, Be Clear, Honest, and Worthy of Trust

In the words of ungrading pioneer Jesse Stommel, "start by trusting students."[9] Begin with the view that students are trustworthy and not trying to

Figure 12.1. Visualization of grades for use with grade adjustments.

| D | D+ | C– | C | C+ | B– | B | B+ | A– | A |

"get away" with something. Genuinely believe that your students can succeed, that they are interested in learning, and that they will act in sensible, trustworthy ways. And tell them so.

Be clear and honest in your communication with students. If you realize something isn't working and needs to be fixed, say so, explain it, and clearly communicate the change. Students appreciate clarity and will recognize when you have their best interests at heart.

Share the Benefits of Your System for Students

Tell students how your assessment system is good for them ("It's okay to struggle early on. That won't hurt you as long as you learn these ideas eventually."). This helps students understand why they will benefit from your system and makes it clear that you care about their success. One benefit that is especially worth sharing is fairness: Students see alternative systems as more fair, because they make expectations clear and reduce competition compared to traditional systems.[10]

Through your words and actions, show students that you're not going to pull the rug out from under them. State your beliefs directly and in plain language, for example by saying, "I want you to succeed, and this class is designed to help you succeed. I believe that everyone in this class can earn an A."

Treat Learning About Your System Just Like Any Other Teachable Topic

Your students are learning something new when it comes to your grading system. This means that you will need to devote instructional time to it, like any other new idea. In fact, since traditional grades are so deeply ingrained in higher education, you may need to address your alternative grading system more than other new ideas.

However, don't try to explain the grading system all at once on the first day of class and then assume everyone understands it, and don't assume that students understand how their grades will work just from reading the syllabus. Plan multiple encounters or explanations. For example:

1. In the week before the semester, email students and ask them to read a short summary of the grading system. Set expectations without getting into details: Give only a brief overview of the main points, reasoning, and benefits of your system.
2. On the first day of class, outline the system in a little more detail, but don't try to cover everything. One of the most helpful things we've

found, both to improve understanding and to provoke questions, is to run students through several concrete examples of how final grades are determined. Share a copy of the syllabus requirements, and ask students to determine what grades various hypothetical students earned. Be sure to include examples that might surprise students (such as a student who fails to complete one requirement in the "A" row of a grade table). Give students opportunities to talk with each other: They can often answer each other's questions.

3. Reexplain key parts of the system as they become relevant. For example, reexplain how standards work just before you hand out the first assignment involving standards. Then review the meaning of your feedback, and how to determine next steps, just after handing back the graded assignment. Expect students to have many questions at these points, and plan some time to answer them.

4. A few weeks before the end of your term, give advice on some common scenarios, such as students who need to complete revisions or reassessments before the end of the semester. The imminent end of the semester tends to focus students and generate new questions. See "How to Assign Midterm Grades and Give Progress Reports" for advice on how to communicate these items.

As LinkedIn CEO Jeff Weiner is fond of saying, "When you are tired of saying it, people are starting to hear it."[11] That's especially true with explaining how grading systems work to students.

Use the Language of Standards

Walk the walk and talk the talk when discussing work with students. A pleasant feature of alternative grading methods is that standards and marks give students language to describe the ways in which they are learning. Model this: Mention relevant standards (and the actions they describe) when students are discussing their work, in class and in office hours. For example, ask students to explain why what they've shown you "demonstrates evidence" of meeting a standard. Nudge conversations about grades toward discussing specific standards and concrete steps to make progress.

Also help students understand when they're working with each standard. Put a full statement of relevant standards on each assessment. Write relevant standards on the board (or slides) before each class and explicitly call out when you're using them. Provide models of meeting, and not meeting, standards. Make it clear that your standards really matter to you and help students understand when they're working with them.

Communicate Progress Clearly

In many alternative systems, students are effectively at an F for most of the semester, until they (at long last) finally earn enough marks to reach up into the higher grades. If your system is like this, make a concrete plan to communicate progress in a way that encourages students.

Ask for Anonymous Feedback

After students have experienced all key parts of your assessments (e.g., receiving feedback, having a chance to reassess), ask for anonymous feedback. You can do this with a short paper form or through an online forum. This is a good idea in general, not just for alternative grading. You could ask, "What is one thing I should continue doing in this class? Why?" and then repeat the question for things you should stop and something you should start doing. Always ask why. Use responses to make real changes as needed, and don't ignore themes that show up.

Call Out Unusual Incentives or Pitfalls

Students are used to the ways that points and percentages incentivize their work (in particular, treating assignments as "one and done" or thinking in terms like "what grade do I need on the final in order to pass?"). Your class is likely to be very different. For example, when using SBG, it is likely you will reach a point where some students have already completed certain standards and don't need to attempt them again. If those standards appear on the next exam, be very clear that it's not necessary to complete problems that deal with those standards, and that this won't hurt them. They will likely need repeated assurances about this and clarifications about what is required.

Similarly, if you have hard deadlines or limits on revisions, remind students early and often about what they should be doing in order to meet those deadlines or avoid being unable to revise something they need.

How to Build Trust and Promote Buy-In With Administrators (and Others)

When instituting big changes in your grading practices, you'll need to build trust not only with your students but with others, including colleagues, your department chair, deans, and so on up the organizational hierarchy. It's difficult for a grading system to be fully effective if this "second level" of stakeholders doesn't understand, or even opposes what you are doing.

Talk to Your Colleagues and Administrators

Many of us teach year after year without ever talking about what we are doing until it's required for review. But when making a major change to your grading system, take initiative to keep your "second level" informed. It's especially good to keep your department chair, who is likely your most immediate supervisor, in the loop about what you are doing, why you're doing it, and what you expect *before you implement anything*. In particular, prepare your chair to get—and help them be ready to address—potential student complaints. It can be helpful to do this with a memo that spells out your plans along with the benefits and potential issues.[12]

Speak the Other Person's Language

When communicating with your "second level" group, remember that they have values and immediate interests that are different from students; the language you use should connect with those values and interests. For example, one concrete and immediate concern for many administrators is enrollment and retention. So when speaking about alternative grading to a dean or provost, explain that alternative grading builds intrinsic motivation, which improves engagement and therefore retention. Equity, in particular, is an important lever for discussing alternative grading with administrators. So emphasize the very real issues with inequity in traditional grading practices that we discussed in chapters 2 and 4 and how your alternative approach should be more equitable. Take any available chance to connect your alternative grading plans with strategic plans and be ready to explain how your plans will help realize the institution's plans.

Prepare Good Answers for Objections

Efforts to change grading systems will draw skeptics out of the woodwork, including (perhaps especially) among your colleagues. Common objections center around "rigor" and grade inflation. Have counter-arguments ready to deploy in case they are needed. See chapter 4 for possible responses to common objections, and familiarize yourself with the ones you're most likely to encounter. Also consider employing analogies to explain how your grading system works, such as comparing it to peer review in academic publishing (see chapter 3).

Show Enthusiasm and Have a Learning Mindset

When talking to colleagues, administrators, and others about your alternative grading plans, be excited about what you are doing. There is good reason for excitement: You are taking a huge step toward improving the intellectual and personal development of your students and doing concrete work toward dismantling an inequitable system. Let that enthusiasm shine through. At the same time, avoid giving a sales pitch. Be ready to explain what you are doing, why you're doing it, and what you hope to accomplish, but also ask for feedback from the people you talk to, and be honest about what might need to change and how you're planning to change it.

This advice is particularly useful for documentation you use for review, whether annual performance evaluations, contract renewal, or promotion or tenure decisions. Most institutions require evidence of teaching effectiveness. Explaining your alternative grading implementations, presenting evidence for their effectiveness, and discussing ways you are seeking out growth and improvement in them present a powerful picture of you as an expert teacher committed to learning and professional growth. Our experience is that institutions want to keep people who are taking intelligent risks to better themselves and their students.

Notes

1. Collins et al., 2019.
2. Nilson, 2014.
3. Phoel, 2009.
4. Phoel, 2009, para. 4.
5. Phoel, 2009, para. 7.
6. You can find extremely detailed advice on using gradebooks on our blog, https://gradingforgrowth.com/p/using-a-gradebook-with-alternative
7. Su, 2020.
8. For much more detailed advice about building trust or "buy-in" with students, see Kelly, 2020.
9. See https://twitter.com/jessifer/status/726424167420145664
10. Buckmiller et al., 2017; Pope et al., 2020.
11. Doerr, 2018, p. 50.
12. Bethany Blackstone and Elizabeth Oldmixon, two political science instructors who use specifications grading, provided a memo to their department chair in advance, giving a simple and student-focused explanation of specs grading and why they were implementing it. By keeping the chair informed, they were able to get his full support, and the chair was able to handle student complaints easily when they arose. See Blackstone & Oldmixon, 2019, for details.

13

WHAT'S NEXT?

Changing your grading system can be fraught with new ideas and decisions. This book has been aimed at helping you make them confidently. As you continue your assessment journey, remember that nobody else knows your situation better than you do.

This final chapter looks a little further ahead. We'll start with some possibly unexpected things to be ready for when first using alternative grading. We'll give some advice about how to revise and improve your classes in future semesters. We'll also step back and think about the limitations that alternative grading has. Finally, we'll review open questions and places where further research is needed.

What to Expect

As you use the workbook to convert a class to use alternative grading, you know what *you're* going to change. It's also important to be ready for other changes that will likely happen in your freshly updated classes. These are mostly positive, but they can surprise you if you aren't expecting them.

Grade Distributions Change

Perhaps this shouldn't be a surprise, but when you change your assessment strategy, final grade distributions change, too. Often, they become bimodal, with a greater number of students earning A's and B's (because they are no longer penalized for taking time to learn) as well as more students earning D's and F's (because they can no longer get by on partial credit). As we described in chapter 4, a higher number of high course grades is not grade inflation; both the high and the low grades are more accurate than the grades reported by traditional methods, because grades are directly connected to concrete evidence of learning.

214

While changes in grade distributions are expected and defensible, it's important to be proactive in addressing them. Talk to your department chair, colleagues, or dean in advance, to help them understand the changes you're making and likely outcomes. Have a plan to quickly identify and reach out to struggling students, who may react by calling your grading "picky" or "too harsh," or by complaining to an administrator. See "How to Build Trust and Promote Buy-In With Students" and "How to Build Trust and Promote Buy-In With Administrators (and Others)" in chapter 12 for further advice.

Office Hours Get Busier

Many instructors are used to quiet office hours. Be ready for that to change. You may find that once students start to understand how important and beneficial reassessments are, they'll come to your office hours in droves. However, some office hours will be busier than others. Office hour visits often increase steadily, with the peak typically coming around two thirds of the way through the semester. If you are used to using office hours to get other work done, that too will change. If you offer "on demand" reassessments during office hours, have a plan in case too many students arrive at once. Is there an overflow room available? Can students schedule specific meeting times?

Office hour conversations often also become more learning-focused. Rather than "Why didn't I do well on this exam?" or "Can I have a point back?," students are ready to focus on specific work and standards. Use the language of standards, "demonstrating evidence," and so on to model this process for students.

Incentives Change on Assessments

In alternative grading, each assessment is beneficial: It's another chance for students to show that they've learned. So students often want—and ask for—more assessments.

Students will also approach assessments differently than they may have in the past. If students know that they will have future opportunities to show their learning without penalty, then skipping a problem isn't a big deal. In traditional grading, deliberately skipping a problem is a terrible mistake; in alternative grading, we should embrace it. In fact, you can encourage students to write "I'm not ready yet" rather than making a poor attempt. This helps students think critically about their readiness, and the work you eventually grade will be of a higher quality. Be prepared to follow up with students who make this choice, to ensure they know what to do next. In particular, watch for students with "magical" thinking: There's always another chance, or they will "get it" eventually without having to change their approach.

Finally, be clear and open with students, and share these insights with them. For example, tell them directly that the incentives will be different on assignments and describe some ways that they will need to think differently when approaching a quiz or exam. Make a big deal about knowing which standards need to be attempted and not trying those that are already completed.

Setting Reasonable Expectations

We've written a lot in this book about the benefits of alternative grading. But we also want to give an honest picture of what alternative grading systems *don't* do. Changing your grading won't cure all ills. For example, as we described in chapter 4, alternative grading can be much more equitable than traditional grading—or not, if implemented blindly, without intentionality and careful reflection.

There are many moving parts in every class, and these each affect students. Assessments are just one part. Class structure, policies, communication, and organization each contribute to the culture and atmosphere of a class, and your choices in these areas send messages. They can reinforce and support each other, or they can send mixed messages and cause confusion.

If students are already confused or concerned about nonassessment portions of your class, then adding in a brand new assessment system could actually make things worse. It can add another layer of confusion and reinforce a negative narrative about the class.

So before you jump feet first into alternative grading, take a careful look at the other parts of your class that you have the power to change. Is your class time structured to support student learning, such as using active learning techniques?[1] Do your communications and LMS page have a clear and consistent organization that helps students understand what to do and when to do it? Reflect carefully on student comments, and how those might translate into concerns about a new grading system.

One of the best ways to help a new grading system succeed is to intentionally and vigorously work to build trust with students. We say much more about how to do this in chapter 12.

Revising Your Work

Feedback loops are not only at the heart of student learning; they are also critical to improving our own courses. Once you've dipped your toe into alternative grading, you'll see new ways to improve things for your students and yourself. That is the time to refine our "keep it simple" advice: You'll know where a little more complexity or clarity is needed. Here is our concrete advice about how to engage in your own course-planning feedback loop.

Take Notes Throughout the Semester

Start a file named "Notes for Next Time." Write a note in the file every time you notice something that you'd like to improve, modify, or clarify. Make notes on worksheets or assignments as well. Don't forget to explain: Write clearly and thoroughly enough so that "future you" can understand.

Survey Students Often Throughout the Semester

Don't wait until the end of the semester to learn from your students how your alternative grading system is or is not working. By that point, it's too late. Instead, just as we give students regular feedback throughout the course, solicit feedback from students early and often.

We suggest doing this at least twice, while the course is still going. You might start with a survey, given after the first few weeks of the semester, with simple, open-ended items such as the following:

- What is something about this class that has helped you learn well so far?
- What is one thing I (the instructor) could change about this class that would improve your learning? How would you suggest changing it?

This midsemester check-in with your students can yield a tremendous amount of actionable ideas and surface student issues and misconceptions long before they become critical. Perhaps most importantly, it allows students to be heard, in case they have something they need to say, and that drives better engagement.

You can follow this up with an end-of-semester survey—*before* the formal course evaluation—in which you ask for the big picture from the students' point of view. You might ask, "Please give your feedback on the grading system used in this class; how did it affect the way you learned or worked, compared to other classes?" As with the midsemester survey, read student responses carefully and objectively. Summarize the results in your "Notes for Next Time" document.

Reflect on Your Own Experience

At the end of the semester, set aside an hour to reflect on the whole course experience. Write in your "Notes for Next Time" document about what you should change and why. Next time you teach the class, believe your "past self." Trust your big-picture view from the end of the semester.

If you're anything like us, you will feel utterly unwilling to go back to teaching a class with points and partial credit. Here's some good news: Once you've figured out a system that you like, you can use it as a basis for future classes.

Open Questions

There is a lot that we currently don't know about alternative grading, at least from the standpoint of peer-reviewed, published research on this subject. The body of literature on alternative grading is still emerging at the time of this writing. Many articles are "action research" studying the implementations on a small, often individual, scale; a few give theoretical frameworks or high-level arguments in favor of general approaches. These are useful for learning purposes, and we encourage you to dive into the literature (maybe with a colleague or a study group). But there is still much room for additional research about alternative grading.

Most important are large-scale studies of the effectiveness of alternative grading. Most previous studies have focused at the level of individual small classes. Large-scale studies could involve larger numbers of students, in many sections, or across disciplines. There is also a need for longitudinal studies.

There are many things that *effectiveness* could mean. Here are just a few:

- *Grades.* How do different implementations of alternative grading affect average class grades? What patterns do student grades show in later classes, especially when those classes don't use alternative grading?
- *Anxiety.* In what situations does alternative grading lower stress? What types of stress or anxiety are most affected?
- *Mindset.* Do students' mindsets about learning change throughout an alternatively graded class?[2] Do those beliefs persist after the class ends? What if they are part of a curriculum including multiple alternatively graded classes?
- *DFW rates.* Does alternative grading affect DFW rates? What specific implementation aspects help improve those rates?
- *Withdrawing versus failing.* Do alternative grading strategies change the likelihood of withdrawing (the "W" part of DFW)? Pulling apart the "grade" part of DFW rates (i.e., D's and F's) from the "withdraw" part (the W's) may reveal interesting results.
- *Retention.* Does alternative grading affect student retention in their major, or in higher education as a whole?

Another major, and very broad, area for study: What helps instructors succeed in alternative grading? Which aspects of implementation or instructor beliefs are most likely to lead instructors to a successful implementation? What are the best ways to introduce and train instructors in using alternative grading?

Most of these questions are wide open and ready for interested faculty to address. Work that addresses these questions will typically fall under the heading of "scholarship of teaching and learning" (SoTL). Most disciplines have at least one journal that focuses on SoTL, and in our experience, editors are very interested in work on alternative grading.

Another way to help support the community of alternative graders is to share materials. Syllabus repositories for a variety of disciplines already exist, and often include lists of standards for various classes.[3]

Next Steps

This is it, the last chapter of the book. You've read about the four pillars of alternative grading and seen a huge variety of practices in the case studies. We hope that you're excited to convert one of your own classes to use improved grading, using the workbook as a guide. Start soon!

As you start your journey with alternative grading, we can't overstate how much you'll benefit from finding a community of support. Ask a colleague to convert a class with you, join a teaching group at your institution, or join an online community.[4] It helps to have people to talk with, and to provide advice and support when you need it.

Welcome to the world of alternative grading!

Notes

1. Mazur, 2022, gives an example of how to implement active learning even in large classes.

2. Two studies of math classes, Harsy et al., 2021, and Lewis, 2022, found little change, possibly due to the effects of students' other classes.

3. See these references: Mattaini, 2022 (biology); Closser, 2022 (chemistry); Weir, 2022 (math); Ramos, 2022 (physics).

4. David and Robert help run a Slack Workspace—an online message board—that supports alternative graders in a huge number of disciplines. Use this link to join it: https://bit.ly/3FC8TJy

APPENDIX

Frequently Asked Questions

Some questions are so frequently asked that we've written entire chapters or sections on them.

If you're wondering how alternative grading can be used in a specific context, the case studies in chapters 5–10 have you covered. In addition to the subject of each chapter, you can find introductory classes in chapters 5 and 7 and advanced classes in chapter 6. If you are curious about how to use alternative grading as an adjunct, contingent, nontenure-track, or pretenure faculty member, see Bender and Freeman's case studies in chapter 8, Link in chapter 9, and Creighton in chapter 10.

Research questions about the effectiveness of alternative grading are addressed in chapter 4. Chapter 4 also includes direct answers to the most common criticisms of alternative grading, including questions about equity, grade inflation, "rigor," and cheating.

Implementation concerns tied to particular methods appear at the end of several case study chapters. For example, concerns about giving away the right approach to a problem, or encouraging synthesis, are addressed in chapter 5 on SBG. Direct implementation advice is concentrated in chapters 11 and 12, including assessing participation, assigning midterm grades, using final exams, and communicating with both students and administrators about your grading system.

The remainder of this appendix is a list of additional commonly raised questions, concerns, and objections to alternative grading methods.

Will I be overwhelmed with grading?

This is possible, but can be avoided if you plan carefully. See the workbook (chapter 11) and "How to Keep Reassessments Reasonable" (chapter 12) for advice about how to avoid common pitfalls and keep your grading load reasonable.

Will reassessments be too much work for students?

Like the preceding, this is possible, but can be avoided with careful planning. See advice about this in the workbook (chapter 11) as well as "How to Keep Reassessments Reasonable" (chapter 12).

Will my students be unprepared for future classes that don't use alternative grading?

No. Preliminary data suggest that when students take prerequisite courses with alternative grading, they on average earn the same or even higher grades in the following classes compared with their peers who took prerequisites with traditional grading.[1] This is true even when the following classes are traditionally graded. Possible explanations include that students in alternatively graded classes have had the opportunity to return to and learn prerequisite materials more deeply, and have also improved their study skills while doing so.

Likewise, a study of student transitions from SBG-based high schools to traditional college classes found no significant issues related to SBG.[2]

How can I encourage creativity and exploration when holding students to specific, concrete standards?

Creativity and specific standards can both exist in the same class. Class time can be fun, creative, and thought-provoking independently of assessment or grading choices. Projects are a good place to give students room for creativity in assessments: Give students clear specifications but don't overly limit their options. That is, give students freedom in how to meet the specifications, what format or medium to use, and so on.

For examples, see Kay C Dee's case study, and "More Examples of Specifications" (both in chapter 6).

Can active learning be used along with alternative grading? Must it be?

Yes and no. Many instructors pair active learning methods such as flipped learning, inquiry-based learning, and others with alternative grading, and they work well together. Both approaches encourage learning and remove demotivational aspects of traditional lecture and grading. While alternative grading can be used successfully with any kind of class structure, including traditional lecture, you'll see the most benefits if your assessments and class structure send the same message.

Many case studies mention specific active learning approaches. See all of chapter 7, plus Momsen and Bender's case studies in chapter 8. See "Standards-Based Testing" in chapter 10 for an example of how to use alternative grading in an otherwise traditional class.

How much time does it take to convert a class to use a new assessment system?

It's possible to change your whole class on extremely short notice (see Robert and David's origin stories in chapter 1). But we recommend beginning your planning at least 1 month before the start of your class. The workbook (chapter 11) is designed with this pacing in mind. We also recommend preparing by reading this book or attending a conference or workshop well before you start planning. That will give you plenty of time to think about the big ideas and begin to sort out what works for you.

What can I do if I make a choice in my system that doesn't work, and I find out halfway through the semester?

If possible, only change grading systems for a course you're familiar with. This will help you better understand which standards are appropriate, where hard parts are (hence additional reassessment pressure), and so on.

But if something needs to be changed halfway through the semester, be ready and willing to adjust. Communicate these changes clearly and in multiple ways (e.g., in class, via email, on your LMS, etc.). Small changes can make big differences; talk with and listen to your students and work with them to find appropriate fixes. Explain your reasoning and be transparent. Students are generally quite understanding if you do this. Examples of common things you might change include removing or regrouping standards and changing final grade requirements. See "Revising Your Work" in chapter 13 for advice on how to catch issues early via student surveys.

If a student earns credit for a standard in the first week of class, how do I know they still retain that knowledge at the end of the semester?

You can require a student to complete each standard two (or more) times. This has the effect of testing their knowledge at multiple points throughout the semester. Or identify a set of "core" standards that must be recertified (completed another time) on the final exam. You can also give a comprehensive final exam whose only purpose is to adjust the student's final grade in a limited way.

Examples of these approaches can be found in the case studies from Bowman (chapter 5), Muchalski (chapter 7), and Freeman (chapter 8).

How can I generate multiple assessments for each standard that are at similar levels of difficulty?

This applies to a system that uses "new attempts" for reassessment. Set aside time before classes start to assemble a collection of reassessment problems. This is also a reason to limit the number of standards you'll assess.

Some disciplines and classes lend themselves to creating questions with minor variations; just change the numbers, name, or graph, and ask the same questions about it. You will likely be able to find multiple variations on a question in the exercises sections of textbooks. Collect several textbooks, find the appropriate sections, and make copies of questions as needed. Another good source is online homework systems, which can autogenerate variations on a core question. Ask colleagues or consult email lists and other online sources.

I'm stuck and I need somebody to talk to!

This is critical. Colleagues can be a good place to begin—find a trusted colleague to talk with, perhaps somebody who is teaching your same class. Even better, ask them to convert their class along with you and meet weekly to discuss your successes and struggles. Your institution's teaching and learning center can help in this way as well. There are also many online communities of practice, small and large, that support alternative grading.[3]

Notes

1. DeKorver et al., 2022.
2. Guskey et al., 2020.
3. One example is the Alternative Grading Slack Workspace that David and Robert help run. Use this link to join it: https://bit.ly/3FC8TJy

REFERENCES

Alley, L. R. (1996). Technology precipitates reflective teaching: An instructional epiphany. *Change, 28*(2), 48. https://doi.org/10.1080/00091383.1996.9937751

Anderman, E. M., & Koenka, A. C. (2017). The relation between academic motivation and cheating. *Theory Into Practice, 56*(2), 95–102. https://doi.org/10.1080/00405841.2017.1308172

Arnaud, C. H. (2021, April 26). How an alternative grading system is improving student learning. *Chemical & Engineering News, 99*(15). https://cen.acs.org/education/undergraduate-education/alternative-grading-system-improving-student/99/i15

Axelson, R. D., & Flick, A. (2010). Defining student engagement. *Change: The Magazine of Higher Learning, 43*(1), 38–43. https://doi.org/10.1080/00091383.2011.533096

Baird, J. S. Jr. (1980). Current trends in college cheating. *Psychology in the Schools, 17*(4), 515–522. https://doi.org/10.1002/1520-6807(198010)17:4<515::AID-PITS2310170417>3.0.CO;2-3

Barth, E., & Higginbottom, R. S. (2021). The Calculus Mastery Exam: A report on the use of gateway-inspired assessment tools at liberal arts colleges. *PRIMUS, 31*(8), 883–899. https://doi.org/10.1080/10511970.2020.1776804

Beatty, I. D. (2013). Standards-based grading in introductory university physics. *Journal of the Scholarship of Teaching and Learning, 13*(2), 1–22. https://scholarworks.iu.edu/journals/index.php/josotl/article/view/3264

Becker, K. A. (2003). *History of the Stanford-Binet intelligence scales: Content and psychometrics.* (Stanford-Binet Intelligence Scales, Fifth Edition Assessment Service Bulletin No. 1). Riverside Publishing. https://citeseerx.ist.psu.edu/document?repid=rep1&type=pdf&doi=184d722e916f41ab3507108a67676a3f78edf7a1

Blackstone, B., & Oldmixon, E. (2019). Specifications grading in political science. *Journal of Political Science Education, 15*(2), 191–205. https://doi.org/10.1080/15512169.2018.1447948

Bloom, B. S. (1968). *Learning for mastery: Instruction and curriculum* (Topical Papers and Reprints, no. 1). Regional Education Laboratory for the Carolinas and Virginia. https://eric.ed.gov/?id=ED053419

Blum, S. D. (2020). *Ungrading: Why rating students undermines learning (and what to do instead).* West Virginia University Press. https://wvupressonline.com/ungrading

Boesdorfer, S. B., Baldwin, E., & Lieberum, K. A. (2018). Emphasizing learning: Using standards-based grading in a large nonmajors' general chemistry survey course. *Journal of Chemical Education, 95*(8), 1291–1300. https://doi.org/10.1021/acs.jchemed.8b00251

Bowen, R. S., & Cooper, M. M. (2021). Grading on a curve as a systemic issue of equity in chemistry education. *Journal of Chemical Education, 99*(1), 185–194. https://doi.org/10.1021/acs.jchemed.1c00369

Brilleslyper, M., Ghrist, M., Holcomb, T., Schaubroeck, B., Warner, B., & Williams, S. (2012). What's the point? The benefits of grading without points. *PRIMUS, 22*(5), 411–427. https://doi.org/10.1080/10511970.2011.571346

Brown, P. C., Roediger, H. L., III, & McDaniel, M. A. (2014). *Make it stick: The science of successful learning.* Harvard University Press.

Buckmiller, T., Peters, R., & Kruse, J. (2017). Questioning points and percentages: Standards-based grading (SBG) in higher education. *College Teaching, 65*(4), 151–157. https://doi.org/10.1080/87567555.2017.1302919

Butler, R., & Nisan, M. (1986). Effects of no feedback, task-related comments, and grades on intrinsic motivation and performance. *Journal of Educational Psychology, 78*(3), 210–216. https://doi.org/10.1037/0022-0663.78.3.210

Carlisle, S. (2020). Simple specifications grading. *PRIMUS, 30*(8–10), 926–951. https://doi.org/10.1080/10511970.2019.1695238

Carpenter, S. K., Cepeda, N. J., Rohrer, D., Kang, S. H., & Pashler, H. (2012). Using spacing to enhance diverse forms of learning: Review of recent research and implications for instruction. *Educational Psychology Review, 24*(3), 369–378. https://doi.org/10.1007/s10648-012-9205-z

Carter, C. E., & Grahn, J. A. (2016). Optimizing music learning: Exploring how blocked and interleaved practice schedules affect advanced performance. *Frontiers in Psychology, 7*, 1251. https://doi.org/10.3389/fpsyg.2016.01251

Cassady, J. C., & Johnson, R. E. (2002). Cognitive test anxiety and academic performance. *Contemporary Educational Psychology, 27*(2), 270–295. https://doi.org/10.1006/ceps.2001.1094

Chamberlin, K., Yasué, M., & Chiang, I. C. A. (2018, December 25). The impact of grades on student motivation. *Active Learning in Higher Education.* Advance online publication. https://doi.org/10.1177/1469787418819728

Chen, L., Grochow, J. A., Layer, R., Levet, M. (2022, July). *Experience report: Standards-based grading at scale in algorithms.* Cornell University. https://arxiv.org/abs/2204.12046

Cilli-Turner, E., Dunmyre, J., Mahoney, T., & Wiley, C. (2020). Mastery grading: Build-a-syllabus workshop. *PRIMUS, 30*(8–10), 952–978. https://doi.org/10.1080/10511970.2020.1733152

Closser, K. (2022). *Mastery grading materials for chemistry courses* [Unpublished manuscript]. *Google Drive.* https://bit.ly/3xhlAUQ

Coles, A. (1999, June 16). Mass-produced pencil leaves its mark. *Education Week.* https://www.edweek.org/teaching-learning/mass-produced-pencil-leaves-its-mark/1999/06

Collins, J. B., Harsy, A., Hart, J., Haymaker, K. A., Hoofnagle, A. M., Kuyper Janssen, M., Stewart, J., Austin, K., Mohr, T., & O'Shaughnessy, J. (2019). Mastery-based testing in undergraduate mathematics courses. *PRIMUS, 29*(5), 441–460. https://doi.org/10.1080/10511970.2018.1488317

Cooper, A. A. (2020). Techniques grading: Mastery grading for proofs courses. *PRIMUS*, *30*(8–10), 1071–1086. https://doi.org/10.1080/10511970.2020.1733151

Crooks, A. D. (1933). Marks and marking systems: A digest. *The Journal of Educational Research*, *27*(4), 259–272. https://www.jstor.org/stable/27525788

DeKorver, B. K., Clark, S., Henderleiter, J., & Barrows, N. J. (2022, July 31–August 4). *Mastery-based grading across a first-year chemistry sequence at Grand Valley State University* [Conference presentation]. Biennial Conference on Chemical Education, West Lafayette, IN, United States.

De Zouche, D. (1945). "The wound is mortal": Marks, honors, unsound activities. *The Clearing House: A Journal of Educational Strategies, Issues and Ideas*, *19*(6), 339–344. https://www.jstor.org/stable/30177988

Doerr, J. (2018). *Measure what matters: How Google, Bono, and the Gates Foundation rock the world with OKRs*. Penguin.

Duker, P., Gawboy, A., Hughes, B., & Shaffer, K. P. (2015, March). Hacking the music theory classroom: Standards-based grading, just-in-time teaching, and the inverted class. *Music Theory Online*, *21*(1). https://mtosmt.org/issues/mto.15.21.1/mto.15.21.1.duker_gawboy_hughes_shaffer.html

Durm, M. W. (1993, September). An A is not an A is not an A: A history of grading. *The Educational Forum*, *57*(3), 294–297. https://doi.org/10.1080/00131729309335429

Elkins, D. M. (2016). Grading to learn: An analysis of the importance and application of specifications grading in a communication course. *Kentucky Journal of Communication*, *35*(2), 26–48.

Elliot, A. J., & McGregor, H. A. (2001). A 2 × 2 achievement goal framework. *Journal of Personality and Social Psychology*, *80*(3), 501. https://doi.org/10.1037/0022-3514.80.3.501

Elsinger, J., & Lewis, D. (2020). Applying a standards-based grading framework across lower level mathematics courses. *PRIMUS*, *30*(8–10), 885–907. https://doi.org/10.1080/10511970.2019.1674430

Evergreen State College. (2023). Evergreen: Making history since 1967. https://www.evergreen.edu/about/evergreen-making-history-1967

Feldman, J. (2018). *Grading for equity: What it is, why it matters, and how it can transform schools and classrooms*. Corwin Press.

Feldman, J. (2019). Beyond standards-based grading: Why equity must be part of grading reform. *Phi Delta Kappan*, *100*(8), 52–55. https://doi.org/10.1177/0031721719846890

Fernandez, O. E. (2021). Second chance grading: An equitable, meaningful, and easy-to-implement grading system that synergizes the research on testing for learning, mastery grading, and growth mindsets. *PRIMUS*, *31*(8), 855–868. https://doi.org/10.1080/10511970.2020.1772915

Freeman, S., Eddy, S. L., McDonough, M., Smith, M. K., Okoroafor, N., Jordt, H., & Wenderoth, M. P. (2014). Active learning increases student performance in science, engineering, and mathematics. *Proceedings of the National Academy of Sciences*, *111*(23), 8410–8415. https://doi.org/10.1073/pnas.1319030111

Guskey, T. R., Townsley, M., & Buckmiller, T. M. (2020). The impact of standards-based learning: Tracking high school students' transition to the university. *NASSP Bulletin, 104*(4), 257–269. https://doi.org/10.1177/0192636520975862

Halperin, A. (2020). Mastery-based testing in calculus with a final exam component. *PRIMUS, 30*(8–10), 1017–1039. https://doi.org/10.1080/10511970.2019.1700575

Hamilton, R. (2012). Elaboration effects on learning. In N. M. Seel (Ed.), *Encyclopedia of the sciences of learning.* Springer (pp. 1103–1105). https://doi.org/10.1007/978-1-4419-1428-6_170

Harsy, A. (2020). Variations in mastery-based testing. *PRIMUS, 30*(8–10), 849–868. https://doi.org/10.1080/10511970.2019.1709588

Harsy, A., Carlson, C., & Klamerus, L. (2021). An analysis of the impact of mastery-based testing in mathematics courses. *PRIMUS, 31*(10), 1071–1088. https://doi.org/10.1080/10511970.2020.1809041

Harsy, A., & Hoofnagle, A. (2020). Comparing mastery-based testing with traditional testing in Calculus II. *International Journal for the Scholarship of Teaching and Learning, 14*(2), Article 10. https://doi.org/10.20429/ijsotl.2020.140210

Hembree, R. (1988). Correlates, causes, effects, and treatment of test anxiety. *Review of Educational Research, 58*(1), 47–77. https://doi.org/10.3102/00346543058001047

Heubach, S., & Krinsky, S. (2020). Implementing mastery-based grading at scale in introductory statistics. *PRIMUS, 30*(8–10), 1054–1070. https://doi.org/10.1080/10511970.2019.1700576

Inoue, A. B. (2019). *Labor-based grading contracts: Building equity and inclusion in the compassionate writing classroom.* WAC Clearinghouse. https://wac.colostate.edu/books/perspectives/labor/

Karpicke, J. D., & Roediger, H. L. III. (2008). The critical importance of retrieval for learning. *Science, 319*(5865), 966–968. https://doi.org/10.1126/science.1152408

Kelly, J. S. (2020). Mastering your sales pitch: Selling mastery grading to your students and yourself. *PRIMUS, 30*(8–10), 979–994. https://doi.org/10.1080/10511970.2020.1733150

Kirschenbaum, H., Napier, R., & Simon, S. B. (1971). *Wad-ja-get? The grading game in American education.* Hart.

Kohn, A. (2006). The trouble with rubrics. *English Journal, 95*(4), 12–15. https://www.alfiekohn.org/article/trouble-rubrics/

Kohn, A. (2011). The case against grades. *Educational Leadership, 69*(3), 28–33. https://www.alfiekohn.org/article/case-grades/

LabWrite. (2004). *What is LabWrite?* North Carolina State University. https://labwrite.ncsu.edu/instructors/what_is_lwr.htm

Lang, J. M. (2016). *Small teaching: Everyday lessons from the science of learning.* Jossey-Bass.

Lewis, D. (2020). Student anxiety in standards-based grading in mathematics courses. *Innovative Higher Education, 45*(2), 153–164. https://doi.org/10.1007/s10755-019-09489-3

Lewis, D. (2022). Impacts of standards-based grading on students' mindset and test anxiety. *Journal of the Scholarship of Teaching and Learning, 22*(2), 67–77. https://doi.org/10.14434/josotl.v22i2.31308

Linhart, J. M. (2020). Mastery-based testing to promote learning: Experiences with discrete mathematics. *PRIMUS, 30*(8–10), 1087–1109. https://doi.org/10.1080/10511970.2019.1695236

Lipnevich, A. A., & Smith, J. K. (2008). *Response to assessment feedback: The effects of grades, praise, and source of information* (Research Report Series, no. 1). ETS. https://doi.org/10.1002/j.2333-8504.2008.tb02116.x

Locke, D. (2022, April 26). The Levels System: An application of mastery learning to the teaching of philosophical writing. *Teaching Philosophy, 46*(1), 1–39. Advance online publication. https://doi.org/10.5840/teachphil2022418166

Lyle, K. B., & Crawford, N. A. (2011). Retrieving essential material at the end of lectures improves performance on statistics exams. *Teaching of Psychology, 38*(2), 94–97. https://doi.org/10.1177/0098628311401

Mangum, A. (2020). Implementation of mastery-based testing in Calculus I. *PRIMUS, 30*(8–10), 869–884. https://doi.org/10.1080/10511970.2019.1709587

Marshall, M. S. (1968). *Teaching without grades*. Oregon State University Press.

Marzano, R. J. (2003). *What works in schools: Translating research into action*. ASCD.

Mattaini, K. (2022). Mastery grading materials for biology courses [Unpublished manuscript]. *Google Drive*. https://drive.google.com/drive/folders/1L-akqa_1BLFQM0ukM_N_Kwr8562yB_gG

Mayfield, K. H., & Chase, P. N. (2002). The effects of cumulative practice on mathematics problem solving. *Journal of Applied Behavior Analysis, 35*(2), 105–123. https://doi.org/10.1901/jaba.2002.35-105

Mazur, E. (2022). *Peer instruction*. Mazur Group. https://mazur.harvard.edu/research-areas/peer-instruction

McCabe, D. L., Treviño, L. K., & Butterfield, K. D. (2001). Cheating in academic institutions: A decade of research. *Ethics & Behavior, 11*(3), 219–232. https://doi.org/10.1207/S15327019EB1103_2

McDaniel, M. A., Thomas, R. C., Agarwal, P. K., McDermott, K. B., & Roediger, H. L. (2013). Quizzing in middle-school science: Successful transfer performance on classroom exams. *Applied Cognitive Psychology, 27*(3), 360–372. https://doi.org/10.1002/acp.2914

McKnelly, K. J., Morris, M. A., & Mang, S. A. (2021). Redesigning a "Writing for Chemists" course using specifications grading. *Journal of Chemical Education, 98*(4), 1201–1207. https://doi.org/10.1021/acs.jchemed.0c00859

New College of Florida. (n.d.). *Office of the provost and vice president for academic affairs*. https://www.ncf.edu/wp-content/uploads/2022/06/2021-Provost-Letter-NCF-Grading-System-Explanation.pdf

Niemiec, C. P., & Ryan, R. M. (2009). Autonomy, competence, and relatedness in the classroom: Applying self-determination theory to educational practice. *Theory and Research in Education, 7*, 133–144. https://doi.org/10.1177/1477878509104318

Nilson, L. B. (2014). *Specifications grading: Restoring rigor, motivating students, and saving faculty time*. Stylus.

Palmer, B. (2010, August 10). E is for fail. *Slate*. https://slate.com/news-and-politics/2010/08/how-come-schools-assign-grades-of-a-b-c-d-and-f-but-not-e.html

Phoel, C. M. (2009, April 7). Feedback that works. *Harvard Business Review*. https://hbr.org/2009/04/feedback-that-works

Pope, L., Parker, H. B., & Ultsch, S. (2020). Assessment of specifications grading in an undergraduate dietetics course. *Journal of Nutrition Education and Behavior*, *52*(4), 439–446. https://doi.org/10.1016/j.jneb.2019.07.017

Post, S. L. (2014, June 15–18). *Standards-based grading in a fluid mechanics course* [Paper presentation]. ASEE Annual Conference & Exposition, Indianapolis, IN, United States. https://doi.org/10.18260/1-2--23032

Prasad, P. V. (2020). Using revision and specifications grading to develop students' mathematical habits of mind. *PRIMUS*, *30*(8–10), 908–925. https://doi.org/10.1080/10511970.2019.1709589

Ramos, G. (2022). *Mastery grading materials for physics courses* [Unpublished manuscript]. *Google Drive*. http://bit.ly/PhysicsMBGRepository

Ring, J. (2017). ConfChem conference on select 2016 BCCE presentations: Specifications grading in the flipped organic classroom. *Journal of Chemical Education*, *94*(12), 2005–2006. https://doi.org/10.1021/acs.jchemed.6b01000

Roediger, H. L., III, & Butler, A. C. (2011). The critical role of retrieval practice in long-term retention. *Trends in Cognitive Sciences*, *15*(1), 20–27. https://doi.org/10.1016/j.tics.2010.09.003

Rundquist, A. (2012, February). Standards-based grading with voice: Listening for students' understanding. *AIP Conference Proceedings*, *1413*(1), 69–72. https://doi.org/10.1063/1.3679996

Ryan, R. M., & Deci, E. L. (2000). Self-determination theory and the facilitation of intrinsic motivation, social development, and well-being. *American Psychologist*, *55*, 68–78. https://doi.org/10.1037/0003-066X.55.1.68

Schneider, J., & Hutt, E. (2013). Making the grade: A history of the A–F marking scheme. *Journal of Curriculum Studies*, *46*(2), 201–224. https://doi.org/10.1080/00220272.2013.790480

Schwarzer, R. (1990). Current trends in anxiety research. *European Perspectives in Psychology*, *2*, 225–244.

Selbach-Allen, M. E., Greenwald, S. J., Ksir, A. E., & Thomley, J. E. (2020). Raising the bar with standards-based grading. *PRIMUS*, *30*(8–10), 1110–1126. https://doi.org/10.1080/10511970.2019.1695237

Shields, K., Denlinger, K., & Webb, M. (2019). Not missing the point(s): Applying specifications grading to credit-bearing information literacy classes. In M. Mallon, L. Hays, C. Bradley, R. Huisman, J. Belanger, & S. Beene (Eds.), *The grounded instruction librarian: Participating in the scholarship of teaching and learning* (pp. 87–97). Association of College and Research Libraries.

Smallwood, M. L. (1935). *An historical study of examinations and grading systems in early American universities: A critical study of the original records of Harvard, William and Mary, Yale, Mount Holyoke, and Michigan from their founding to 1900* (Vol. 24). Harvard University Press.

Stange, K. E. (2018). Standards-based grading in an introduction to abstract mathematics course. *PRIMUS*, *28*(9), 797–820. https://doi.org/10.1080/10511970.2017.1408044

Stone, N. J. (2000). Exploring the relationship between calibration and self-regulated learning. *Educational Psychology Review*, *12*, 437–475. https://doi.org/10.1023/A:1009084430926

Stutzman, R. Y., & Race, K. H. (2004). EMRF: Everyday rubric grading. *The Mathematics Teacher*, *97*(1), 34–39. https://doi.org/10.5951/MT.97.1.0034

Su, F. (2020, April 28). *7 exam questions for a pandemic (or any other time)* Francis Su. https://www.francissu.com/post/7-exam-questions-for-a-pandemic-or-any-other-time

Taylor, K., & Rohrer, D. (2010). The effects of interleaved practice. *Applied Cognitive Psychology*, *24*(6), 837–848. https://doi.org/10.1002/acp.1598

Toledo, S., & Dubas, J. M. (2017). A learner-centered grading method focused on reaching proficiency with course learning outcomes. *Journal of Chemical Education*, *94*(8), 1043–1050. https://doi.org/10.1021/acs.jchemed.6b00651

Townsley, M. (2019). Walking the talk: Embedding standards-based grading in an educational leadership course. *Journal of Research Initiatives*, *4*(2), Article 2. https://digitalcommons.uncfsu.edu/jri/vol4/iss2/2

Townsley, M., & Buckmiller, T. (2016). *What does the research say about standards-based grading?* Matt Townsley. http://mctownsley.net/standards-based-grading-research/

Weir, R. J. (2020). Rethinking precalculus and calculus: A learner-centered approach. *PRIMUS*, *30*(8–10), 995–1016. https://doi.org/10.1080/10511970.2019.1686669

Weir, R. J. (2022). *Mastery grading materials for mathematics courses* [Unpublished manuscript]. *Google Drive*. http://goo.gl/6wMAHb

Williams, K. (2018). Specifications-based grading in an introduction to proofs course. *PRIMUS*, *28*(2), 128–142. https://doi.org/10.1080/10511970.2017.1344337

Zimmerman, J. K. (2020). Implementing standards-based grading in large courses across multiple sections. *PRIMUS*, *30*(8–10), 1040–1053. https://doi.org/10.1080/10511970.2020.1733149

ABOUT THE AUTHORS

David Clark is an associate professor in the Department of Mathematics at Grand Valley State University. As a classroom teacher, his classes are active, engaging, and highly student-centered. His research also centers on students, especially projects that introduce them to mathematical research through puzzles and games. Over his 17-year teaching career, David has won numerous teaching awards, including the Mathematical Association of America's national Alder Award. He lives with his wife Sarah in Grand Rapids, Michigan, where he hikes, gardens, and plays board games (usually losing).

Robert Talbert is a professor in the Department of Mathematics at Grand Valley State University. Robert has experimented with and advocated for innovation in teaching and learning throughout his 25-year career in higher education. Primarily a classroom instructor, he has also served as scholar-in-residence at Steelcase, Inc., and held an appointment as Presidential Fellow for the Advancement of Learning in the GVSU President's Office, where he coordinated large-scale initiatives on teaching innovation and built communities of practice around alternative grading. Robert lives in Allendale, Michigan, with his wife, two teenage children, and three cats. He aspires to spend more time kayaking or playing bass guitar than being in front of a computer.

in General Biology II (North Dakota
State University), 101
hands-on technique video as, 125
incentive changes on, 215–216
lab notebook as, 125
live, 115
of participation, 201–202
portfolios for, 96
postlab report as, 125
prototype of, 177–181
purpose of, 24
sharing benefits of, 209
simplification of (workbook for
alternative grading), 167
summative, 101
in Teaching and Learning
Innovations (California State
University-Channel Islands),
77–78
assessment check, in Introduction
to World Art (University of
Pittsburgh), 106–107
assessment-level objectives, 157–158,
163
assignments
application/extension problem (AEP)
as, 85–86
in Engineering Physics course
(Grand Valley State University),
89–90, 94
in hybrid classes, 98
mechanism portfolio as, 83, 86, 88
in Regulatory Affairs-Medical
Devices course (Rose-Hulman
Institute of Technology), 67–68
science literacy, 76
in Teaching and Learning
Innovations (California State
University-Channel Islands),
77–78
weekly video, 94
asynchronous online courses, 66
autonomy, 36
auxiliary tasks, 51–52, 53, 60

Barre, Betsy, 144–145
bell curve, 21
Bender, Gretchen, 105–114
Best Practices, in Electromagnetism
and Thermodynamics course
(Citrus College), 134–135
bias, in grading, 21, 44–46
Big Ideas, at College of Charleston, 61
biomedical engineering course,
specifications (specs) grading in,
65–71
blocked practice, 35
Bloom's taxonomy, 160, 161
Bowman, Joshua, 51–58, 62
build your own final (BYOF) exam,
in Calculus class (Colorado State
University), 115–116

Calculus 1 (Pepperdine University),
51–58
Calculus Center (Colorado State
University), 116
Calculus class (Colorado State
University), 105–114
calibration, 35
categorical data, 20
challenge problems, in
Electromagnetism and
Thermodynamics course
(Citrus College), 137–138
cheating, reduction of, 40
checkpoints, 83–89
communication, 101–104, 190, 211,
212
community development, in General
Biology II (North Dakota State
University), 103
competence, 35–36
concept/process-focused courses, 166
conditions, for standards, 160
content/skills-focused courses, 166
core standards, in Engineering Physics
course (Grand Valley State
University), 90–92